W9-BRE-527

A Year of Puzzles, Fun Facts, Jokes, Crafts, Games, and More!

The 2021 ALMANAC of FUN

HIGHLIGHTS PRESS

Honesdale, Pennsylvania

SUNDAY	MONDAY	TUESDAY	WEDNESDAY

BIRTHSTONE
GARNET

ZODIAC SIGNS

CAPRICORN: DECEMBER 22–JANUARY 19

AQUARIUS: JANUARY 20–FEBRUARY 18

FLOWERS
CARNATION AND SNOWDROP

Festival of Sleep Day

Get some shut-eye after staying up until midnight to ring in 2021!

3

WORLD BRAILLE DAY

4

Harbin International Ice and Snow Sculpture Festival (China) starts

This annual event is the largest ice and snow festival in the world!

5

Feast of the Epiphany

Around the world, this day is also known as Three Kings' Day, Theophany, Dehna, and Little Christmas.

6

NATIONAL HOUSEPLANT APPRECIATION DAY

10

Step in a Puddle and Splash Your Friends Day

Don't forget your rain boots!

11

Avengers, assemble! Timely Comics (later called Marvel) was founded on this day in 1939.

12

MAKE YOUR DREAMS COME TRUE DAY

13

Bundle up! In 1773, Captain James Cook became the first to cross the Antarctic Circle.

17

MARTIN LUTHER KING JR. DAY

18

On your mark, get set, go! In 1903, the now popular bicycle race Tour de France was announced.

19

U.S. Presidential Inauguration

20

Global Belly Laugh Day / National Gorilla Suit Day

24 / **31**

NATIONAL OPPOSITE DAY

Definitely forget this day and *don't* celebrate.

25

Up Helly Aa (Scotland)

At Europe's largest fire festival, a full-scale replica of a Viking ship is burned!

26

INTERNATIONAL HOLOCAUST REMEMBRANCE DAY

27

THURSDAY	FRIDAY	SATURDAY

| | **NEW YEAR'S DAY** 1 | **World Introvert Day** Studies show that introverts make up 30 to 50 percent of the U.S. population. 2 |

| **NATIONAL BOBBLEHEAD DAY** 7 | *Extra, extra!* In 1656, the oldest surviving commercial newspaper began in Haarlem, the Netherlands. 8 | **NATIONAL APRICOT DAY** 85 percent of our nation's apricots are grown in California. 9 |

| **National Dress Up Your Pet Day** Take pictures and share them with your friends! 14 | **National Bagel Day** Why does a seagull fly over the sea? *Because if it flew over the bay, it would be a bagel!* 15 | **APPRECIATE A DRAGON DAY** 16 |

| **International Sweatpants Day** Get comfy! 21 | **National Answer Your Cat's Questions Day** "Meow?" 22 | *Catch!* In 1957, the toy company Wham-O produced the first Frisbees. 23 |

| **National Kazoo Day** No kazoo? No problem! Make your own with a comb and waxed paper. 28 | *Care for a drink?* The Coca-Cola Company began in Atlanta, Georgia, in 1892. 29 | **NATIONAL CROISSANT DAY** 30 |

JANUARY

GET ORGANIZED MONTH
5 QUICK WAYS TO GET ORGANIZED

1. Keep a daily planner. Write down all the tasks you need to finish each day. Don't forget to check off each item as you complete it!

2. Clean out your backpack every Friday after school.

3. Keep all of your important papers in one place.

4. Each school night, get your backpack ready and lay out your clothes for the next day.

5. Use shoeboxes to store small knickknacks.

The first Get Organized Month was held **January 2005**.

A book never written: **How to Be Neat** by Mac K. Mess

PENCIL MEMO BOARD

For a fun way to store important messages, make this craft!

1. Cut a large rectangle from **corrugated cardboard**. Cut a point at one end. Trace around the shape twice onto corrugated cardboard and cut out the pieces. Stack all three and glue them together.

2. For the pencil's tip, wood, body, metal band, and eraser, cut out **felt** pieces wide enough to wrap over the sides. Glue them on. Add details with a **marker**.

3. Tape **yarn** to the back for a hanger.

Use thumbtacks to post important memos on your board!

Meet at library 4:00 pm

NATIONAL OATMEAL MONTH

To celebrate, ask an adult to help you make a bowl of plain oatmeal, then choose a recipe for the toppings. See how many variations you can try this month!

BANANA SUNDAE

Top with banana slices, a spoonful of yogurt, and a sprinkle of sunflower seeds.

MAPLE NUT

Stir in a handful of cashews or almonds, then decorate with raisins and a drizzle of maple syrup.

PEACHY KEEN

Stir in a drop of almond extract and a drizzle of honey, then top with peach slices and another drizzle of honey.

RING AROUND THE MOON

Put a small scoop of frozen yogurt on top and surround it with a circle of blueberries.

CINNAMON APPLE

Peel and core an apple, then grate it over the oatmeal. Add a sprinkle of cinnamon and a drizzle of honey.

GREAT GRANOLA

Sprinkle granola over the top, then add milk.

INTERNATIONAL CREATIVITY MONTH

Get your creative juices flowing this month by tackling each of these prompts.

CREATE YOUR OWN GAME

On January 6, 1975, the game show **Wheel of Fortune** debuted. There have been more than **7,000 episodes** since!

Let's play! If you could create your own game, what would it be? It could be an outdoor game, a board game, a video game, or any other kind of game. The sky's the limit!

DRAW YOUR OWN EMOJI

If you could draw your own emoji, what would it look like? When would you use it? Draw a picture of it or turn it into a sticker.

January 13 is National Sticker Day!

PUT YOUR BEST FOOT FORWARD

January 23 is Measure Your Feet Day. If you didn't have a ruler or measuring tape, how would you tell how long something is? What's the silliest way you can think of to measure your feet?

WHAT'S HIDING IN THE CAVE?

Did you see that? There's something hiding in the cave! Grab a piece of paper and draw what you think the rest of it looks like.

January 7 is Old Rock Day. What can old rocks like fossils tell us about the past?

CREATE YOUR OWN MUSICAL INSTRUMENT

What do violins, kazoos, bagpipes, and tubas have in common? They all started as an idea that turned into a musical creation. And now it's your turn! If you could design a musical instrument, what would it look like? What would it sound like? What kind of music would it play? Draw or create a model of your instrument.

Famed composer Mozart was born on **January 27, 1756**.

ALPHABET ART

The **letter J** was the last letter to be introduced into the alphabet. It was added in 1524, almost **500 years** ago!

Art can be found anywhere—even in your own name! Write the first letter of your name on paper, like the yellow *Y* in the drawing below. Then create a drawing around that letter.

YOU'RE THE INVENTOR!

On **January 3, 1496,** Leonardo da Vinci unsuccessfully tested a flying machine, 407 years before the Wright brothers flew the first successful airplane.

Kid Inventors' Day is January 17. If you could create your own invention, what would you make? Come up with your best idea, then draw it out or build a prototype.

125 YEARS AGO, UTAH BECAME THE 45th U.S. STATE.

Some of the country's most popular national parks are in Utah. In fact, they make up 66 percent of the state! Put the names of these Utah parks and other places into the crisscross puzzle. Each word fits into the grid in only one way. Use the number of letters in each word as a clue to where it might fit.

4 LETTERS
ZION

5 LETTERS
DIXIE
OURAY

6 LETTERS
ARCHES

8 LETTERS
DINOSAUR

10 LETTERS
GLEN CANYON
MANTI-LA SAL

11 LETTERS
CANYONLANDS
CAPITOL REEF
CEDAR BREAKS

12 LETTERS
FLAMING GORGE
GOBLIN VALLEY

Arches National Park has over 2,000 natural arches. The Delicate Arch is featured on Utah license plates.

January 15, 2001

20 YEARS AGO, WIKIPEDIA WENT ONLINE.

Wikipedia is an online encyclopedia. What makes it so unique is that anyone can edit the entries. That means it's a good idea to check original sources for school research papers. In the past 20 years, it has become one of the most popular websites on the internet. Can you match each fact to its corresponding number?

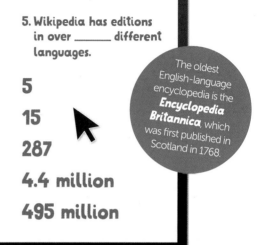

1. Over _____ people visit Wikipedia each month.

2. In 2019, Wikipedia ranked number _____ in most-visited websites.

3. The English edition of Wikipedia has over _____ articles.

4. About _____ percent of internet users visit it each day.

5. Wikipedia has editions in over _____ different languages.

5

15

287

4.4 million

495 million

The oldest English-language encyclopedia is the *Encyclopedia Britannica*, which was first published in Scotland in 1768.

WHAT SILLY THINGS DO YOU SEE?

These people are using computers at a library. Where else can you find a computer?

HARLEM GLOBETROTTERS DAY

On January 7, 1927, the Harlem Globetrotters played their first game. Although they played regular basketball at first, the exhibition basketball team has since become famous for entertaining crowds with their amazing basketball skills and tricks. **Can you find 18 hidden objects in this picture?**

bell

ruler

fish

artist's brush

fishhook

sailboat

nail

crescent moon

magnet

snake

envelope

scarf

canoe

saw

sock

heart

flashlight

pennant

The Globetrotters have played in front of **148 million fans** in more than 123 countries.

The team did not actually play in Harlem until 1968!

The name is a combination of the words *University* and *olympiad*.

January 21–31, 2021

WINTER UNIVERSIADE

The 30th Winter Universiade will be held in Lucerne, Switzerland.

WNTR SPRTS are the words *winter sports* with the vowels taken away. Can you figure out the names of the 10 WNTR SPRTS that will be played in Lucerne?

SKI ORIENTEERING

SK RNTRNG

SNWBRDNG

C HCKY

FGR SKTNG

CRLNG ← ------- HINT

BTHLN

SHRT TRCK SPD SKTNG

CRSS-CNTRY SKNG

LPN SKNG

FRSTYL SKNG

It is the largest university winter multi-sport competition in the world.

Athletes from more than 50 countries will compete.

University students between ages 17 and 25 are eligible to compete.

January 2

NATIONAL SCIENCE FICTION DAY

Read the letters in green to find out what term Isaac Asimov coined in his 1941 short story "Liar!"

Many science-fiction fans celebrate this unofficial holiday on the birthdate of famous science-fiction author Isaac Asimov. Use one of these story starters or your own idea to write a science-fiction story.

As Dad twisted knobs on the panel, the rocket started to shake and . . .

_____

_____

_____

_____

Knock, knock, knock. The door burst open, and . . .

_____

_____

_____

_____

We looked at the strange metallic substance, which suddenly started to . . .

_____

_____

_____

_____

January 18

NATIONAL THESAURUS DAY

Celebrate by spotting eight synonyms hidden in this scene. Can you find the words SMART, BRAINY, INTELLIGENT, BRILLIANT, WISE, GENIUS, BRIGHT, and CLEVER?

January 4

NATIONAL SPAGHETTI DAY

Make these bite-sized spaghetti nests to celebrate!

Wash your hands before and after handling food.

1. Mix together 4 ounces of cooked **spaghetti**, ¼ cup shredded **Parmesan cheese**, ¼ cup shredded **mozzarella cheese**, and ⅔ cup **marinara sauce** in a large bowl.

2. Grease a nonstick 6-cup **muffin tin** with vegetable-oil spray.

3. Use tongs to evenly fill the muffin cups with the spaghetti mixture. Make a dent in the center of each cup to create the nest.

4. Sprinkle ¼ cup cooked **bacon bits** or **vegan-sausage crumbles** on top of the nests.

5. Add ¼ cup shredded **Parmesan cheese** over the nests.

6. Bake at 375°F for 13–15 minutes or until set. Serve with extra sauce, if you wish.

Ask an adult to help with anything sharp or hot.

The word **spaghetti** comes from the Italian word *spaghetto*, meaning "thin string" or "twine."

NATIONAL SOUP MONTH

Celebrate all month long with these soup jokes!

What is a duck's favorite meal?

Soup and quackers

If you leave alphabet soup on the stove and go out, it could spell disaster.

NATIONAL POPCORN DAY

What's popping in this pot besides popcorn? See if you can find at least 22 items among the kernels.

Why are you eating alphabet soup?

Because if I were eating number soup, I'd be a cow-culator.

Knock, knock.
Who's there?
Jupiter.
Jupiter who?
Jupiter fly in my soup?

Martin Luther

Read the poem, then write your own poem to honor Dr. King.

The holiday is observed on the third Monday of January each year.

Sonnet for a King

This January day was set aside

to celebrate the birthday of a man,

a gentle man, who bravely lived and died

too soon, but left a challenge and a plan.

He was a man of strength and grace and will

who stood for honor, character, and grit,

a man who sought and fought for freedom till

he gave his life, in faith, defending it.

He had a dream of hope, a dream that we,

though different in creed, belief, and race,

could live, as friends, in peace and harmony

and make the world a better place.

"Hold fast to dreams": together we must strive

to understand, and keep the dream alive.

The line *Hold fast to dreams* is from the poem "Dreams" by Langston Hughes.

MLK DAY OF SERVICE
Corporation for
NATIONAL &
COMMUNITY
SERVICE ★★★

The MLK Day of Service was created to inspire Americans to turn Martin Luther King Jr. Day into a day of citizen action volunteer service in King's honor.

Talk with your parents about ways you can volunteer. Here are some ideas:
- Walk a neighbor's dog or wash their car.
- Help do yardwork for people who can't.
- Make welcome kits for new kids at school.
- Read books to others during your library's story hour.

King Jr. Day

The Martin Luther King Jr. Memorial opened in Washington, D.C., in 2011. It features a granite statue of the civil rights leader called the *Stone of Hope*.

Martin Luther King Jr. was born on **January 15, 1929.**

January 20, 1986, was the first time Martin Luther King Jr. Day was observed.

- Why do we build memorials?
- Name some people and events with memorials built in their honor.
- How else do we remember important people and events?
- Are there any memorials or monuments near where you live? If so, what do they honor?

What is your New Year's resolution?

January 1
NEW YEAR'S DAY

Happy 2021! Celebrate by watching the Philadelphia Mummers Parade, the oldest continuous folk parade in the U.S. It was also voted the best holiday parade. Can you find 17 differences between these two photos of saxophone players in a Fancy Brigade?

PASS THE LUCK, PLEASE!

Many countries around the world have foods that they consider to bring good luck when eaten at the start of the new year. Can you match each food with the country it belongs to?

1

Black-eyed peas and collard greens: The peas represent coins, while the greens stand for "folding money."

Saint Basil's Day cake: The cook sprinkles coins and other trinkets into the cake before baking. Whoever finds the treasure in their slice of cake gets good luck!

2

Pork sausages and lentils: The fat, rich sausage is a symbol of plenty, while the green, coin-shaped lentils represent money.

3

4

Grapes: As the clock strikes midnight, 12 grapes are eaten for each chime of the clock, in hopes of 12 months of prosperity.

Soba noodles: To ensure a long life, noodles must be sucked up and swallowed without breaking or chewing them.

5

 Italy

 Japan

United States

Spain

Greece

January 9

STATIC ELECTRICITY DAY

KIDS' SCIENCE QUESTIONS

Why do we sometimes feel shocks when we touch things?

zap!

That ZAP happens when static electricity gets moving! As you scuff across a rug, your socks may pick up a charge. That's from electrons, negatively charged bits that are part of all atoms. Usually they stay with their atoms, nicely balanced by positive charges. But if they rub onto an object, it gets extra negativity!

Robert Van de Graaff, an American physicist, invented the Van de Graaff generator in 1931. A Van de Graff generator is an electrostatic generator that can create static electricity for experiments.

Negative charges push away from each other. So the extra electrons move away from that charged sock. Destination: Earth's big surface, where they can spread out (or *ground*). To get there, they need *conductors*—things that a charge can easily move across. Unlike your socks and rug, YOU are a conductor. A charge can flow across you, but it's *static*; it can't keep going until you are almost touching another conductor. Then, ZAP! Electrons leap through the air as a spark. Shocking, huh?

January 11
LEARN YOUR NAME IN
MORSE CODE DAY

Morse code uses dots and dashes to represent letters. Morse code was first demonstrated on January 11, 1838, by Samuel Morse and Alfred Vail. The first telegraphic message was transmitted in 1844 on an experimental line between two American cities. To figure out the names of the two cities, decipher this code.

• — — / • — / ••• / •••• / •• / — • / — — • / — / — — — / — •

— ••• / • — / • — •• / — / •• / — — / — — — / • — • / •

What is your name in Morse code? Write it here.

International Morse Code

A • —	Q — — • —
B — •••	R • — •
C — • — •	S •••
D — ••	T —
E •	U •• —
F •• — •	V ••• —
G — — •	W • — —
H ••••	X — •• —
I ••	Y — • — —
J • — — —	Z — — ••
K — • —	
L • — ••	
M — —	
N — •	
O — — —	
P • — — •	

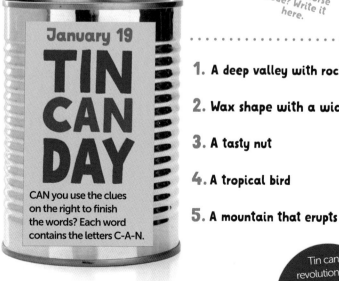

January 19
TIN CAN DAY

CAN you use the clues on the right to finish the words? Each word contains the letters C-A-N.

1. **A deep valley with rock sides**   CAN__ __ __

2. **Wax shape with a wick**   CAN__ __ __

3. **A tasty nut**   __ __CAN

4. **A tropical bird**   __ __ __CAN

5. **A mountain that erupts**   __ __ __CAN__

Tin cans revolutionized how people stored food by keeping it from spoiling.

Before the can opener's invention in 1858, tin cans were opened with a hammer and chisel.

What did the can say to the can opener?

"You really flip my lid!"

January 4
NATIONAL TRIVIA DAY

Celebrate by testing out your world knowledge.

1. The average thickness of Antarctica's continental ice sheet is _____.
   a. about four Empire State Buildings deep (more than a mile)
   b. about two Empire State Buildings deep (less than a half mile)

2. During what season in Norway does the sun stay up past midnight?
   a. Summer
   b. Winter

3. Ocean covers more of the planet than land, but we still have what percent of the sea to explore?
   a. 50 percent
   b. 95 percent

4. Most of this island country's plant and animal species, including the lemur, are native nowhere else.
   a. Madagascar
   b. Greenland

January 15
NATIONAL HAT DAY

A brisk breeze just blew everyone's hats off. Put on your thinking cap and help match each hat with its owner!

January 29
NATIONAL PUZZLE DAY

Can you find these hidden jigsaw pieces in this photo of rubber ducks?

Jigsaw puzzles were invented in 1767 by mapmaker John Spilsbury. He glued maps onto wood and cut them into pieces.

January 13 is National Rubber Ducky Day!

Puzzles became a popular hobby during the Great Depression as an affordable, reusable activity. In 1933, over **10 million puzzles** were sold per week!

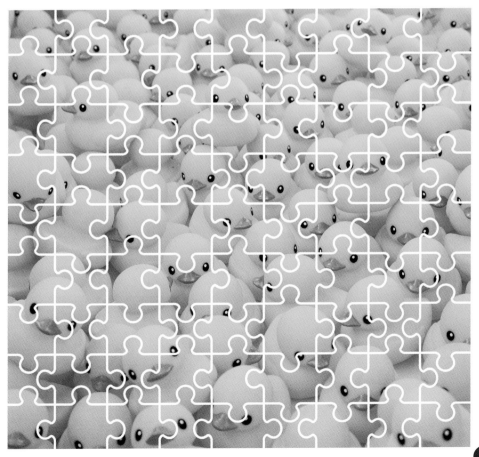

January 13

SAINT KNUT'S DAY

In Sweden, Saint Knut's Day is the day to get rid of Christmas trees. Swedes eat any edible ornaments, smash gingerbread houses, and put away decorations. In Swedish, this is called *julgransplundring*, which translates to "Christmas tree plundering."

Can you match these other Swedish words with their English translation? *God jul!* (Merry Christmas!)

SWEDISH	ENGLISH
julstjärna	Christmas stocking
julklappsstrumpa	Christmas star
julgranskula	Christmas tree lights
julgransbelysning	Christmas ornament

January 14–15, 2021

PONGALO PONGAL!

In Sri Lanka, Tamil Thai Pongal Day is a two-day harvest festival dedicated to the Sun God. On the first day of the festival, Sri Lankans make rice in large clay pots, outside under the sun. They boil the rice in milk and spices. As the milk boils over, people shout, "Pongalo pongal!" An overflowing pot brings good luck.

The second day of the festival honors the oxen who provide milk, transportation, and help with harvesting rice and other crops. The oxen are bathed and given special food to eat. Then they have their horns painted beautiful colors and are given garlands to wear.

This ox is ready for Tamil Thai Pongal Day!

THE WORLD

January 18

HAPPY BIRTHDAY, LIMA!

On January 18, 1535, the conquistador Francisco Pizarro founded Lima, Peru, as "Ciudad de los Reyes" (City of the Kings). Major celebrations and civic events take place across Lima to mark the capital's foundation, including parades, food, dancing, and fireworks!

January 27-28, 2021

HAPPY NEW YEAR, TREES!

Tu BiShvat is a Jewish holiday that is celebrated in Israel. It is a celebration for trees as they begin to grow again for the season. To celebrate, people eat fruits such as grapes, pomegranates, and olives. Many people will also get out into nature and plant a tree. In fact, over a million Israelis take part in the Jewish National Fund's Tu BiShvat tree-planting activities!

Israel is home to many different types of trees. Can you find the 10 here hidden in these letters?

Cypress
Eucalyptus
Fig
Jujube
Juniper
Mulberry
Oak
Olive
Palm
Sycamore

H	O	I	C	Y	P	R	E	S	S
F	C	D	V	R	M	K	F	U	T
E	E	G	R	R	J	W	T	S	L
O	L	I	V	E	D	P	K	P	P
A	P	F	S	B	Y	C	E	A	Z
K	M	Q	O	L	Z	C	V	X	M
C	I	L	A	U	Y	X	J	H	B
S	Y	C	A	M	O	R	E	U	M
J	U	N	I	P	E	R	Y	J	D
E	B	U	J	U	J	T	K	M	V

SUNDAY	MONDAY	TUESDAY	WEDNESDAY

Robinson Crusoe Day

Imagine what you'd do if you found yourself alone on a deserted island—with no Wi-Fi.

1

GROUNDHOG DAY

Will Punxsutawney Phil o Staten Island Chuck see their shadows?

2

Is it cold, or is it me? In 1947, Snag, Yukon, snagged the record for the coldest temperature ever recorded in North America: 81°F below 0!

3

Send a Card to a Friend Day

Just because.

7

Checkmate! In 1958, 15-year-old Bobby Fischer won the match that made him the then-youngest international chess grandmaster.

8

Read in the Bathtub Day

Add bubbles, and soak up one of your favorite stories.

9

Take a message, then take a bow! In 1933, the singing telegram was introduced.

10

Valentine's Day

Wear your heart on your sleeve—or anywhere else.

14

WASHINGTON'S BIRTHDAY

George often shares his birthday celebration with Abe and others.

15

Fat Tuesday

No, it doesn't weigh more than the other days. But it does sound better in French: Mardi Gras!

16

Ash Wednesday (first day of Lent)

It's also Random Acts of Kindness Day. Nice!

17

In 1828, the first issue of the *Cherokee Phoenix*, the first Native American newspaper, was published.

21

BE HUMBLE DAY

Aw, shucks!

22

Chew on this! In 1896, Leo Hirschfield gave us the Tootsie Roll, named after his five-year-old daughter Clara, whose nickname was "Tootsie."

23

National Tortilla Chip Day

What's this chip's favorite type of dance? Salsa, of course!

24

Dord is the word. In 1939, a *Webster's Dictionary* editor discovered the book's second edition included *dord*—a word that doesn't exist!*

*It was mistakenly defined as a scientific term for density.

28

BIRTHSTONE
AMETHYST

FLOWERS
PRIMROSE AND VIOLET

THURSDAY	FRIDAY	SATURDAY

National Sweater Day (Canada)

Bundle up and turn down the heat to tackle climate change.

4

In 1869, the biggest gold nugget ever, called the "Welcome Stranger," was found in Australia. It weighed nearly 157 pounds!

5

National Frozen Yogurt Day

Don't forget the toppings!

6

Don't Cry Over Spilled Milk Day

Instead, think positive and mop up that milk with some cookies!

11

Blades of glory! In 1879, skaters glided on North America's first artificial ice rink, set up in New York City's Madison Square Garden.

12

WORLD RADIO DAY

Tune in! Did you know that radio reaches more people around the globe than any other media?

13

PLUTO DAY

In 1930, Clyde Tombaugh discovered the tiny, distant dwarf planet, using a cool tool called a blink microscope.

18

International Tug-of-War Day

Grab a rope and some friends, then dig in your heels!

19

Out of this world! In 1962, John Glenn became the first American to orbit the Earth.

20

PURIM BEGINS

25

Tell a Fairy Tale Day

Make up your own! (Add an ogre or two.)

26

INTERNATIONAL POLAR BEAR DAY

27

FEBRUARY

ZODIAC SIGNS

AQUARIUS: JANUARY 20– FEBRUARY 19

PISCES: FEBRUARY 20– MARCH 20

Psst! Polar bear fur isn't really white. Each hair is a clear, hollow tube that looks white because of reflected light.

Frederick Douglass

Harriet Tubman

Madam C.J. Walker

W.E.B. Du Bois

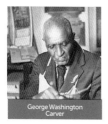
George Washington Carver

Jackie Robinson

Rosa Parks

BLACK HISTORY MONTH

Travel through this timeline of influential African Americans

1847 Abolitionist, author, and orator **Frederick Douglass** publishes the antislavery newspaper the *North Star*.

1849 **Harriet Tubman** escapes from slavery and leads others to freedom through the Underground Railroad.

1905 **Madam C.J. Walker** launches a business creating hair-care products, eventually becoming the first black woman millionaire.

1909 **W.E.B. Du Bois** co-founds the NAACP (National Association for the Advancement of Colored People).

1921 Inventor **George Washington Carver** addresses Congress about the hundreds of uses he discovered for peanuts, including flour, milk, dyes, and cheeses.

1947 **Jackie Robinson** joins the Brooklyn Dodgers, a Major League Baseball team.

1955 **Rosa Parks** takes a stand against segregation and is arrested for refusing to give up her bus seat.

1967 **Judge Thurgood Marshall** is appointed to the Supreme Court.

1986 **Oprah Winfrey** first goes on the air with her national TV show.

1992 Astronaut **Mae Jemison** blasts off on the space shuttle Endeavor.

1993 Author **Toni Morrison** wins the Nobel Prize in Literature.

2001 Four-star general **Colin Powell** is appointed U.S. secretary of state.

2008 **Barack Obama**—a senator from Illinois, born in Hawaii—is elected the 44th president of the United States.

2015 **Misty Copeland** is named a principal dancer with the American Ballet Theatre.

Judge Thurgood Marshall

Oprah Winfrey

Mae Jemison

Toni Morrison

Colin Powell

Barack Obama

Misty Copeland

NATIONAL BIRD-FEEDING MONTH

Give your feathered friends a treat! Then find 12 objects in this Hidden Pictures puzzle.

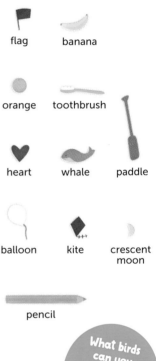

flag

banana

orange

toothbrush

heart

whale

paddle

balloon

kite

crescent moon

pencil

What birds can you see in your neighborhood this month?

BIRD SEARCH

The Great Backyard Bird Count takes wing February 12–15, 2021. Grab your binoculars and add to the count online, with a parent's permission. Below are the names of the 2019 most spotted species. Find the uppercase words in the grid. Can you spot those that are also in the Hidden Pictures puzzle?

Northern **CARDINAL**

Dark-eyed **JUNCO**

Mourning **DOVE**

Downy **WOODPECKER**

BLUE JAY

American **CROW**

House **FINCH**

House **SPARROW**

Black-capped **CHICKADEE**

White-breasted **NUTHATCH**

```
Y W C L I Q M G H S C P
N O X L D X J A A Y H U
E O Y A J E U L B C T V
V D K O P D M P N E H L
M P Y J E V K I E V A N
E E A U P T F D E N S U
V C J N Z R A D I P L T
O K R C O K V D A Q H H
D E P O C K R R N B R A
N R D I W A R N R Q I T
P Z H U C O L B I L S C
T C W Z W I M T C V D H
```

NATIONAL LIBRARY LOVERS' MONTH

Why did the fish go to the library?

To find some bookworms

Find 12 bookworms hidden in the library.

The Library of Congress, the largest library in the world, has more than **167 million** items on about 838 miles of bookshelves—nearly the distance from Washington, D.C., to Cape Canaveral, Florida.

In 2016, there were **1.4 billion** in-person visits to public libraries across the U.S., the equivalent of about 4 million visits each day. That's 2,664 per minute.

CHECK-OUT

DUE

AUTHOR AUTHOR!

Match up "Books Never Written" with their authors.

_____ 1. **Face to Face with a Bear**

_____ 2. **How to Catch Worms**

_____ 3. **Running the Mile**

_____ 4. **Strong Bones**

_____ 5. **Two Kinds of Numbers**

_____ 6. **What Dogs Do**

_____ 7. **Tasty Squash**

_____ 8. **All About Atoms**

_____ 9. **Sing Out Loud**

_____ 10. **Summer School**

A. **Evan N. Odd**

B. **Heidi Bones**

C. **Otto Breath**

D. **Terry Fied**

E. **Earl E. Byrd**

F. **Cal C. Uhm**

G. **Mike Rofone**

H. **Nova Kayshon**

I. **Sue Keeney**

J. **Molly Cule**

SPELL CHECK

_Uh-oh!_ Someone misprinted the titles of these classic children's books. Can you fix them?

Where the Mild Things Are

The Phantom Trolltooth

The Cat in the Hut

Green Eggs and Him

Goodnight Noon

Harriet the Shy

Winnie-the-Pooch

CHILDREN'S DENTAL HEALTH MONTH

Sink your teeth into this! Can you find the 20 non-beaver teeth hidden in this scene?

RIDDLE SUDOKU

Fill in the squares so that the six letters appear once in each row, column, and 2 x 3 box. Then read the yellow squares to find out the answer to the riddle.

Letters: **C N O R S W**

				W	
		N		O	
S	W				
				S	O
	S		R		
	N			C	

RIDDLE: Why do kings and queens go to the dentist?

ANSWER: To get ___ ___ ___ ___ ___ ___

What time do you go to the dentist?

Tooth-hurty

The first toothbrushes were tree twigs. Chewing on the tips of the twigs spread out the fibers, which were then used to clean the teeth.

50 YEARS AGO, APOLLO 14 LANDED ON THE MOON.

Commander Alan Shepard and lunar module pilot Edgar Mitchell are 2 of only 12 astronauts who have walked on the moon. All of their names can fit in this grid in just one way. Use the number of letters in each person's name as a clue to where it might fit.

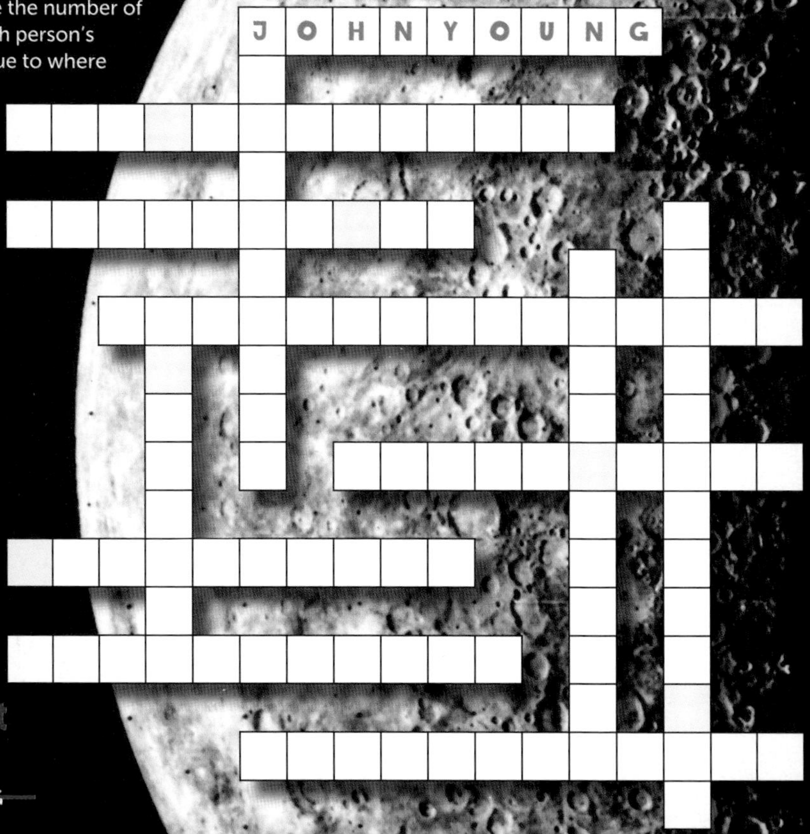

J O H N Y O U N G

Word List

ALAN BEAN

~~JOHN YOUNG~~

BUZZ ALDRIN

DAVID SCOTT

PETE CONRAD

JAMES IRWIN

ALAN SHEPARD

CHARLES DUKE

EUGENE CERNAN

NEIL ARMSTRONG

EDGAR MITCHELL

HARRISON SCHMITT

BONUS!
Unscramble the six shaded letters to spell the name of the space program that sent these men to the moon.

February 23, 1836
185 YEARS AGO, THE SIEGE OF THE ALAMO BEGAN.

A fortified mission known as The Alamo, in San Antonio, Texas, was the site of an important battle in the fight for Texas's independence from Mexico. The Mexican army led by General Antonio López de Santa Anna surrounded two hundred Texian rebels in the fort for 13 days.

The rebels didn't win that battle, but the rallying cry "Remember the Alamo!" inspired them to keep up their fight. Two months later, Texas did become free.

Can you find the 15 objects in this Hidden Pictures puzzle?

Texas was an independent country for nine years before it joined the U.S. in 1845.

The Alamo was a Spanish mission at first and later became a fort.

The famous frontiersman Davy Crockett fought and died at The Alamo.

toothbrush · ice-cream cone · fish · arrow

dog · apple · envelope · thimble · screwdriver

 wrench · key · canoe · artist's brush · comb · acorn

February 3, 2021

NATIONAL GIRLS & WOMEN IN SPORTS DAY

Since 1987, National Girls & Women in Sports Day has spotlighted the history of women's athletics. Held the first Wednesday of February, it also recognizes the progress made since the passing of Title IX of the Education Amendments of 1972, which ensures that students receive educational—and athletic—opportunities free from discrimination based on gender.

Alex, Brooke, and Claire are about to dive into the pool. Circle the correct answers to the questions below about famous female firsts. Then for each answer, shade in a square in the matching swim lane (A, B, or C). The first swimmer to reach the end of her lane wins!

	A	B	C
1. At age 13, Donna de Varona was the youngest to compete on the 1960 U.S. Olympic _____ team.	discus	swimming	boxing
2. Fore! In 2014, 11-year-old Lucy Li was the youngest girl to qualify to compete in the Women's U.S. Open _____ tournament.	snowboard	polo	golf
3. Goal! In 1987 at age 15, Mia Hamm became the youngest member ever of the U.S. women's national ___ team.	soccer	ice hockey	judo
4. Tatyana McFadden was 15 when she won two gold medals at the Paralympics on the U.S. _____ team.	wheelchair racing	wheelchair rugby	wheelchair boccia
5. In 1904, teenager Amanda Clement became baseball's first paid female _____.	cheerleader	quarterback	umpire
6. In 1948, Alice Coachman became the first African American woman to win an Olympic track-and-field gold medal for the _____.	beanbag toss	high jump	bobsled
7. Nadia Comăneci of Romania was the first female to be awarded a perfect score of ___ in an Olympic gymnastics event.	100	10	25
8. Wilma Rudolph, once considered the fastest woman in the world, was the first American woman to win three gold medals in a single Olympics for _____.	running	skiing	curling
9. Janet Guthrie was the first woman racecar driver to earn a starting spot in both the Daytona 500 and the _____ 500.	Cincinnati	Peoria	Indianapolis
10. Tara Lipinski glided into history as the youngest person ever to hold the titles of world and Olympic champion in _____.	ice-skating	basketball	canoeing

February 7, 2021

SUPER BOWL LV

It's been a windy day in the stadium. With the game tied and just a few seconds left on the clock, Chase Gridiron must get to the end zone to score the winning touchdown. Help him find his way around the other players and also the objects that have blown onto the field.

BONUS! Unscramble the letters on the 10 foam fingers to answer the riddle: What do football champions put their cereal in?

_____

SNACK BOWL

Super Bowl Sunday is second only to Thanksgiving as America's biggest food holiday. Maybe that's why February is also National Snack Food Month! Here's what people have eaten, by the numbers, on recent Super Bowl Sundays:

More than **1.35 billion** wings

More than **12.5 million** takeout pizzas

29 million pounds of chips (with dip)

160 million avocados (Holy guacamole!)

3.8 million pounds of popcorn

That's 55 Super Bowls since the first in 1967. Each year, the two winningest teams of the American Football Conference and the National Football Conference face off in a championship game. This year, Super Bowl LV kicks off at Raymond James Stadium in Tampa, Florida.

SUPER BOWL
SUPER
STATS

Tackle this quiz!

1. Which city has hosted the most Super Bowls?

    a. Los Angeles

    b. New Orleans

    c. Miami

2. Which team has competed at the most Super Bowls?

    a. New England Patriots

    b. Pittsburgh Steelers

    c. Dallas Cowboys

3. Which was the most watched Super Bowl of all time?

    a. XLV (2011)

    b. XLIX (2015)

    c. LIII (2019)

4. Who has appeared at the most halftime shows?

    a. World Famed Tiger Marching Band

    b. Justin Timberlake

    c. Beyoncé

OPERA DAY

The first opera was Jacopo Peri's *Dafne*, first performed in Italy in 1597.

An opera is like a play, except all the words are sung, not spoken. Opera singers are known for their powerful voices that can be heard at the back of the opera house without a microphone. Some—including Enrico Caruso, Maria Callas, Luciano Pavarotti, Kiri Te Kanawa, and Jessye Norman—have become as famous around the world as rock stars.

Match the famous opera house to its home country.

Bolshoi Theatre	Argentina
La Scala	Australia
Metropolitan Opera House	Austria
Nhà hát lớn Hà Nội	France
Palais Garnier	Italy
Sydney Opera House	Russia
Teatro Colón	United States
Wiener Staatsoper	Vietnam

KIDS' SCIENCE QUESTIONS

Can a voice get loud enough and high enough that glass can break?

Yes! A singing voice can create sound waves that crack glass. When you tap the side of an empty drinking glass, the sides of the glass bend back and forth—very slightly and very quickly—at the same speed each time and make a sound. This is the natural frequency of the glass. A thicker glass will have a slower natural frequency, and a deeper sound, than a thin glass. When a singer's voice matches the natural frequency of the glass, each sound wave gives a little push; each push adds a little more bend to the glass. If each bend becomes bigger and bigger until the glass cannot bend any farther, it breaks. But you can listen to an opera without worrying about your goldfish bowl! This works only on very thin glass.

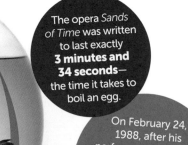

Do Re Mi...

The opera *Sands of Time* was written to last exactly **3 minutes and 34 seconds**—the time it takes to boil an egg.

On February 24, 1988, after his performance in Berlin, Italian opera singer Luciano Pavarotti received **165 curtain calls,** and was applauded for 1 hour and 7 minutes.

February 11
GET OUT YOUR GUITAR DAY

Study these two jam sessions at the B.B. King Museum in Indianola, Mississippi, the hometown of the master blues guitarist. Can you find at least 20 differences?

NAME THAT GUITAR

Some instruments are nearly as famous as the musician who played them. Which guitarist plucked which guitar?

Willie Nelson	**Blackie**
B.B. King	**Red Special**
Eric Clapton	**Frankenstrat**
Eddie Van Halen	**Lucille**
Brian May	**Trigger**

ANATOMY OF A GUITAR

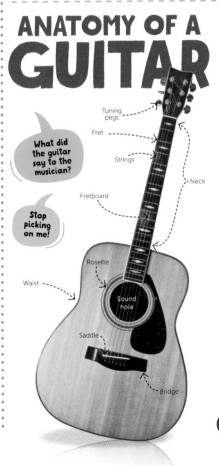

What did the guitar say to the musician?

Stop picking on me!

37

February 16, 2021
PANCAKE DAY

What kind of exercises do pancakes do?
JUMPING JACKS*FLAP

Call it Pancake Tuesday, Shrove Tuesday, Fat Tuesday, or Mardi Gras (French for "Fat Tuesday"), this moveable holiday is celebrated 47 days before Easter Sunday. It started as a way to use up rich foods (eggs, sugar, butter) before the Christian season of Lent, which begins the next day, Ash Wednesday.

You'll flip for these jokes, once you unflip and unscramble each answer!

The world's tallest stack of pancakes was a whopping 213 pancakes, measuring 3 feet and 4 inches!

Who flies through the air covered with maple syrup?
PANCAKE PETER

How is a baseball team like a pancake?
They both need a BATTER GOOD.

What do cowboys put on their pancakes?
MAPLE SIRUP

INTERNATIONAL EATS

On the day or week before Lent, other seasonal specialties are served up around the world, including:

Shrove Tuesday, Australia: Pikelets—small buttermilk pancakes, usually topped with jam, whipped cream, or butter

Día de la Tortilla (Day of the Omelet), Spain: Potato omelet

Mardi Gras, New Orleans: King cake, with a tiny baby-shaped charm baked in to represent Jesus

La Chandeleur (Candlemas, February 2), France: Crepes

Pączki Day, Poland: Pączki (pownch-key), sugar-dusted fried dough filled with jam or custard

CHILI DAY

Chili peppers have more vitamin C than oranges.

What better way to warm up on a chilly February day than with chili? There are many variations, but all chili recipes include peppers. This word grid is peppered with fifteen different kinds. Each will fit into the grid only one way. Use the number of letters in each word as a clue to where it might fit.

Word List

3 letters
AJI

4 letters
BELL
PUYA

5 letters
ANCHO
DATIL
HATCH

6 letters
ROCOTO

7 letters
CAYENNE
POBLANO
SERRANO
TABASCO

8 letters
CHIPOTLE
HABANERO
JALAPEÑO
PIRI PIRI

A chili pepper's heat is ranked on a special scale called the Scoville scale. Bell peppers are up to 100 Scoville heat units, while habanero peppers can be up to **350,000 SCOVILLE** heat units.

Chili Cookoff

Try these on the road.

TEXAS: BOWL O' RED
Leave out the beans or tomatoes; this chili is meat and peppers only.

NEW MEXICO: CHILI VERDE Simmer pork in a verde (green) sauce made from tomatillos and jalapeños.

ILLINOIS: SPRINGFIELD CHILLI
Yes, with two L's

Stir up ground beef, canned tomato sauce, a spice mix that includes chili powder, and a dash of Tabasco.

OHIO: CINCINNATI CHILI It may have a dash of chocolate and cinnamon, but it's almost always on top of spaghetti! Order it "five-way," with spaghetti, chili, onions, beans, and shredded cheddar.

GROUNDHOG DAY

According to German lore, if a hibernating badger sees his shadow on Candlemas Day (a holiday 40 days after Christmas), six more weeks of winter chill are in store. But German immigrants in Pennsylvania soon discovered that badgers are not native to the area, and so groundhogs took over the powers of prognostication.

If Candlemas be fair and bright,

Come, Winter, have another flight;

If Candlemas brings clouds and rain,

Go Winter, and come not again.

—OLD ENGLISH SONG

Punxsutawney Phil is the best-known weathercritter, but he has rivals (and some are more accurate), including Unadilla Bill of Nebraska, Staten Island Chuck of New York, Chuckles of Connecticut, and Pierre C. Shadeaux of Louisiana.

GHD HAT

Since 1887, folks have trekked to Gobbler's Knob to await Phil's prediction. They love to dress up like their favorite forecaster. Now you can too!

1. Cut out eyes, ears, a nose, and teeth from **felt**. To make the ears and teeth stiffer, glue a second piece of felt to each. Draw a line on the teeth with a **marker**.

2. Attach the felt pieces to a **brown hat** using fabric glue. Use **clothespins** to keep the ears in place until they're dry.

Phil is late for his annual appearance on Gobbler's Knob in Punxsutawney, Pennsylvania. Can you help him find the right path aboveground?

The groundhogs' species name *monax* comes from a Native American word that means "the digger."

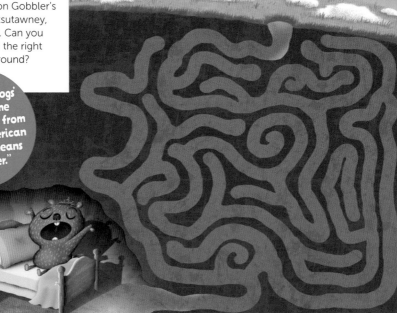

VALENTINE'S DAY

Originally a festival day in ancient Rome, Valentine's Day is still celebrated in Italy, as well as in the United States, Canada, Mexico, the United Kingdom, France, Australia, and Denmark.

February is also American Heart Month. Eat healthily and exercise to keep yours ticking!

Among this Valentine's card-maker's supplies, find:

8 sequins
7 crayons
6 wiggle eyes
5 markers
4 glue sticks
3 paintbrushes
2 pairs of scissors
1 heart-shaped button

BONUS! Find 11 letters and unscramble them to answer this riddle: What kind of flower should you *not* give on Valentine's Day?

_____

What do you call two birds in love?

Tweet-hearts

VALENTINE'S DAY "FORTUNE" HEARTS

1. Cut out a pair of hearts from **cardstock**. Glue the edges together.

2. Write a Valentine's Day "fortune" on a narrow strip of **paper**.

3. Cut the heart down the center, leaving a small connection at the point.

4. Glue the left side of the fortune into the left half of the heart. Fold the fortune and insert it into the right half of the heart.

5. Write a name on a small strip of paper. Glue it to the heart to hold the left and right sides together.

Natalie

Sam

Ryan

May you always be surrounded by good friends. Valentine!

About 145 million greeting cards are exchanged every Valentine's Day in the U.S. alone.

WASHINGTON'S BIRTHDAY

Since 1885, this federal holiday has honored the February 22 birthday of the first U.S. president. The date was later moved to the third Monday of the month to give government workers—and schoolkids—a three-day weekend. Today it is often called Presidents' Day and celebrates Abraham Lincoln (born February 12) and all U.S. presidents, past and present. However, officially, it still is just George Washington's day.

Spell out the last name of each U.S. president below to find something that was named for him or built in his honor. Start each name on a letter in the yellow column, then move in any direction, including diagonally. We've found HOOVER for you.

Two other presidents were also born in February: William Henry Harrison (February 9, 1773) and Ronald Reagan (February 6, 1911).

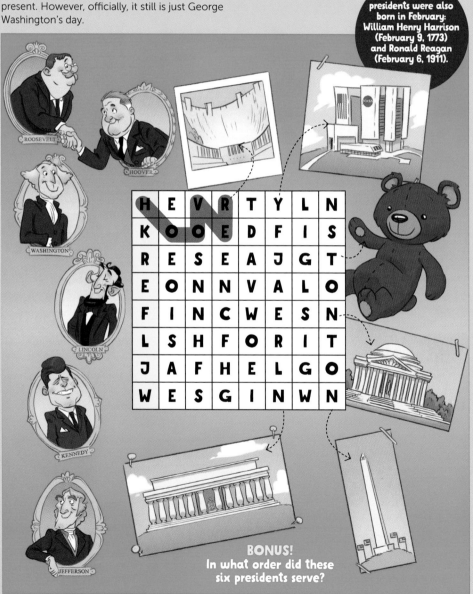

BONUS!
In what order did these six presidents serve?

PURIM

This Jewish holiday honors Queen Esther, who persuaded her husband, King Ahasuerus, to save the Jewish people of Persia from the villain Haman. It's a festive day, during which people dress up in costumes, exchange gifts, and give to the poor.

From the Middle Ages onward, actors have performed funny plays called *spiels* that tell the Purim story, known as the Megillah. (*Spiel* means "play" or "skit" in Yiddish, the language Jews spoke in Central and Eastern Europe.) To this day, the name *Haman* is met with boos and the sounds of *groggers* (noisemakers) during these plays— and even during religious services.

MAKE HAMANTASCHEN

Hamantaschen, which means "Haman's pockets" in Yiddish, are traditional treats eaten at Purim. This three-sided pastry looks like the hat that Haman supposedly wore.

Ask an adult for help using the stove, food processor, and oven.

FILLING*

1. Place 1 package (16 ounces) **pitted prunes** in a saucepan and cover with water. Add ½ teaspoon **cinnamon**, 1 tablespoon **sugar**, and 1 tablespoon **lemon juice**. Simmer until fruit is soft and mushy. (Add more water if needed.) Let cool.

2. With an adult's help, chop 1 cup **shelled walnuts or other nuts** in a food processor or blender. Add prune mixture and mix well. Set aside.

    * Prune butter or apple butter can be substituted for prune-nut filling

DOUGH

1. With a mixing bowl, cream together 1 stick **softened butter or margarine** and ¾ cup **sugar.**

2. Beat 3 **egg yolks** in a separate bowl and add to the butter-sugar mixture. Add 1 cup **sour cream**. Mix well.

3. In a large bowl, sift together 3 cups **flour**, 2 teaspoons **baking powder**, and ¼ teaspoon **baking soda**. Add to the butter-sugar mixture. Then add 1 teaspoon **vanilla** and ½ teaspoon **grated orange rind**. Mix well.

4. On a floured board, roll out the dough about ¼-inch thick. If the dough is too sticky, cover and refrigerate for a few hours before rolling out.

5. Cut into 3-inch circles with a cookie cutter or a drinking glass turned upside down.

6. Place a teaspoon of filling in the center of each circle. Fold up two sides of the circle and pinch together. Fold up the third side and pinch together with the other two sides to form a triangle, leaving the center open.

7. Place the hamantaschen on greased baking sheets and into the oven. Bake for about 20 minutes at 350°F, until lightly browned.

WORLD WETLANDS DAY

Wetlands are complex habitats found all over the planet, from the polar regions to the tropics, inland and along the coast. They include marshes, swamps, bogs, and lagoons. These valuable resources protect against flooding, help maintain water quality, and provide a habitat to wildlife.

Find the one path from START to FINISH. Then use the letters along the correct path to spell the name of an endangered Everglades animal.

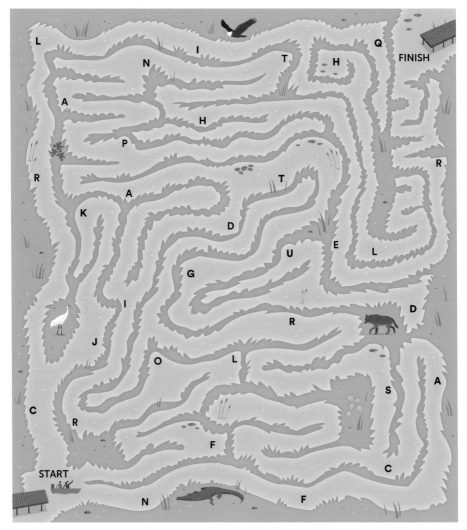

WETLANDS YOU CAN VISIT

Kenai National Wildlife Refuge, Alaska

White River National Wildlife Refuge, Arkansas

Merced National Wildlife Refuge, California

Saratoga Springs (Death Valley National Park), California

Everglades National Park, Florida

Okefenokee National Wildlife Refuge, Georgia/Florida

Cumberland Island National Seashore, Georgia

Klamath Marsh National Wildlife Refuge, Oregon

Congaree National Park, South Carolina

Great Dismal Swamp, Virginia/North Carolina

NATIONAL PERIODIC TABLE DAY

Using the periodic table, combine these elements' symbols to make a word.

barium + cobalt + nitrogen =
_____

barium + sodium + sodium =
_____

calcium + neodymium + yttrium =
_____

molybdenum + uranium + selenium =
_____

americium + erbium + iodine + calcium =
_____

helium + lithium + cobalt + platinum + erbium =
_____

fluorine + uranium + nitrogen =
_____

hint

OMg! (That's oxygen and magnesium, to scientists.) Today marks the publication date of chemist John Newlands's first periodic table of elements in 1863. It's also the day before the birthday of Dmitri Mendeleev, a Russian chemist who, in 1869, came up with a way to organize the periodic table by each element's atomic mass (the weight of one atom of the element).

Now, make up your own elemental equation!

We would have put a chemistry joke here, but we didn't think we'd get a reaction.

1 H Hydrogen																	2 He Helium
3 Li Lithium	4 Be Beryllium											5 B Boron	6 C Carbon	7 N Nitrogen	8 O Oxygen	9 F Fluorine	10 Ne Neon
11 Na Sodium	12 Mg Magnesium											13 Al Aluminium	14 Si Silicon	15 P Phosphorus	16 S Sulfur	17 Cl Chlorine	18 Ar Argon
19 K Potassium	20 Ca Calcium	21 Sc Scandium	22 Ti Titanium	23 V Vanadium	24 Cr Chromium	25 Mn Manganese	26 Fe Iron	27 Co Cobalt	28 Ni Nickel	29 Cu Copper	30 Zn Zinc	31 Ga Gallium	32 Ge Germanium	33 As Arsenic	34 Se Selenium	35 Br Bromine	36 Kr Krypton
37 Rb Rubidium	38 Sr Strontium	39 Y Yttrium	40 Zr Zirconium	41 Nb Niobium	42 Mo Molybdenum	43 Tc Technetium	44 Ru Ruthenium	45 Rh Rhodium	46 Pd Palladium	47 Ag Silver	48 Cd Cadmium	49 In Indium	50 Sn Tin	51 Sb Antimony	52 Te Tellurium	53 I Iodine	54 Xe Xenon
55 Cs Caesium	56 Ba Barium	57–71 Lanthanides	72 Hf Hafnium	73 Ta Tantalum	74 W Tungsten	75 Re Rhenium	76 Os Osmium	77 Ir Iridium	78 Pt Platinum	79 Au Gold	80 Hg Mercury	81 Tl Thallium	82 Pb Lead	83 Bi Bismuth	84 Po Polonium	85 At Astatine	86 Rn Radon
87 Fr Francium	88 Ra Radium	89–103 Actinides	104 Rf Rutherfordium	105 Db Dubnium	106 Sg Seaborgium	107 Bh Bohrium	108 Hs Hassium	109 Mt Meitnerium	110 Ds Darmstadtium	111 Rg Roentgenium	112 Cn Copernicium	113 Nh Nihonium	114 Fl Flerovium	115 Mc Moscovium	116 Lv Livermorium	117 Ts Tennessine	118 Og Oganesson

57 La Lanthanum	58 Ce Cerium	59 Pr Praseodymium	60 Nd Neodymium	61 Pm Promethium	62 Sm Samarium	63 Eu Europium	64 Gd Gadolinium	65 Tb Terbium	66 Dy Dysprosium	67 Ho Holmium	68 Er Erbium	69 Tm Thulium	70 Yb Ytterbium	71 Lu Lutetium
89 Ac Actinium	90 Th Thorium	91 Pa Protactinium	92 U Uranium	93 Np Neptunium	94 Pu Plutonium	95 Am Americium	96 Cm Curium	97 Bk Berkelium	98 Cf Californium	99 Es Einsteinium	100 Fm Fermium	101 Md Mendelevium	102 No Nobelium	103 Lr Lawrencium

February 3, 2021
SETSUBUN

Setsubun (節分, or "seasonal division") marks the day before the start of spring according to the Japanese lunar calendar. For many centuries, the people of Japan have been performing these Setsubun rituals to chase away evil spirits, or *oni*, at home and in temples to ensure good luck in the year ahead. Here's how to get into the non-evil spirit:

***ONI* IT!** One family member wears the demon mask.

TOSS IT! In the *mamemaki* (bean-throwing) ceremony, roasted soybeans, gathered in an *asakemasu* (a wooden box), are thrown at the oni.

SHOUT IT! While flinging, chant *"Oni wa soto! Fuku wa uchi!"* ("Demons out! Happiness in!")

CHASE IT! Once the oni is outside, slam the door!

CHEW IT! Afterward, pick up and eat the number of beans equal to your age, plus one.

QUIET! Eat an entire uncut sushi roll, *in silence*, facing toward the year's "lucky direction." (The direction depends on the zodiac sign of the year. For 2021, it's south-southeast!)

February 6
NATIONAL CHOPSTICKS DAY

The earliest chopsticks were likely in use around 5,000 years ago!

Today, try eating all your meals (okay, maybe not a bowl of soup or a sandwich) with chopsticks. Here's how.

1 Tuck the first (lower) chopstick in the nook between your thumb and your index (pointer) finger. Hold it against your thumb and bent ring finger. This chopstick does not move while eating.

2 Hold the second (upper) chopstick between your index finger and thumb, as you would if holding a pencil—only higher up. Brace this chopstick against your middle finger.

Hold the chopsticks near the tops, toward the wider ends, with the tips lined up.

3 Open up the chopsticks by moving just the upper chopstick with your index and middle finger.

4 Moving the upper chopstick down with your index and middle fingers, close the chopsticks over your morsel of food.

February 21, 2021
WORLD WHALE DAY

Thar she blows! The third Sunday of February is a great time to spout off your knowledge of these magnificent marine mammals.

What do you call a whale that talks a lot?

To solve the riddle, use the fractions of the words below.

First ¾ of BLUE

Middle ⅓ of BUBBLE

First ⅖ of ERASE

First ½ of MOON

Last ⅓ of YOU

Last ½ of WITH

A _ _ _ _ _ _ _

_ _ _ _ _

This ocean giant is not just the biggest whale; it's the biggest creature on Earth ever. It can grow up to 100 feet long—more than the length of two school buses.

Whirled Whales

There are dozens of species of whales. Unscramble each set of letters to reveal the names of a few.

elbu _____

gabule _____

thirg _____

phabmuck _____

argy _____

inf _____

kenim _____

rawlhan _____

February 23
INTERNATIONAL DOG BISCUIT APPRECIATION DAY

Before 1860, dogs ate whatever was tossed their way. Then American electrician James Spratt baked up a cake-like mix of grains, beetroot, vegetables, and "the dried unsalted gelatinous parts of Prairie Beef." He called these first dog biscuits by the not-very-appetizing name Meat Fibrine Dog Cakes, but they were a hit with dogs and their owners.

Follow the biscuits and other doggie items to help Pugsley find the right path to his doghouse. The symbols will tell you which way to move.

| RIGHT | UP | DOWN | LEFT |

PATH 1	PATH 2	PATH 3	PATH 4	PATH 5

Take a spin around the globe to see how

February 6
WAITANGI DAY

On this day in 1840, the British government and 540 Māori chiefs signed the Treaty of Waitangi (named after the region where this took place) to create the nation of New Zealand. Māori cultural performances, speeches from Māori and Pakeha (European) dignitaries, and a naval salute are part of the activities.

1. Roll **polymer clay** into a 9-inch-long "snake," wide at one end and thin at the other.

2. On **foil** on a **baking sheet**, arrange the shape into a spiral. With an adult's help, bake the clay according to the instructions. Let the spiral cool.

3. Loop **string** or **cord** to make a lanyard.

Make a Māori koru pendant, inspired by the art of the Māori people of New Zealand.

Red is the Chinese color of luck!

February 12, 2021
CHINESE NEW YEAR

Happy 4719—the Year of the Ox! This holiday, known as the Spring Festival in China, celebrates the beginning of a new year on the Chinese calendar and lasts for 15 days. People celebrate by visiting their families, decorating their houses, and setting off fireworks and firecrackers. Kids often receive a gift of money in a red envelope.
Join the dragon-dance parade and find the 12 hidden objects in this Hidden Pictures puzzle.

THE WORLD

To celebrate Fastelavn, Danes eat fastelavnsboller, sweet buns filled with cream.

February 14, 2021

📍 FASTELAVN

One popular tradition to celebrate this pre-Lenten festival is for Danish children to dress up in fanciful costumes and try to "beat the cat out of the barrel." Don't worry—the wooden barrel only has images of black cats, which represent evil spirits. The person who knocks out the bottom of the barrel is crowned *Kattedronning* (Cat Queen), and the person who knocks down the last piece of the barrel is crowned *Kattekonge* (Cat King).

February 27, 2021

📍 NAVAM FULL MOON POYA DAY

This Buddhist holiday usually takes place on the first full moon in February. The tiny country of Sri Lanka, a raindrop-shaped island off the tip of India, celebrates in a big way: Its capital, Colombo, hosts a joyous parade, or *perahera*, featuring thousands of fire dancers, flag bearers, traditional dancers, musicians, and dozens of dazzlingly dressed elephants. Can you find where the 3 jigsaw pieces fit into this photo of a typical Navam Perahera sight?

Dr. Seuss Day

Celebrate the birthday of Theodor Seuss Geisel by reading one of the 60+ books he wrote.

2

"If Pets Had Thumbs" Day

This day gets four thumbs up!

3

NATIONAL PIG DAY

Oink, oink, oink!

1

Ring, ring, ring! On this day in 1876, Alexander Graham Bell received a patent for the telephone.

7

INTERNATIONAL WOMEN'S DAY

8

Hello, dolly! In 1959, the Barbie doll debuted at the American Toy Fair.

9

INTERNATIONAL BAGPIPE DAY

10

Daylight Saving Begins

Don't be late! "Spring" forward your clocks one hour today.

14

National Napping Day

You snooze, you ̶l̶o̶s̶e̶ win!

15

Day of the Book Smugglers (Lithuania)

In the 1800s, *knygnešiai* smuggled books into the country to help preserve the Lithuanian language.

16

SAINT PATRICK'S DAY

17

Harmony Day (Australia)

The message of this day, which celebrates diversity and inclusiveness, is "Everyone belongs."

21

World Water Day

How many times did you use water today?

22

National Chip and Dip Day

23

National Cheesesteak Day

As they say in Philly, do you want yours "wit" or "witout" (onions)?

24

Palm Sunday

28

Youth Day (Taiwan)

This day commemorates the victims of the Second Guangzhou uprising in 1911.

29

3, 2, 1, blastoff! In 2021, the James Webb Telescope is scheduled to launch.

30

NATIONAL CRAYON DAY

Is it "cran," "cray-ahn," "cray-awn," or "crown"?

31

MARCH

THURSDAY

Marching Band Day

Today's the perfect day to grab an instrument and "march forth!"

4

FRIDAY

Swing those hips! In 1963, the Hula-Hoop—named after the famous Hawaiian dance—was patented.

5

SATURDAY

NATIONAL OREO DAY

6

Moshoeshoe Day (Lesotho)

This holiday honors King Moshoeshoe I, the founder and national hero of Lesotho.

11

GIRL SCOUTS' BIRTHDAY

Girl Scouts was founded on this day in 1912.

12

Keep those ears warm! In 1877, earmuffs, known then as "ear mufflers," were patented.

13

Far out! In 1965, Alexei Leonov became the first man to walk in space.

18

NATIONAL LET'S LAUGH DAY

19

First Day of Spring

What is the best smell in spring?

20

Ciao, Venezia! In 421—1,600 years ago!—the city of Venice was founded at the stroke of noon.

25

Make Up Your Own Holiday Day

You know what to do!

26

PASSOVER

begins at sunset.

27

The weather in

_____
(WHERE YOU LIVE)

on March 20, 2021, is

_____ .

BIRTHSTONES
AQUAMARINE

BLOODSTONE

FLOWER
DAFFODIL

ZODIAC SIGNS

♓ PISCES: FEBRUARY 19–MARCH 20

♈ ARIES: MARCH 21–APRIL 19

Kathryn Bigelow

Marie Curie

Mo'ne Davis

Amelia Earhart

WOMEN'S HISTORY MONTH

Celebrate by matching each pioneering woman with her historic achievement.

Aretha Franklin

1. Who was the first woman to win a Nobel Prize (1903)?

2. Who was the first woman to make a nonstop solo airplane flight across the Atlantic Ocean (1932)?

3. Who was the first woman to fly into outer space (1963)?

4. Who was the first woman to reach the summit of Mount Everest (1975)?

5. Who was the first woman to serve on the Supreme Court (1981)?

Sandra Day O'Connor

6. Who was the first woman to be inducted into the Rock & Roll Hall of Fame (1987)?

7. Who was the first woman to win an IndyCar Series race (2008)?

Danica Patrick

8. Who was the first woman to win an Academy Award for Best Director (2010)?

9. Who was the first girl to pitch a shutout in the Little League World Series (2014)?

INTERNATIONAL WOMEN'S DAY IS MARCH 8. This global day celebrates women's achievements and calls for gender equality.

Junko Tabei

Valentina Tereshkova

NATIONAL UMBRELLA MONTH

Knock, knock.
Who's there?
Butter.
Butter who?
Butter bring an umbrella— it looks like rain.

Can you tell what's alike in each row of umbrellas, across, down, and diagonally?

Since the invention of the basic umbrella more than four thousand years ago, umbrellas have been made from lots of different materials. Handles and frames have been made from:

WHALEBONE
ALUMINUM
BAMBOO
FIBERGLASS
STEEL

Canopies have been made from:

FEATHERS
SILK
GINGHAM
OILCLOTH
NYLON
PLASTIC

Read the letters in blue from top to bottom to reveal an American slang term for *umbrella*.

NATIONAL MUSIC IN OUR SCHOOLS MONTH

Celebrate by finding these six WORDS (not pictures) hidden in the scene below. Can you find BEAT, CHORUS, CONDUCT, MUSICIAN, NOTE, and PIANO?

The most popular instruments to play are:
1. Piano
2. Guitar
3. Violin
4. Drums
5. Saxophone

NATIONAL NOODLE MONTH

No one knows for sure where noodles were first invented, but they are believed to have existed in some form in ancient China and Greece. Today, there are all noodles of all shapes and sizes, including gluten-free and wheat-free versions and even noodles made from vegetables.

Use your noodle to take this quiz and figure out which facts are true and which are impastas!

T F In Italian, *orecchiette* means "little ears" and *linguine* means "little tongues."

T F Noodles that are cooked *al dente* means they were cooked in a pot without any dents in it.

T F Thomas Jefferson helped popularize macaroni and cheese by serving it to his dinner guests.

T F Although used interchangeably, pasta and noodles are technically two different foods.

T F The name *macaroni* comes from the song "Yankee Doodle."

T F In Japan, somen noodles are hung outside to dry in the sun.

T F It is scientifically impossible to eat spaghetti and meatballs without making a mess.

T F In 1848, the first commercial pasta plant in the U.S. was founded in Brooklyn.

NATIONAL PEANUT MONTH

Make these Peanutty Sesame Noodles to celebrate!

Ask an adult to help with anything hot or sharp.

1. Peel and cut 1 **cucumber** into matchsticks. Wash and chop 2 **green onions**.

2. Toast 4 teaspoons **sesame seeds** in a small pan over medium heat, shaking occasionally, until they darken and become fragrant.

3. Put ½ cup **peanut butter**, 2 tablespoons **brown sugar**, 3 tablespoons **low-sodium soy sauce**, 2 tablespoons **sesame oil**, 2 tablespoons **distilled white vinegar**, and ¼ cup **water** into a blender. Blend until smooth, 20–30 seconds.

4. Put 8 ounces of **cooked spaghetti** into a large bowl and add the peanut sauce. Stir.

5. Divide the noodles into four bowls. Top with the cucumber, green onions, and sesame seeds.

Wash your hands before and after handling food.

NATIONAL CRAFT MONTH

Get crafty and make some spring things!

TULIP PENCIL BOX

1. For flower stems, **paint** several **cardboard tubes** green.

2. For a window box, cut the top off a **snack box**. Cover it with **paper**.

3. Cut leaves and tulips from paper. Glue them to the stems. Glue

4. Store **pencils** in the stems.

FLYING CARDINAL

Here's how you put it together:

1. Fold red **poster board** in half. Cut out a cardinal's body, keeping part of the fold uncut at the top.

2. Use a **marker** to draw the bird's face. Add **wiggle eyes**.

3. Cut out wings from poster board. Cut a slit in the body. Insert the wings. Use two small pieces of poster board to cover the ends of the slit.

4. Find the center of balance by holding the top of the bird with two fingers. Punch a hole in that spot. Tie on a **yarn** hanger.

"FEED THE FROG" GAME

Use a plastic spoon to flick the fly!

1. Cover a **large round container** with green **paper**.

2. Draw a frog with a large mouth on **poster board**. Cut out the frog. Decorate it with colored paper and **markers**. Glue the frog to the container.

3. To make "flies," crinkle small pieces of black paper.

To Play:
Play with a friend. Whoever gets a fly into the frog's mouth in the fewest flicks wins.

March 3, 1931

90 YEARS AGO, "THE STAR-SPANGLED BANNER" BECAME THE OFFICIAL NATIONAL ANTHEM.

This silly version has some WRONG words.
Can you circle the 10 words that are incorrect?
Then sing the real words.

O say, can you see, by the dawn's early flight,
What so proudly we hailed at the flashlight's last gleaming?
Whose broad pipes and bright stars, through the perilous fight,
O'er the sheepdogs we watched, were so gallantly streaming?
And the rockets' gray glare, the bombs bursting in air,
Gave foolproof through the night that our flag was still there.
O hey, does that star-spangled banana yet wave
O'er the land of the three and the comb of the brave?

Written as a poem by Francis Scott Key in 1814 and set to a melody from an English song, "The Star-Spangled Banner" was popular throughout the nineteenth century. But it wasn't until President Herbert Hoover signed a bill into law on March 3, 1931, that it became the official national anthem.

Although the presidential inauguration is now January 20, March 4 was the official inauguration date until 1933.

Here are some inauguration firsts:

March 4, 1801

220 YEARS AGO, the Marine Band played at its first inauguration: Thomas Jefferson's.

March 4, 1841

180 YEARS AGO, William Henry Harrison set the record for the longest inaugural address with a nearly two-hour-long speech.

March 4, 1921

100 YEARS AGO, Warren G. Harding was the first president-elect to ride to his inauguration in an automobile.

Beyoncé sang the national anthem at Barack Obama's second inauguration in 2013.

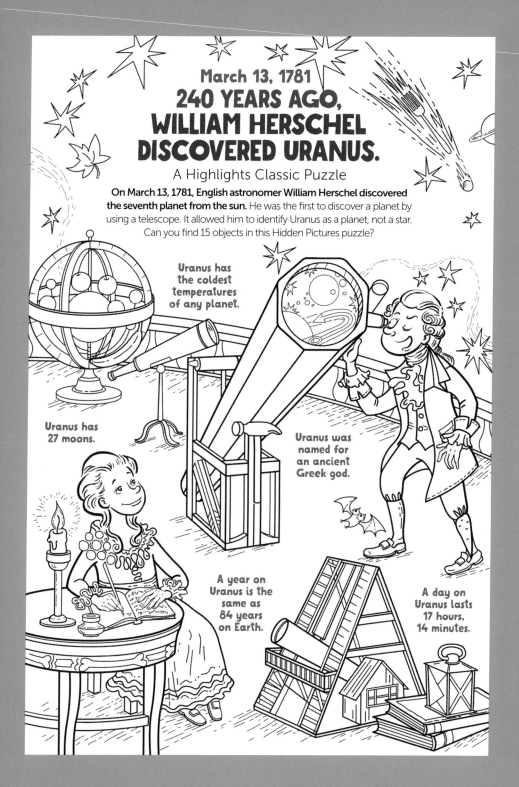

March 13, 1781
240 YEARS AGO, WILLIAM HERSCHEL DISCOVERED URANUS.
A Highlights Classic Puzzle

On March 13, 1781, English astronomer William Herschel discovered the seventh planet from the sun. He was the first to discover a planet by using a telescope. It allowed him to identify Uranus as a planet, not a star. Can you find 15 objects in this Hidden Pictures puzzle?

Uranus has the coldest temperatures of any planet.

Uranus has 27 moons.

Uranus was named for an ancient Greek god.

A year on Uranus is the same as 84 years on Earth.

A day on Uranus lasts 17 hours, 14 minutes.

In this picture, find the arrow, banana, candle, carrot, cherries, dog bone, envelope, fishhook, fork, french fries, grapes, hammer, leaf, paper airplane, and ruler.

MARCH MADNESS

Throughout the month of March, 64 women's teams and 68 men's teams will play in a single-elimination **National Collegiate Athletic Association (NCAA) Division I Basketball Tournament**, also known as March Madness. The men's championship game will take place on April 5, 2021, at the Lucas Oil Stadium in Indianapolis, Indiana. The women's championship game will take place on April 4, 2021, at the Alamodome in San Antonio, Texas.

TOP CHAMPS

These teams have won the most championships:

Men's NCAA Division I (since 1939)
1. UCLA Bruins (11 wins)
2. Kentucky Wildcats (8)
3. North Carolina Tar Heels (6)

Women's NCAA Division I (since 1982)
1. UConn Huskies (11 wins)
2. Tennessee Lady Vols (3)
3. Baylor Lady Bears (3)

BASKETBALL OR BASEBALL?

Which sport is each clue about? Take a shot or a swing, and circle the correct answer.

1. Gym-class variations of this sport include "H-O-R-S-E" and "Around the World."

2. Two teams of five players oppose each other in this sport.

3. This sport's championship series was first played in 1903.

4. James Naismith invented this sport in 1891.

5. There's no clock on during this sport.

6. This sport has plays called alley-oop, pick and roll, and V-cut.

7. German teams that play this sport include the Mainz Athletics and the Solingen Alligators.

8. Chinese teams that play this sport include the Beijing Ducks and the Shanghai Sharks.

What made the chicken good at basketball?

He was great at fowl shots.

March 2021

WORLD BASEBALL CLASSIC

To warm up for the 2021 World Baseball Classic, write each set of colored letters on the corresponding lines to find out the winners of the 2017 series.

UPNNEUJIETRTEAHDPETRSOLTRAAATINECDSONS

1: _____

2: _____

3: _____

4: _____

READ ACROSS AMERICA DAY

These four friends love to read! Using the clues below, can you figure out what book subject each person likes and how many books he or she checked out of the library?

Use the chart to keep track of your answers. Put an X in each box that can't be true and an O in boxes that match.

	Darryl	Keiko	Gunner	Ximena
Sports				
History				
Outer Space				
Animals				
Two				
Four				
Six				
Eight				

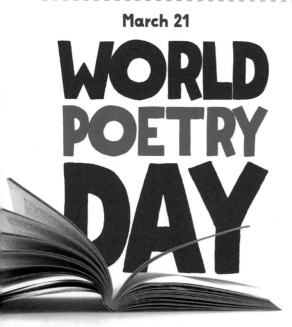

- Darryl checked out twice as many books as Gunner.
- Keiko checked out six fewer books than Darryl.
- All of Ximena's books are about horses.
- Keiko showed her soccer stories to the boy whose four books were about astronauts.

WORLD POETRY DAY

Poetry Superlatives

The **LONGEST** poem ever written—a Sanskrit epic called the *Mahābhārata*—is more than **200,000 lines**. That's **1.8 million words**!

The **OLDEST** poem ever written—*The Epic of Gilgamesh* from ancient Mesopotamia—was written in Sumerian around 2150–1400 BCE. That's **more than 3,000 years ago**!

The **OLDEST** surviving poem written in English is *Beowulf*, which was composed between 700 to 750 AD in Old English.

WORLD THEATER DAY

Have you been to a theater? If so, what did you see?

If you could write your own play, what would it be about?

World Theater Day is celebrated annually on March 27 with theater events around the world. Theater people can be pretty superstitious, so read up on these seven tips to avoid bad luck in the theater.

1. **"Good luck" is bad luck!** Say "break a leg" to wish someone in theater well.

2. **Leave the ghost light on.** A single lit bulb upstage center helps ward off theater ghosts—and helps the crew see in the dark!

3. **Don't say "Macbeth!"** To avoid saying the famous Shakespeare play's title, which supposedly brings bad luck, theater people call it "The Scottish Play."

4. **Mirror, mirror, on the wall—not on stage.** If a mirror breaks on stage, it brings bad luck, so most sets don't include real mirrors.

5. **Don't whistle while you work!** Stagehands once communicated with coded whistles, so whistling backstage could lead to accidents.

6. **What's under your pillow?** Superstitious performers sleep with a script under their pillow to help them memorize lines faster. Just don't try it for your next history exam!

7. **Lucky lefty.** In theater, the left foot is luckier than the right foot, so actors should always walk left foot first into a dressing room.

Top Act

Here's a list of the top 10 most frequently performed musicals in North American high schools, with a twist—we replaced one word in six of the titles with a synonym in blue. Can you figure out the real names of the six silly musicals?

What performances did your school do this year?

1. **Beauty and the Monstrosity**

   _____

2. **The Addams Clan**

   _____

3. **The Miniature Mermaid**

   _____

4. **Into the Forest**

   _____

5. **Cinderella**

6. **Shrek**

7. **Seussical**

8. **Little Boutique of Horrors**

   _____

9. **The Magician of Oz**

   _____

10. **Annie**

NATIONAL PI DAY

The largest pumpkin pie ever made weighed 3,699 pounds and was 20 feet across.

March 14 (3/14) is celebrated as Pi Day because 3, 1, and 4 are the first three digits of the mathematical symbol π.

Seventeen types of pie are hidden up, down, across, backwards, and diagonally. Dig in!

```
        C O C O N U T
      Y I C E C R E A M
    Y P M I N C E M E A T
  U O E P R U N E W H I P R
  T U A Y E L E M O N C E T
H C R N R E Q B N A P E A R B
Q H T U R T R K E Y L I M E P
Y E E T E A M Y     N A C E P
U R E B B L P L           E O
M R T U Q O U F             S
Y H T A C M O
R A T P O P O T
  H E P H K H B
    R L C I S L
    E A N E X
```

What's the best thing to put in a pie?

WORD LIST:

APPLE	MINCEMEAT
BERRY	PEACH
CHERRY	PEANUT BUTTER
CHOCOLATE	PEAR
COCONUT	PECAN
ICE CREAM	PRUNE WHIP
KEY LIME	PUMPKIN
LEMON	RHUBARB
	SHOOFLY

A Never-Ending Number

The number pi is infinitely long, but that hasn't stopped people from trying to calculate it. A new record was set in March 2019 when Emma Haruka Iwao calculated pi to 31,415,926,535,897 digits! Why is that number significant? Here are the first 100 digits:

3.14159265358979323846264338327950288419716939937510582097494459230781640628620899862803482534211706 7

More Treats for Your Tongue

Say these tongue twisters three times, fast!

Three slices of pumpkin pie, please!

Pecan pie is perfect for a party.

Crisscrossed crispy piecrust.

March 25

INTERNATIONAL WAFFLE DAY

Here are four meals you can make to celebrate. Rate each recipe you try by filling in the stars.

☆☆☆☆
Cornbread-and-Chili Dinner

Pour cornbread batter onto a waffle iron. Cook until lightly browned, about 1½–2 minutes. Top with chili, cheese, lettuce, and sour cream.

☆☆☆☆
Waffled-Egg Breakfast

Beat 3 eggs. Add salt and pepper. Pour the eggs onto a waffle iron. Cook through, about 2–3 minutes.

☆☆☆☆
Mini-Pizza Lunch

Add pizza sauce, cheese, and mini pepperoni to the bottom half of a refrigerated biscuit. Put on the top half and squeeze the edges together. Cook in a waffle iron for 1–1½ minutes.

☆☆☆☆
S'more Dessert

Mix chocolate chips and mini marshmallows into waffle batter. Cook until the waffles are done.

We hope you're hungry! There are lots of fun food holidays in March. Here are just a few:

March 1
NATIONAL PEANUT BUTTER LOVERS' DAY

There are about 540 peanuts in a 12-ounce jar of peanut butter.

March 7
NATIONAL CEREAL DAY

Most Americans eat around 160 bowls of cereal per year.

March 16
NATIONAL ARTICHOKE HEARTS DAY

Artichokes are flowers. They're part of the daisy family.

March 26
NATIONAL SPINACH DAY

If you see *Florentine* on a menu or in a recipe, there's probably spinach in the dish.

SAINT PATRICK'S

Follow the rainbow that leads to the leprechaun's pot of gold.

DID YOU KNOW?

Chicago holds one of the largest Saint Patrick's Day parades in the United States. Each year, the Chicago River is dyed a brilliant shade of emerald green as part of the city's celebration.

DAY

Saint Patrick's Day is celebrated in more countries than any other national festival.

The chance of finding a four-leaf clover is said to be 1 in 10,000!

Míle

Céad

Fáilte

Double-the-Luck Necklace

1. Cut a long piece of **ribbon**. Glue the middle around a **plastic bottle cap**. Knot the ribbon at the top of the cap. Tie the ends to make a necklace.

2. Glue a **penny**, heads up, to the inside of the bottle cap.

3. For the clover, glue four **craft gems** to the outside of the cap. Use a **marker** to draw a stem.

Legend says that four-leaf clovers and heads-up pennies are lucky!

Irish Welcome Sign

Céad míle fáilte (kade meel-a fall-cha) means "a hundred thousand welcomes" in Irish. Irish is one of the oldest written languages in the world. Today, Irish is still spoken and it is one of the official languages of Ireland and Europe. The word shamrock comes from an Irish word for "clover."

1. Draw and cut out matching shamrock shapes from **craft foam** and **cardboard**. Glue them together.

2. Use **glitter glue** to write *Céad Míle Fáilte* on the foam. Decorate the shamrock with craft-foam shapes.

3. Tape a **yarn** hanger to the back.

KIDS' SCIENCE QUESTIONS

How do you find the end of a rainbow?

A rainbow is sunlight that has been bent and reflected to you by raindrops. As drops fall through the sunlight, they bend light that enters them, separating it into its different colors—red, orange, yellow, green, blue, indigo, and violet. Some of this light is reflected inside the drops and heads toward you.

A rainbow you see is not the same one seen by your friend. Because you're in different positions, the colors reflected to your eyes and to your friend's eyes come from different drops. It appears to you that the rainbow forms an arch that ends, but where you can't see the rainbow anymore and where your friend can't see the rainbow anymore are different places.

A complete rainbow would be a full circle if the earth weren't in the way. You would have to be high above the earth to see more than half a rainbow. Pilots report seeing complete circular rainbows if the conditions are just right, but it's not very common.

March 20, 2021

COUNTDOWN TO SPRING

What is your favorite flower?

How do you welcome spring?

6 POPULAR SPRING FLOWERS

crocus

daffodil ----->

tulip

lilac

lily

iris

5 CUTEST RABBIT BREEDS

lionhead rabbit

Netherland dwarf rabbit

mini lop rabbit

rex rabbit -------->

Polish rabbit

4 WAYS TO CELEBRATE SPRINGTIME CRITTERS

Sing back to the robins.

Sketch the creatures that live near your home.

Write a story from a toad's point of view.

Invent dance moves inspired by inchworms.

3 SPRING IDIOMS

"full of the joys of spring"

"spring chicken"

"spring fever"

2 SPRING TONGUE TWISTERS

Parker planted plenty of peas.

Spring makes Spike and Mike want to bike.

1 FIRST DAY OF SPRING

In the Northern Hemisphere, the vernal equinox signals the beginning of spring. On this day, the amount of daylight is almost exactly the same as the amount of darkness. The word equinox comes from the Latin for "equal night."

March 27–April 4, 2021
PASSOVER

Every spring, a special meal called a *seder* occurs on the first night of the Jewish holiday of Passover. At the seder, everyone at the table takes part in telling the story of how the Jewish people escaped slavery, using a guide called the *Haggadah*. There is food and song. There are prayers for remembering what happened long ago and prayers that there will be no slavery anywhere at any time for any people.

In the 1930s, a rabbi lobbied Coca-Cola to make a kosher version of its soda for Passover. He was successful, and the company still makes Kosher Coca-Cola today.

1 ROASTED EGG The roasted egg symbolizes life.

2 MAROR This bitter root represents the bitterness of slavery. Horseradish is often used.

3 ROASTED LAMB BONE This bone symbolizes the lamb eaten quickly when the Jews fled Egypt.

4 CHAROSET (hah-ROH-set) An apple-and-nut mixture represents the mortar made by the Jews when they toiled as slaves in Egypt. The sweetness of the apple symbolizes the promise of a better world.

5 KARPAS These greens, usually parsley, symbolize freedom. The parsley is dipped in salt water, which stands for the tears of slavery. In addition, karpas represents spring, because Passover is also a celebration of the spring harvest.

6 PESACH These three Hebrew letters spell *Pesach*, or *Passover*.

The youngest child traditionally asks four questions at a Passover seder. The last one is "Why do we lean on pillows tonight during dinner?" In ancient times, only free people reclined while eating. Using pillows reminds everyone of freedom's gifts and the end of the Jews' enslavement in ancient Egypt.

MAKE A MATZO PILLOW

1. Trace around a large **cereal box** twice onto **muslin fabric**. Cut out the two rectangles.

2. Thread **brown yarn** through a **large-eyed needle**. Knot the end of the yarn. Sew the two pieces of muslin together on three sides. Make a second knot. Cut off the extra yarn.

3. Fill the pocket with **polyester fiberfill**. Sew the open end closed.

4. Draw lines on the pillow with a **marker**.

WORLD METEOROLOGICAL DAY

Want to be a meteorologist? You'll study advanced math, chemistry, and physics to get your degree.

Meteorology is the study of weather and forecasting. The word comes from the Greek word *meteoros*, which means "high in the air." The letters in **METEOROLOGY** can be used to make many other words. Use the clues below to think of some of these words.

The 2021 theme for World Meteorological Day is "The Ocean, Our Climate, and Weather."

1. The opposite of *less* ___ ___ ___ ___

2. A small organism that causes disease ___ ___ ___ ___

3. A mythical ugly giant ___ ___ ___ ___
There's one of these in "Puss in Boots."

4. A machine that makes power ___ ___ ___ ___ ___

5. A man who is getting married ___ ___ ___ ___ ___

6. Wet and sticky ___ ___ ___ ___ ___
Only 6.1% of weddings take place in March.

7. Similar to a hotel ___ ___ ___ ___ ___

8. Dark and dreary ___ ___ ___ ___ ___ ___
This certainly describes some March weather!

There are over 100 ways to prepare an egg!

9. An egg dish with a filling ___ ___ ___ ___ ___ ___

10. Math that studies shapes ___ ___ ___ ___ ___ ___ ___ ___

Between snowstorms, thunderstorms, and tornadoes, **March weather is unpredictable!** Thanks to extremely warm temperatures, **more than 20,000 weather records** were broken across the U.S. in March 2012.

MON TUE WED

What's the weather like in March where you live?

What's the difference between weather and climate?

You can't weather a tree, but you can climate.

March 27, 2021

EARTH HOUR

Earth Hour is a global environmental event that encourages people to turn off their lights for one hour. Earth Hour started in 2007 in Australia and is now celebrated in more than 180 countries and territories around the world. Famous landmarks, including **Big Ben**, the **Statue of Liberty**, the **Eiffel Tower**, and the **Sphinx and Great Pyramids of Giza** have all participated in Earth Hour.

Earth Hour starts at 8:30 p.m. local time on the last Saturday in March.

The Statue of Liberty is modeled after the sculptor's mother.

The Eiffel Tower first opened to the public on March 31, 1889.

Big Ben is actually the 13-ton bell at the top of the clock tower.

The more than 4,500-year-old Sphinx was originally painted in bright colors like red, yellow, and blue.

AM PM PM PM

While getting ready for Earth Hour, Bethany notices that all the country labels have fallen off the world clocks. Using the clues below, help her match each country label with the correct clock.

NEPAL

UKRAINE

MALI

CHINA

Mali is 8 hours behind China.
Nepal is 5 hours and 45 minutes ahead of Mali.
Ukraine is 6 hours behind China.

Which continent has the most time zones? Asia (11 time zones)

March 14

LEARN ABOUT BUTTERFLIES DAY

Spread your wings and take this butterfly quiz.

1. What is the study of butterflies called?
a. Lepidopterology
b. Ornithology
c. Flutterology

2. About how many species of butterflies are there in the world?
a. 175
b. 1,750
c. 17,500

3. What is the smallest butterfly?
a. Western pygmy blue
b. Small tortoiseshell
c. Zebra longwing

4. Where are a butterfly's taste sensors?
a. On their antennae
b. On their legs
c. On their wings

5. Which of these is not a butterfly?
a. Eastern comma
b. Question mark
c. Western semicolon

March 23

NATIONAL PUPPY DAY

Popular Male Dog Names
1. Max
2. Charlie
3. Cooper

Popular Female Dog Names
1. Bella
2. Lucy
3. Luna

70% of people sign their pet's name on greeting cards.

These new puppy owners got their leashes terribly tangled. Who is walking each dog?

March 27, 2021

BLOSSOM KITE FESTIVAL

Kite makers and fliers from around the world come to Washington, D.C., for competitions and demonstrations.

Find what's silly in this What's Wrong? puzzle. It's up to you!

March 30

TAKE A WALK IN THE PARK DAY

Grab your boots and take a walk in these national parks. Can you match each park to its superlative?

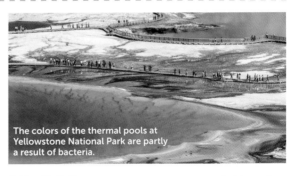

The colors of the thermal pools at Yellowstone National Park are partly a result of bacteria.

1. **Death Valley**
2. **Great Smoky Mountains**
3. **Hot Springs**
4. **Mount Rainier**
5. **Wrangell-St. Elias**
6. **Yellowstone**

A. **biggest**
B. **smallest**
C. **most-visited**
D. **oldest**
E. **hottest**
F. **snowiest**

The United States has 60 national parks and 8,565 state parks.

Take a spin around the globe to see how

March 6

INDEPENDENCE DAY

In 1957 Ghana gained its independence from the United Kingdom. Although English is Ghana's official language, about 80 languages are spoken in the country. The names of government-sponsored Ghanaian languages are listed here. Use the number of letters in each word as a clue as to where it might fit in the grid.

AKAN
DAGAARE
DAGBANI
DANGME
EWE
GA
GONJA
KASEM
MFANTSE
NZEMA

Happy 1,400th! According to the Persian calendar, March 21, 2021, is the first day of the year 1400.

March 21, 2021

HAPPY NEW YEAR!

March 21 is Nowruz, or Iranian New Year.
To symbolize rebirth and growth, Iranians prepare *sabzeh* (sab-ZAY), sprouted seeds grown in a dish.

THE WORLD

people around the world celebrate in March.

Farion (fez) has the Greek coat of arms.

Tsarouchi (clogs) have 60 nails on the sole and weigh more than 3 pounds each!

Fustanella (kilt) has 400 pleats to represent the years of Ottoman occupation.

March 25

⦿ GREEK BICENTENNIAL

The Greek War of Independence started on March 25, 1821. On Greek Independence Day, the national holiday is celebrated with a miltary parade in Athens, the capital city. Children also march in local parades, waving Greek flags and wearing traditional costumes with symbolic significance.

March 28–29, 2021

⦿ HOLI

During Holi, people in northern India wear new white clothes. They toss colored powder called *gulal* (goo-LAHL) and colored water on one another. The streets soon fill with children and adults, their new white clothes blooming in wild bouquets of color. Can you find the jigsaw pieces below in this photo of kids holding colored powder during Holi?

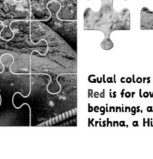

Gulal colors hold special meaning. Red is for love, green is for new beginnings, and blue represents Krishna, a Hindu deity.

SUNDAY	MONDAY	TUESDAY	WEDNESDAY

EASTER

4

Sikmogil (South Korea)

Although it is no longer a public holiday, Koreans still celebrate trees, forests, and gardening on this day. The name means "tree-planting day."

5

NATIONAL CARAMEL POPCORN DAY

6

National Walking Day

It's recommended that we walk at least 10,000 steps a day. Can you reach that goal today?

7

National Submarine Day

(The ship, not the sandwich.)

11

RAMADAN
begins at sunset and continues for 30 days.

12

Teachers' Day (Ecuador)

This day takes place on the birthday of Juan Montalvo, an popular Ecuadoran writer in the 1800s.

13

Iceberg, straight ahead!
In 1912, the supposedly unsinkable ship *Titanic* hit an iceberg off Newfoundland and sank the next day.

14

Do, re, mi wins!
In 1966, *The Sound of Music* won the Academy Award for Best Picture of the Year.

18

National Garlic Day

A vampire's least favorite day.

19

National Look-Alike Day

"You look familiar!"

20

Kartini Day (Indonesia)

This holiday commemorates the 1879 birthday of Raden Ajeng Kartini, a national hero and a pioneer in fighting for women's rights.

21

Great move!
In 1950, Chuck Cooper became the first African American hoopster drafted into the NBA.

25

An atomic tragedy.
A nuclear reactor disaster took place at the Chernobyl atomic power station in the U.S.S.R. in 1986.

26

Morse Code Day

Learning the code is as easy as

.—. .
. .
.

27

Out-of-this-world vacation!
American Dennis Tito became the first person to pay for a trip into space when he rocketed to the International Space Station in 2001.

28

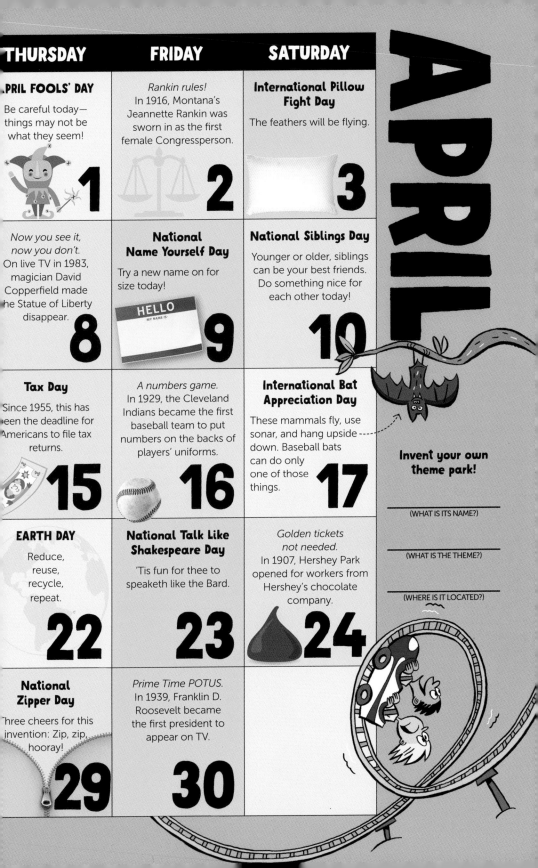

THURSDAY	FRIDAY	SATURDAY

APRIL

APRIL FOOLS' DAY

Be careful today—things may not be what they seem!

1

Rankin rules!
In 1916, Montana's Jeannette Rankin was sworn in as the first female Congressperson.

2

International Pillow Fight Day

The feathers will be flying.

3

Now you see it, now you don't.
On live TV in 1983, magician David Copperfield made the Statue of Liberty disappear.

8

National Name Yourself Day

Try a new name on for size today!

HELLO
MY NAME IS

9

National Siblings Day

Younger or older, siblings can be your best friends. Do something nice for each other today!

10

Tax Day

Since 1955, this has been the deadline for Americans to file tax returns.

15

A numbers game.
In 1929, the Cleveland Indians became the first baseball team to put numbers on the backs of players' uniforms.

16

International Bat Appreciation Day

These mammals fly, use sonar, and hang upside down. Baseball bats can do only one of those things.

17

Invent your own theme park!

_____
(WHAT IS ITS NAME?)

_____
(WHAT IS THE THEME?)

_____
(WHERE IS IT LOCATED?)

EARTH DAY

Reduce, reuse, recycle, repeat.

22

National Talk Like Shakespeare Day

'Tis fun for thee to speaketh like the Bard.

23

Golden tickets not needed.
In 1907, Hershey Park opened for workers from Hershey's chocolate company.

24

National Zipper Day

Three cheers for this invention: Zip, zip, hooray!

29

Prime Time POTUS.
In 1939, Franklin D. Roosevelt became the first president to appear on TV.

30

NATIONAL KITE MONTH

As the weather begins to get warmer, celebrate the joy and happiness that come from flying a kite by going out and . . . flying a kite! Invite friends and family to join you as you let your kites soar high into the sky.

Each of these colorful kites has an exact match. Can you find all 9?

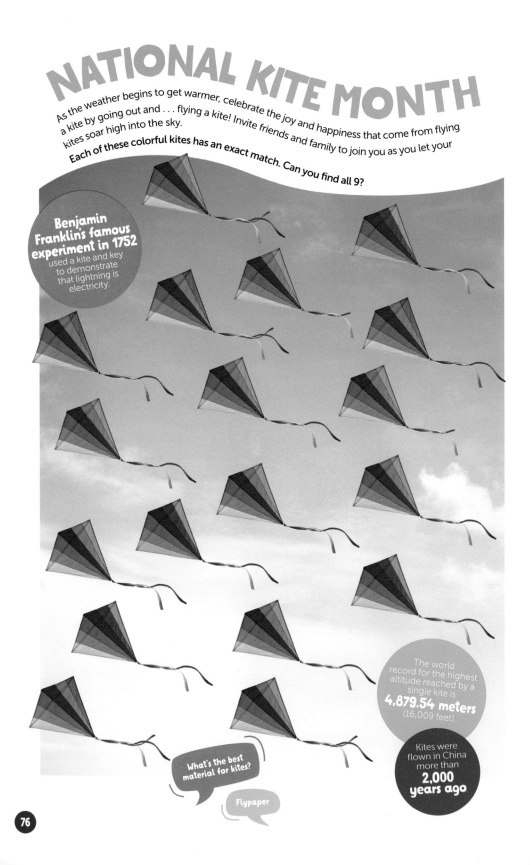

Benjamin Franklin's famous experiment in 1752 used a kite and key to demonstrate that lightning is electricity.

The world record for the highest altitude reached by a single kite is **4,879.54 meters** (16,009 feet).

Kites were flown in China more than **2,000 years ago.**

What's the best material for kites?

Flypaper

NATIONAL HUMOR MONTH

PUNCH-LINE CONFUSION

There's a communications goof-up in outer space: the astronauts' jokes don't make sense! Can you match the correct punch lines on the right to their set-ups on the left?

1. Get ready for launch.

2. Can you telephone from a space shuttle?

3. If you look down, I think you can see China.

4. What's that thing in the frying pan?

a. You've got to be kidding. The next thing I know, you'll tell me I can see knives and forks too.

b. Of course I can tell a phone from a space shuttle.

c. It's an unidentified frying object.

d. But I haven't had breakfast yet.

GOOD FOR A LAUGH!

These jokes are missing their punch lines! Come up with your best answers and share them with your friends.

What's a dentist's favorite chair?

_____

Why did the ballerina quit?

_____

What kind of nut can sneeze?

_____

What did one wall say to the other?

_____

CAPTION ACTION

See if you have what it takes to be a cartoonist! Write your funniest caption for each panel.

NATIONAL POETRY MONTH

A poet once described the difference between poetry and prose: prose is walking, poetry is dancing. Here are a few famous lines of poetry. What kind of dance do you think they're doing?

Shall I compare thee to a summer's day? Thou art more lovely and more temperate.
—WILLIAM SHAKESPEARE

'Tis better to have loved and lost Than never to have loved at all.
—ALFRED, LORD TENNYSON

I wandered lonely as a cloud.
—WILLIAM WORDSWORTH

MAKE-A-POEM KIT

Arrange the words on these refrigerator magnets to create your own poetry. Move over, Shakespeare!

SKUNK • OVER • OF • A • FIRE • YOU • EARTH • ME • TREE • TOES • LOVE • HAIR • CLOUDS • UNDER • THE • SEA • FISH • OVER • TO • IS • WATER • US • FLOWER • WE • NEAR • HANDS • SMILE • EYE • SKIES • HEAR • SKY • TRY

Poems can be serious, silly, or sappy, super long or super short. And guess what? They don't have to rhyme! What are your favorite kinds of poems to read? Maybe you'll enjoy this one— it's one of our favorites!

Singer-songwriter Bob Dylan won the **NOBEL PRIZE** for Literature in 2016.

The first African American book of poems, *Poems on Various Subjects, Religious and Moral,* was written by Phillis Wheatley in 1773.

How do poets say hello?

"Hey, haven't we metaphor?"

ANGLERFISH

The anglerfish
is rather odd.
Its dorsal fin's
a fishing rod.
And dangling
from that line—
a lure—
resembling
a worm for sure.
Imagine
if you think you can:
A fish
both fish
and fisherman.
—EILEEN SPINELLI

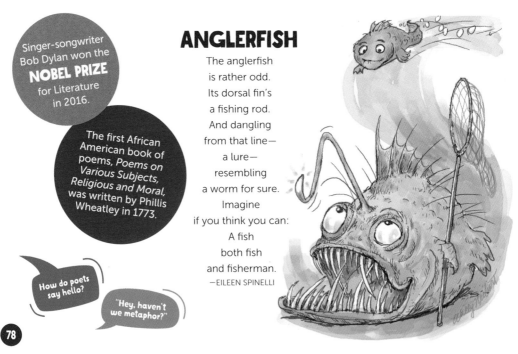

NATIONAL
MATHEMATICS AND STATISTICS
AWARENESS MONTH

S	M	T	W	T	F	S
		1	2	3	4	5
6	7	8	9	10	11	12
13	14	15	16	17	18	19
20	21	22	23	24	25	26
27	28	29	30	31		

CALENDAR
MATH-A-MAGIC!

Hand a friend an old calendar, a calculator, and a pencil. Tell your friend to draw a box around any group of nine dates that form a three-by-three square, like the example above.

Explain that you can magically add the numbers in the box faster than your friend can, even though you won't use a calculator yourself.

The trick? Multiply (in your head or on paper) the middle number in the box by 9. In the example above, multiply 15 x 9. The answer is the same as when adding all nine numbers in the red box.

If you add up the numbers on any opposite sides of a dice, the numbers will always add up to seven.

The number four is the only number with the same number of letters as its meaning.

Why was the math book sad?

It had too many problems.

24 TO THE DOOR

Matt Amatics will step only on tiles with equations that equal 24. Can you help him get to his apartment door? He can move up, down, left, or right.

24

FINISH

9 + 12	2 x 11	15 + 9	17 + 7
7 + 15	35 - 11	8 x 3	25 - 2
3 x 4	6 x 4	20 + 3	18 + 7
18 + 6	40 - 16	5 x 7	33 - 10

START

SUM FUN!

Write the correct answer to each question in the blanks.

1. _____ Number of red stripes in the U.S. flag

2. _____ Number of Harry Potter movies

3. _____ Number of days in February during a leap year

4. _____ Number of squares on a chessboard

5. _____ Number of continents

6. _____ Number of seconds in an hour

7. _____ Number of U.S. states that have two words in their name

Add the above answers together to find out how many pounds the world's largest box of chocolates weighed.

125 YEARS AGO, the first modern Olympic games were held in Athens, Greece.

OTTER-LY OUTSTANDING OLYMPICS

Go for the gold by searching for 20 objects hidden at this Olympic meet. Can you find an adhesive bandage, arrowhead, candle, domino, drumstick, envelope, heart, kite, megaphone, paper clip, party hat, paw print, pencil, question mark, ruler, slice of bread, slice of pizza, tea bag, tennis ball, and worm?

OLYMPIC NUMBERS
Go for the gold by matching the Olympic fact with the correct number.

1. Since 1896, the youngest Olympian to compete was _____ years old.

2. The first Winter Olympics was held in _____.

3. In the 2016 Games in Rio de Janeiro, more than _____ athletes competed.

4. The earliest record of the original Greek Olympics was from _____ BCE.

5. Only _____ continents have not hosted an Olympics.

6. There were _____ sports represented at the first modern-day Olympics.

7. Swimmer Michael Phelps has won _____ medals, more than any other Olympic athlete.

8. Women began competing in the Olympics in _____.

A. 776

B. 9

C. 10

D. 1900

E. 1924

F. 2

G. 22

H. 11,000

The 2022 Winter Olympics will begin **FEBRUARY 4** in Beijing, China.

The 2024 Summer Olympics will begin **JULY 26** in Paris, France.

ODDITIES AT THE OLYMPICS

The Olympics has seen many different events in its long history—and some of them have been a little unusual. Below is a list of events: some have been featured at the Olympics games and some haven't. Can you tell which events never made Olympic status? Cross off each sport that hasn't made the cut.

1. tug of war
2. croquet
3. billiards
4. rope climbing
5. cornhole
6. Wiffle ball
7. roller hockey
8. horse long jump
9. video gaming
10. breakdancing

April 12, 1961
60 YEARS AGO, Russian cosmonaut Yuri Gagarin became the first human to travel into space.

Yuri Gagarin

For many years, the U.S. and the U.S.S.R. (a group of Soviet countries, including what is now Russia) were rivals in space exploration. The U.S. responded to Yuri Gagarin's flight: a month later, Alan Shepard became the first American to reach space. Which of the two—the U.S. or U.S.S.R.—achieved each of these space-race firsts?

1. _____ First artificial satellite to orbit Earth

2. _____ First animal to orbit Earth

3. _____ First reusable space shuttle

4. _____ First human-made object to land on the moon's surface

5. _____ First space traveler to go on a spacewalk

6. _____ First probe to land on Venus

7. _____ First space station sent into orbit

8. _____ First probe to successfully land on Mars

9. _____ First manned spacecraft to circle the moon

10. _____ First human-made object to leave the solar system

Alan Shepard

AN OUT-OF-THIS-WORLD
WORD SEARCH

There are 34 space terms inside the rocket. Circle all the words that you find. They can be vertical, horizontal, or diagonal. Write the leftover letters in order in the spaces below the rocket. They will give you an important message from mission control.

About
600 MILLION
people worldwide watched a live broadcast of Neil Armstrong stepping on the moon's surface in 1969.

WORD LIST

ARMS
CARGO
FORCE
MOONS
ORBIT
SALVO
APOGEE
ATOMIC
COSMOS
FUNDED
LANDER
RAMJET
RANGER
CAPSULES
CONTROL
MISSION
PERIGEE
NECK-WRENCHING G-FORCES

RE-ENTRY
BOOSTERS
FAIL-SAFE
MOMENTUM
MOUNTAIN
NOSE CONE
THRUSTER
CELESTIAL
ASTRONAUTS
SPLASHDOWN
SPACE DEBRIS
CAPE CANAVERAL
GUIDANCE SYSTEMS
MANNED SPACESHIP
ZOOM
ZERO

```
            S
        A   I   O
      P   R   B   S   M   E   E   S
      Z   R   E   E   D   T   S   S
      P   I   G   E   S   S   E   C
      I   H   E   C   A   Y   S   C   R
      H   S   E   A   P   E   C   R   O
      E   E   E   L   P   E   O   F
      C   L   S   C   A   U   N   G   T
      R   A   A   P   N   L   A   G   B   I
    O   S   P   N   L   A   G   B   I
  F   H   S   S   D   E   D   N   U   F   B
  Z   D   N   L   D   E   S   I   I   O   A   A   R
  B   O   O   S   T   E   R   S   U   H   A   I   S   E   O
  W   O   R   E   G   N   A   R   G   C   S   L   S   T   L
N   M   M   M   O   U   N   T   A   I   N   T   S   A   S   A   M
R   C   A   P   E   C   A   N   A   V   E   R   A   L   U   I   O
E   O   O   A   A   T   O   M   I   C   J   R   O   F   V   R   T   M
N   C   C   E   S   O   N   M   T   W   N   E   O   H   S   E   M
T   R   O   T   M   G   A   F   K   A   T   E   N   E
R   O       O   R   S   F       C   U       T   L   E   C
Y   L       S   F   C       N   T   S       C   M
```

Mission control says, " _ _ _ _ _ _   _ _ _ !"

OPENING DAY OF THE MAJOR LEAGUE BASEBALL SEASON

PLAY BALL!
Use the clues to fill in the batting order on each player's card.

CLUES
A. The kids wearing glasses do not bat 1st or 9th.

B. The boy with braces bats 1st.

C. The 8th and 9th batters have the same first initial.

D. The number on the jersey of the boy batting 2nd is twice as much as the number of the kid batting 4th.

E. Batter 6, a girl, has the same color hair as batter 7.

F. The girl outfielder bats 3rd.

Player cards:
- 60 — Lindsey, pitcher
- 22 — Seth, center field
- 47 — Cody, 3rd base
- 55 — Laura, 1st base
- 10 — Claudia, right field
- 44 — Hector, catcher
- 20 — Ariel, shortstop
- 35 — Jacob, 2nd base
- 29 — Troy, left field

The first recorded baseball game took place in 1845 between teams from New York and Brooklyn.

"TAKE ME OUT TO THE BALL GAME"

Write the words below in any order in the blank spaces to create silly lyrics to this famous baseball song:

house, car, pigeons, cheese, football, crayons, email, turtle, sneaker, eyeball

Take me out to the ball_____,

Take me out to the _____.

Buy me some_____ and cracker_____,

I don't care if _____ never get back.

So it's root, root, root for the _____ _____,

If they don't _____ it's a shame.

For it's one, two, three _____ you're out

At the old _____ game.

HOME RUN!
Batter up! Can you find the right path to home plate? The symbols will tell you which way to move.

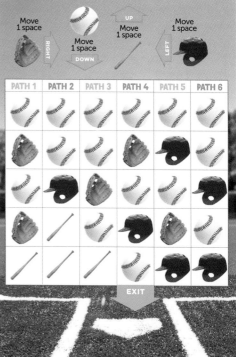

- Move 1 space
- UP — Move 1 space
- Move 1 space
- RIGHT — Move 1 space
- DOWN
- LEFT — Move 1 space

PATH 1	PATH 2	PATH 3	PATH 4	PATH 5	PATH 6

EXIT

WORLD TABLE TENNIS DAY

Your serve! Todd and Samantha have been playing so long, they're starting to see double! Can you find at least 20 differences between these two pictures?

April 19, 2021
THE BOSTON MARATHON

The Boston Marathon takes place on Patriots' Day. Only a few states celebrate this holiday, including Massachusetts. The holiday commemorates the Battles of Lexington and Concord, which were the first battles of the Revolutionary War.

THE RUNDOWN These five racers are poised and ready to race for their prize. Who will get the first-place trophy? Follow each runner's path to find out, and to see what the other runners place.

NATIONAL LIBRARY WEEK

National Librarian Day is on April 16.

This is a weeklong celebration of all that libraries have to offer. And there are plenty of them to celebrate: the U.S. has about 116,000 libraries of all kinds.

SHELF SHUFFLE

Figure out what the library books in each row (vertically, horizontally, and diagonally) have in common.

BOOK SMART

The head librarian wants to order 10 popular books for the library, but someone jumbled up the titles on her list. Can you figure out the correct titles?

1. *Anne of Witch*
2. *Charlotte's Stone*
3. *A Wrinkle in Chocolate*
4. *Diary of a Wimpy Prairie*
5. *The Lion, the Web and the Wardrobe*
6. *Harry Potter and the Sorcerer's Underpants*
7. *Charlie and the Sidewalk Factory*
8. *The Adventures of Captain Time*
9. *Where the Kid Ends*
10. *The Little House on the Green Gables*

April 8
DRAW A BIRD DAY

This day was inspired by a little British girl who visited an uncle wounded in World War II. To cheer him up, she asked him to draw a picture of a bird. Soon after, whenever the girl visited, the uncle and other wounded soldiers competed to see who could draw the best picture of a bird.

THERE ARE ABOUT 9,000 DIFFERENT SPECIES OF BIRDS. About 1,200 of those species may become extinct by the end of the century.

JUST WING IT Fill in the squares by drawing or writing the name of each bird. Every type of bird should appear only once in each row, column, and 2 x 3 box.

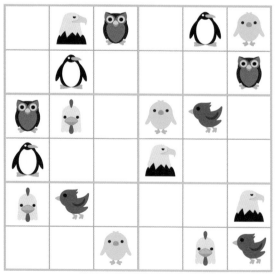

April 15
WORLD ART DAY

The birthday of Leonardo da Vinci is the perfect day to celebrate art and creativity, in all its forms. Da Vinci was not only a great painter, he was an incredible mathematician, architect, engineer, and inventor.

The *Mona Lisa*, one of da Vinci's most popular paintings, was done using oil paint. Use your favorite coloring tool and draw a portrait of yourself or a friend.

Leonardo da Vinci devised plans for such inventions as an armored car, a flying ship, a parachute, and an underwater breathing device.

CRAYON HUNT
Mr. Hall's classroom is coloring pictures, but they've spilled their crayons all over! Can you find all 25 around the room?

April 1, 2021
NATIONAL BURRITO DAY

Made in Mexico in 2010, the world's largest burrito weighed 12,785 pounds. It was wrapped in a flour tortilla that measured nearly a mile and a half.

BOBBIE'S BURRITOS

Bobbie the Burrito Maker wanted to share the recipe for her famous fiery-hot burritos. She drew pictures of the steps involved, but as she was hanging the pictures, the wind blew them onto the floor. **Can you help Bobbie put these pictures back in order?**

The word *burrito* means "little donkey" in Spanish. Some say that long ago a food vendor carried the food on his donkey, and customers asked for his burrito, meaning the donkey holding the food. Others say it got the name because it looks like the bedrolls carried on a donkey. Either way, this sandwich of rice, vegetables, cheese, and meat wrapped in a tortilla is a popular taste sensation.

April 4
INTERNATIONAL CARROT DAY

Carrots have more natural sugar than any other vegetable except beets!

Carrots are orange because they contain the chemical beta-carotene, which our bodies turn into Vitamin A.

CARROT-RAISIN SALAD

1. Put 1 pound of **shredded carrots** into a bowl. Add 1 cup of **raisins**.

2. Squeeze the juice from half of a **lemon** and half of an **orange** into the carrot-and-raisin mixture.

3. Add ¼ cup **brown sugar** and a pinch of **salt**. Mix well. Refrigerate until you're ready to eat.

How can you make a soup rich?

Add 14 carrots (carats) to it.

April 5

NATIONAL DEEP DISH PIZZA DAY

How do you fix a broken pizza?

With tomato paste

CHICAGO VS. NEW YORK PIZZA

Pizza experts believe deep dish pizza originated in Chicago around 1943. The thinner, more traditional kind of pizza is associated with New York. There is a lot of debate over which is better. Which is your favorite? What stuff do you like on it?

CHICAGO STYLE

A thick crust that absorbs lots of oil.

Topped with huge amount of ingredients.

The cheese goes on first, and then the tomato sauce.

A slice is so thick, you can't fold it.

NEW YORK STYLE

A thin crust.

The cheese goes on top of the sauce.

Slices keep their shape.

There are often fewer toppings.

You can fold a slice.

Italy wasn't the first to make pizza. In ancient times, Egyptians, Israelis, and Babylonians were already making pizza-like flatbreads. But Italy was the first to add tomatoes to their pies.

April 26

NATIONAL PRETZEL DAY

HOW TO TAKE PRETZELS TO THE NEXT LEVEL

Dip into: yellow mustard, cheddar cheese, pizza sauce, or caramel

Top with: parmesan cheese, ranch dressing, garlic, cinnamon sugar, raisins, or jalapeño peppers

Stuff with: hot dogs, cheese, or bacon

PRETZEL PATH Find your way around the pretzels from START to FINISH.

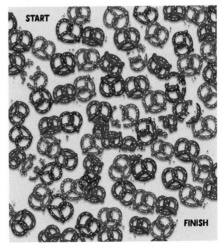

START

FINISH

APRIL FOOLS' DAY

Here's one theory on how April 1 became April Fools' Day. New Year's Day was once celebrated on April 1 in Europe. In 1582, it was decided that New Year's would start on January 1. The people who hadn't heard about this switch continued to celebrate the holiday on April 1, which gave them the reputation of being foolish and easy to trick.

Because they just finished a 31-day March

CUP O' LAUGHS

Build the perfect prank for April Fools'. If someone fills this cup too high, it will spill all over them. Whoops!

1. Use a pushpin to make a small hole in the bottom of a plastic cup.

2. Widen the hole with a pencil until a bendy straw can just fit through.

3. From the bottom, pull the straw partway through the hole. Bend the short section of the straw so it stays down.

4. Cut off the end that sticks out of the bottom of the cup.

5. To test it, fill the cup with water over a sink.

Why do eggs like April Fools' day?

They love practical yolks.

What monster plays the most April Fools' jokes? Prankenstein.

❶ Just right. ❷ Too much! ❸ Everything spills.

OLD-SCHOOL PRANKS

Yum!

- Place vanilla pudding in an empty mayonnaise jar. Eat a big scoop in front of other people and watch their expressions of horror.

- Put a piece of plastic wrap under the lid of a saltshaker. Screw the lid back on, trim off any extra wrap, and watch your family try to shake out the salt.

- Glue a coin to the ground and grin as people try to pick it up.

- Place a leek in your sink and tell your family, "Oh, no! There's a leek in the sink."

- Call a friend and ask for Jess a few times. At the end of the day, call your friend, pretend you're Jess, and ask for messages.

EARTH DAY

Earth Day is celebrated every year to show support for the different ways we can protect our planet and everything that lives on it.

ENVIRONMENTAL IQ TEST

1. **When was Earth Day first celebrated?**
   a. 1904
   b. 1970
   c. 2000

2. **Which is a nonrenewable source of energy?**
   a. Oil
   b. Hydropower
   c. Biomass

3. **Which country uses the most energy in the world?**
   a. U.S.
   b. Russia
   c. China

4. **Where does geothermal energy come from?**
   a. Earth's core
   b. Lava
   c. The moon's gravitational pull

5. **How much has the average temperature in the world risen since 1880?**
   a. 0.3°F
   b. 1.4°F
   c. It has not risen at all.

6. **The Marine Mammal Protection Act protects which of these animals?**
   a. Whale fish
   b. Manatees
   c. Pelicans

7. **How many plastic bottles do people buy every minute across the globe?**
   a. 10,000
   b. 100,000
   c. 1,000,000

8. **How long does it take a plastic bottle to decompose?**
   a. 4 years
   b. 45 years
   c. 450 years

9. **Which of these is not a greenhouse gas?**
   a. Carbon dioxide
   b. Nitrogen
   c. Methane

10. **How much trash does the average American produce in one day?**
    a. 4.4 pounds
    b. 10.5 pounds
    c. 50.3 pounds

One billion people worldwide take part in Earth Day.

EARTH DAY CLEANUP

Can you find 13 differences between these two scenes? Then research what you can do to keep your neighborhood looking beautiful.

EASTER

Easter is the most important holiday in the Christian religion. This holiday celebrates the day Christians believe Jesus Christ rose from the dead on the third day after he was crucified on Good Friday. Western churches celebrate Easter on a Sunday between March 22 and April 25. The exact date depends on the date of the first full moon after the first day of spring.

READY TO ROLL

Since Rutherford B. Hayes was president in 1878, it has been a tradition to hold the Easter Egg Roll on the White House lawn the Monday after Easter. Here are some highlights.

1974: Kids were given spoons to push the eggs along a path in the grass.

1977: President Jimmy Carter added a circus to the egg-roll fun.

1981: President Ronald Reagan replaced hard-boiled eggs with wooden eggs signed by celebrities.

1998: The roll was broadcast live over the Internet for the first time.

2009: The egg roll was so popular, the White House had to give out lottery tickets to kids around the U.S. to limit participants.

A VERY YUMMY EASTER

Four cousins—Carly, Dan, Anthony, and Kiera—each made a dessert for Easter dinner. Using the clues below, can you figure out which dessert each cousin baked and what flavor it was?

	Pie	Muffins	Tart	Cupcake	Apple	Lemon	Coconut	Strawberry
Carly								
Anthony								
Kiera								
Dan								

1. Dan never bakes with coconut.
2. The girl who made muffins put strawberries in them.
3. Anthony made something with apples that was not a pie.
4. Kiera baked her favorite kind of cupcake.

Use the chart to keep track of your answers. Put an X in each box that can't be true and an O in boxes that match.

WHY ARE THESE EASTER SYMBOLS?

Rabbits: They produce so many babies, they are a symbol of new life, or resurrection.

Easter Eggs: Babies hatching from their shells are another symbol of new life.

Lamb: Lambs are also a symbol of Easter because Jesus was called the "lamb of God" and lambs were sacrificed to God in ancient Israel as a symbol of Jesus's future crucifixion.

SUNDAY

SIDEWALK-CHALK EASTER EGGS

1. In a bowl, mix together 1 cup of **baking soda**, 1 cup of **flour**, ½ cup of **white glue**, and 3 tablespoons of **water**.

2. Divide the mixture into several **cups**. Mix a few drops of **food coloring** into each.

3. Press the mixture into **plastic eggs**, filling both halves. Close them.

4. Let them dry for a day. Remove the chalk from the eggs, and let it dry until it hardens.

JELLY BEAN PIECES

Jelly beans are a popular Easter treat. Can you find the jigsaw pieces in this photo of jelly beans?

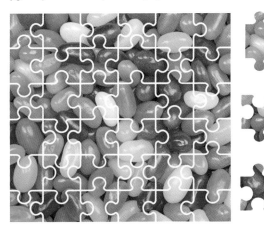

GLOBAL EASTER TRADITIONS

Nine of these are real Easter traditions—but one is made up. Can you figure out which tradition is false?

1. **Australia:** Eating chocolate Easter bilbies (rabbit-eared bandicoots) instead of bunnies

2. **Florence, Italy:** Setting off a cart full of fireworks in front of a church

3. **Finland:** Children dressing up like witches

4. **Manchester, England:** Tossing hard-boiled eggs at each other on the field of Manchester United's stadium

5. **Poland:** Pouring water over each other

6. **Haux, France:** Eating a giant omelet made of 4,500 eggs in the town square

7. **Corfu, Greece:** Throwing pots and pans out their windows so they smash on the street

8. **Norway:** Reading crime novels

9. **Verges, Spain:** Walking through the streets dressed in skeleton costumes

ZOO LOVERS' DAY

ZOOKEEPER'S BYE-BYE

When he left for home, the head zookeeper accidentally scrambled the names of the animals he said goodbye to. Help him straighten out their names. When you do, each name will rhyme with his goodbye phrase.

1. After awhile, DOCCOREIL
2. See you soon, you big NABBOO
3. Got to go, FABFULO
4. Time to sleep, bighorn PEESH
5. Cheerio, KECGO
6. Bye-bye, FEBLUTTRY
7. Toodle-oo, AKNARGOO
8. Take good care, RAPLO EBAR
9. That's all for me, PENCHEZAMI
10. Take a break, TRANTELSAKE

FIVE MOST-VISITED ZOOS IN THE U.S.

1. San Diego Zoo, San Diego, CA
2. Lincoln Park Zoo, Chicago, IL
3. Saint Louis Zoo, Saint Louis, MO
4. Columbus Zoo and Aquarium, Columbus, OH
5. Brookfield Zoo, Brookfield, IL

The oldest zoo in the world was founded in 1752 in Vienna, Austria.

NATIONAL *VELOCIRAPTOR* AWARENESS DAY
KIDS' SCIENCE QUESTIONS

Could a *Velociraptor* pack really kill a *T. rex*?

Velociraptor could not have killed *T. rex*. For one thing, the two never met. *Velociraptor* lived in Asia about 80 million years ago. *T. rex* lived in North America about 65 million years ago. But even if they had met, a *Velociraptor* pack probably couldn't have even scared a forty-foot-long *T. rex*. That carnivore could have swallowed two of those wolf-sized raptors in a single bite!

Velociraptor is Latin for "swift robber."

What do you call a sleeping dinosaur?

A dino-snore

92

April 30, 2021

ARBOR DAY

There weren't a lot of trees in Nebraska in the 1800s, so J. Sterling Morton proposed a holiday called Arbor Day that called for people to plant them. They would provide fuel, building material, and shade. More than one million trees were planted in Nebraska on the first Arbor Day in 1872.

The Arbor Day Foundation hopes to plant 100 MILLION TREES by 2022.

THAT'S ONE OLD TREE!

The oldest living organism that doesn't clone itself is a bristlecone pine located in the White Mountains of California, in Inyo National Forest. Scientists estimate that the tree is more than five thousand years old. It started growing around the time humans invented writing and the wheel! Its location is kept secret to keep people away from it. That way, it might live another five thousand years!

What did the tree wear to the pool party?

Swimming trunks

There are about 5.5 BILLION trees in urban areas of the U.S.

TREEMONTON TOWERS

The animals of Treemonton are celebrating in their town's twin treehouses after a day of planting trees. Can you figure out how to go from the ground to the top floor without waking any bats?

NATIONAL UNICORN DAY

While these unicorns enjoy the aftermath of April showers, can you find the ladybug, plum, jug, peanut, sun, cup, cracker, and mug hidden in this scene?

April 13

NATIONAL SCRABBLE DAY

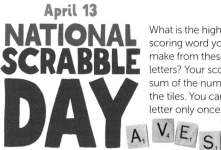

What is the highest-scoring word you can make from these Scrabble letters? Your score is the sum of the numbers on the tiles. You can use each letter only once.

10 TRICKY HIGH-SCORING SCRABBLE WORDS

1. Oxyphenbutazone
2. Muzjiks
3. Zax
4. Quetzals
5. Quixotry
6. Gherkins
7. Quartzy
8. Xu
9. Syzygy
10. Za

April 22, 2021
TAKE OUR DAUGHTERS AND SONS TO WORK DAY

More than 37 million Americans at over 3.5 million workplaces take part in this special day. The object is for kids to think about their careers. It also helps them appreciate what their parents do every day to help their family.

At this job fair, the participants brought things to help show kids what they do at work. Your job is to match each person to the correct object. When you're done, one object will be left. Use it to guess who hasn't arrived yet.

April 28
NATIONAL SUPERHERO DAY

This day was created in 1995 by workers at Marvel Comics. It honors the people who protect us from the bad guys, whether comic-book superheroes or real, everyday heroes.

SUPER SAVERS
This fantastic four can save the day—with a little help from you. Lead each superhero along the path to the person who needs assistance.

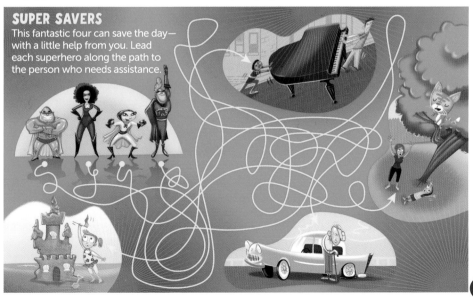

Take a spin around the globe to see how

April 13–15, 2021
◉ SONGKRAN

For three days, people in Thailand and other countries in Southeast Asia get wet to celebrate the New Year. People sprinkle water on statues of Buddha for good luck and on the hands of older relatives and friends as a sign of respect. It is a Buddhist tradition to drizzle water on people; it symbolizes rinsing away the bad luck of the old year and starting over pure for the new one.

April 23, 2021
◉ ST. GEORGE'S DAY

Legend has it that a knight named George killed a dragon to free the city of Silene, which is in modern-day Libya. For that feat of derring-do, George was made a saint and is honored not only in England, but in parts of Italy, Portugal, and Spain.

Do You Know That Dragon?
Match the dragon to the movie or book it appears in.

1. Toothless
2. Haku
3. Smaug
4. Maleficent
5. Mushu
6. Falcor
7. Draco
8. Hungarian Horntail

a. *Sleeping Beauty*
b. *Dragonheart*
c. *Spirited Away*
d. *Mulan*
e. *The Hobbit*
f. *How to Train Your Dragon*
g. *Harry Potter and the Goblet of Fire*
h. *The Neverending Story*

These real animals may have inspired the belief in dragons:
- Dinosaur fossils
- Nile crocodile
- Goanna
- Whales

An Australian lizard

THE WORLD

April 27
📍 KONINGSDAG

Koningsdag means "King's Day", a Netherlands' national holiday that celebrates the birthday of King Willem-Alexander. Before it was King's Day, the holiday was called Queen's Day to honor the female rulers of the Netherlands. Dutch people celebrate by wearing orange and riding through Amsterdam's canals on boats.

Somalian Flag

Gabonese Flag

Nigerian Flag

April 27
📍 INDEPENDENCE DAY

On this day, Sierra Leone celebrates its independence from Great Britain in 1961. Back then, the new nation unveiled its own flag, and today citizens are encouraged to wave it proudly.

Fly It High

Can you figure out the three colors of the Sierra Leone flag?

Clues:

1. The top stripe of the flag has a color found in the flags of both Nigeria and Gabon, but not in Somalia's flag.

2. The middle stripe has a color found in both the Nigerian and Somalian flags, but not in the Gabonese flag.

3. The bottom stripe has a color found in the flags of both Somalia and Gabon, but not in the Nigerian flag.

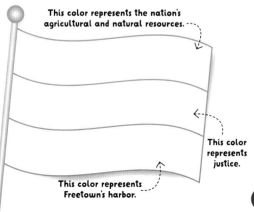

This color represents the nation's agricultural and natural resources.

This color represents justice.

This color represents Freetown's harbor.

SUNDAY	MONDAY	TUESDAY	WEDNESDAY

BIRTHSTONE
EMERALD

ZODIAC SIGNS
TAURUS:
APRIL 20–MAY 20

GEMINI:
MAY 21–JUNE 20

2
Root, root, root for the home team! In 1908, "Take Me Out to the Ball Game" was registered with the U.S. Copyright Office.

3
Święto Konstytucji 3 Maja (Poland)
Polish Parliament passed the country's Constitution on May 3, 1791. Today, Poles celebrate with parades, concerts, and speeches.

4
Star Wars Day
May the Fourth be with you!

5
CINCO DE MAYO

9
Mother's Day
Whatever you do for her, she'll love it!

10
All aboard! In 1869, a golden spike was driven into the track at Promontory Summit, Utah, to complete the first coast-to-coast railroad in the United States.

11
Compute this! In 1997, IBM's Deep Blue became the first computer to win a match against a world chess champion.

12
EID AL-FITR
begins at sunset.

16
National Love a Tree Day
Give your favorite oak, pine, or redwood a hug. Just watch out for splinters!

17
Off to see the Wizard! In 1900, the first copy of *The Wonderful Wizard of Oz*, by L. Frank Baum, was printed.

18
International Museum Day
The theme for 2021 is "Museums Inspiring the Future."

19
Commemoration of Atatürk, Youth and Sports Day (Turkey)
This national holiday celebrates Turkey's youth and the republic's founder.

23
World Turtle Day

30
National Water a Flower Day

24
National Scavenger Hunt Day

31
MEMORIAL DAY

25
National Brown-Bag-It Day
What's your favorite packed lunch? Make it and take it.

26
. . . Now you don't. Stay up to watch the moon disappear—the first total lunar eclipse since January 2019.

THURSDAY	FRIDAY	SATURDAY

MAY

FLOWERS
LILY OF THE VALLEY AND HAWTHORN

Mother Goose Day

Reread a favorite story, then write your own.

1

Mailed it!

In 1840, Great Britain began to use the first adhesive postage stamp, called the Penny Black.

6

INTERNATIONAL TUBA DAY

7

Parents' Day (South Korea)

On 어버이날 (*Eobeonial*), kids write letters of thanks to their parents and give them red carnations to express gratitude.

8

Who are the people in your family?

_____
_____
_____
_____
_____
_____

One of the greats. The Great Comet of 1861 was first spotted by amateur Australian astronomer John Tebbutt. It was visible around the world for three months.

13

INTERNATIONAL CHIHUAHUA APPRECIATION DAY

14

International Day of Families

Learn about families that may be different than yours.

15

Yippee, dungarees! In 1873, Levi Strauss and Jacob Davis patented the first blue jeans—work pants reinforced with metal rivets.

20

National Pizza Party Day

Share with friends—and save a slice for us.

21

National Solitaire Day

Go old school—pick up a deck of cards. How many variations do you know?

22

National Cellophane Tape Day

Stick with it!

27

Slug Appreciation Day

Look how cute!

28

Put a Pillow on Your Fridge Day

Based on an old custom of putting a cloth in the food pantry, it's said to ensure good luck.

29

Kalpana Chawla

George Takei

ASIAN/PACIFIC AMERICAN HERITAGE MONTH

Pay tribute to the generations of Asian/Pacific Americans who have uplifted American history, society, and culture. Match each person to their historic accomplishment.

1. At 17, she was the youngest woman to win a snowboarding gold medal, at the 2018 Winter Olympics in PyeongChang.

2. At the age of 21, this architect and sculptor designed the Vietnam Veterans Memorial in Washington, D.C.

3. This actor was the first Asian American to play a major character on an American TV show, as the original Mr. Sulu on Star Trek.

4. This two-time Olympian is the most-decorated figure skater in U.S. history.

5. This Pulitzer Prize–winning journalist, filmmaker, and immigration activist was born in the Philippines and raised in the U.S.

6. This Olympic gold medalist, who was considered the greatest freestyle swimmer in the world, helped popularize surfing.

7. An advocate for equal rights, this lawyer and politician was the first woman of color and the first Asian American elected to Congress.

8. This astronaut was the first Indian American woman to go into space.

The U.S. Pacific Islands region includes our 50th state, Hawaii, as well as the territories of Guam, the Commonwealth of the Northern Mariana Islands, the Republic of the Marshall Islands, the Federated States of Micronesia, the Republic of Palau, and American Samoa.

Duke Kahanamoku

Michelle Kwan

Jose Antonio Vargas

Patsy Mink

Maya Lin

Chloe Kim

NATIONAL BIKE MONTH

You rode here on a WHAT? Eight early names for bicycles are listed here. Use the number of letters in each word as a clue as to where it might fit in the grid.

The first bicycle, created by German baron Karl von Drais in 1817, was made of wood. It had no chain, brakes, or pedals. Riders pushed off from the ground with their feet.

B O N E S H A K E R S

DRAISINES
ORDINARIES
BONESHAKERS
HOBBY HORSES

VELOCIPEDES
SWIFT WALKERS
PENNY-FARTHINGS
RUNNING MACHINES

National Bike to School Day is during the second week of May. Why not organize a **Bike Train**? Gather a group of friends to bicycle to and from school together, led by an adult riding in front and another at the end. Make stops along your route to pick up and drop off other students.

On May 21, 1819, the first bicycles in the United States were seen in New York City.

What flavor ice cream do bikers like the least?

Rocky road

INTERNATIONAL DRUM MONTH

Drums have been played for centuries all over the world. Early drums were sections of hollowed tree trunks covered at one end with reptile, fish, or other animal skins. Today, drum "skins" are usually made of a plastic called *Mylar*.

The oldest drum was found in China. Made from clay and alligator hides, it dates back as early as **5500 BCE**.

The largest drum—**18 feet 2 inches** in diameter, **19½ feet** tall, and weighing **15,432 pounds**—was created in South Korea in 2011. The drum is a traditional Korean CheonGo drum.

crash cymbal

ride cymbal

snare drum

hi-hat cymbals

high tom

mid tom

floor tom

bass drum

drum throne (seat)

DRUM MATCH

Match each of these drums to its region of origin.

1. **Adufe**
2. **Bodhrán**
3. **Conga**
4. **Djembe**
5. **Pandeiro**
6. **Steel Pan**
7. **Taiko**

A. **Brazil**
B. **Cuba**
C. **Ireland**
D. **Japan**
E. **Portugal**
F. **Trinidad and Tobago**
G. **West Africa**

ANIMAL ACTS

- **Rabbits, kangaroo rats, and other rodents** use their paws to drum the ground, warning others of approaching predators.

- **Palm cockatoos** of Australia break off a stick or seedpod, hold it in their feet, and rap against a hollow tree branch to attract a mate.

- **Macaque monkeys** drum objects to show strength. The louder the drumming, the bigger and stronger the macaque probably is.

NATIONAL PET MONTH

Can you spot at least **20 differences** between these pictures at the vet's office?

More than 63 million households own dogs. More than 42 million have cats. And 6 out of 10 households have more than one pet. Circle sets of four emojis together that have two cats and two dogs. One side of each square must touch a side of another square in the same set. You are done when all the squares are circled.

Dogs keep cool by panting. They also sweat through their foot pads.

Cats can spend up to half their awake time grooming themselves.

A goldfish named Tish lived 43 years. It was won at a fair in 1956.

Underwater, iguanas can hold their breath for up to a half hour.

A group of ferrets is called a *business*.

Christopher Columbus brought back two parrots as pets for Queen Isabella when he returned from his journey to the Americas.

What did the cat say when the dog ran away from home?

"This is the best dog-gone day ever!"

Where do cats and dogs go on vacation?

Pets-ylvania

Pigs are really clean animals and only roll in the mud to cool off. They're also smarter than other pets.

May 1, 1931

90 YEARS AGO, THE EMPIRE STATE BUILDING
OPENED ON THE CORNER OF FIFTH AVENUE AND 34TH STREET IN NEW YORK CITY.

In 1931, President Herbert Hoover pressed a button in Washington, D.C., and on came the lights in what was then the world's tallest skyscraper. **Can you find the jigsaw pieces below in the photo of the Empire State Building?**

The mast at the top, now a TV tower, was a mooring for dirigibles, or airships, in the 1930s.

The Empire State Building has 102 stories and is 1,454 feet tall.

Since 1994, more than 250 couples have been married on Valentine's Day on the 86th Floor Observation Deck.

The Empire State Building has its own zip code: 10118.

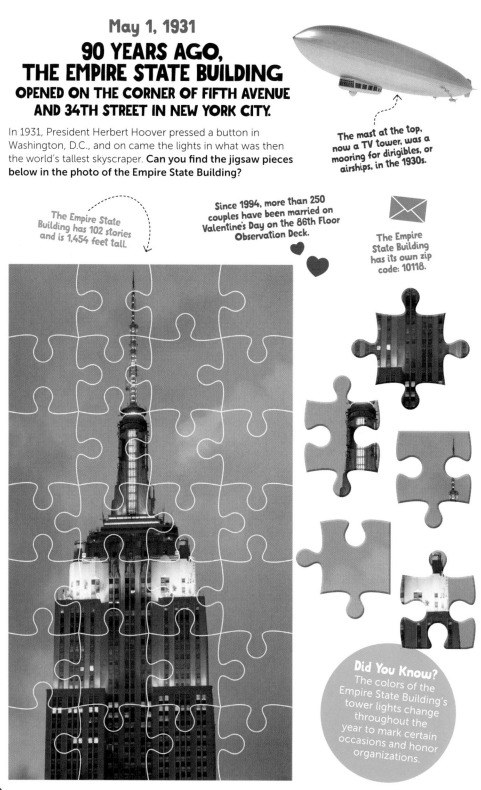

Did You Know?
The colors of the Empire State Building's tower lights change throughout the year to mark certain occasions and honor organizations.

115 YEARS AGO, ORVILLE AND WILBUR WRIGHT WERE GRANTED A PATENT FOR THEIR FLYING MACHINE.

A HIGHLIGHTS CLASSIC PUZZLE

Can you find 24 objects in this Hidden Pictures puzzle?

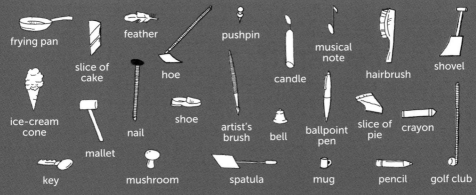

frying pan

slice of cake

feather

hoe

pushpin

candle

musical note

hairbrush

shovel

ice-cream cone

mallet

nail

shoe

artist's brush

bell

ballpoint pen

slice of pie

crayon

key

mushroom

spatula

mug

pencil

golf club

- -

MAKE A WRIGHT FLYER

1. Cut out five rectangles from **poster board** in the sizes shown.

11" 9" 4"
3" 1" 1"

2. Glue the largest rectangle to the middle of a medium rectangle. Glue a short rectangle to one end of the medium rectangle as the airplane's front.

3. Glue the second medium rectangle on top of the first. Glue a **large craft stick** under the front end of the plane. Add two **large paper clips**. Let dry.

4. Make a ½-inch cut in the back end of the plane. Glue the second short rectangle into the slot, as shown. Let dry.

HOW TO LAUNCH

Rest your thumb on the craft stick, with your pointer and middle fingers on either side of the body, behind the wings. Throw it straight—and not too hard.

KENTUCKY DERBY

Every first Saturday in May since 1875, the Churchill Downs racetrack in Lexington, Kentucky, has hosted a special Thoroughbred-horse race, the Kentucky Derby. The Derby is the first of three races known as the Triple Crown of Racing, which also includes the Preakness Stakes race and the Belmont Stakes race. **What do the horses in each row—down, across, and diagonally—have in common?**

HATS ON!

Since the 1960s, spectators at the Kentucky Derby have been known for their fancy hats.

What would your Kentucky Derby hat look like? Draw it here.

INDY 500

May 30, 2021

Called the "Greatest Spectacle in Racing," this competition at the Indianapolis Motor Speedway takes place on the last Sunday of May. Thirty-three drivers zoom 200 laps around a 2½-mile track for a total of 500 miles.

Which things in this picture are silly? It's up to you!

In 2013, Tony Kanaan had the fastest average winning speed: **187.433 MPH.** He had the fastest time, too: 2 hours, 40 minutes and 3.4181 seconds.

INDY TRADITIONS

Drink the Milk: Three-time Indianapolis 500 winner Louis Meyer drank a glass of buttermilk after winning the 1936 race. Except for the years between 1947 and 1955, a bottle of milk has been presented to the winner ever since.

The first Indy 500, in 1911, took winner Ray Harroun **6 HOURS, 42 MINUTES.**

Kiss the Bricks: The Speedway became known as "the Brickyard" after it was paved with 3.2 million paving bricks in 1909. Later, asphalt was laid over the track, except for one yard of brick at the start-finish line. After NASCAR champion Dale Jarrett won a race in 1996, he knelt down and kissed the Yard of Bricks. Now other winners do it, too.

NATIONAL CARTOONISTS DAY

Today marks the first appearance of a newspaper comic strip: *Hogan's Alley*, created by Richard Felton Outcault in 1895. This Sunday comic featured Mickey Dugan, known as the Yellow Kid, who starred in various versions of the strip until January 1898.

Find the funny! Write a caption for each cartoon.

How to Draw a Grumpy Cartoon Bear

1. Start with a circle for the skull. Draw a large oval behind it for the jaw. Add the nose.

2. Define the snout by drawing a circle around the nose. Add eyes.

3. Draw a downturned mouth and slanting eyebrows. Don't forget ears!

4. Flatten the top of the head a little bit. Finish up with a furry coat and other details. Ta-da!

Do cartoons make you laugh? Good news— **WORLD LAUGHTER DAY** is the first Sunday in May. Try laughing in a different language. Instead of texting *hahaha*, type *55555* (Thai, because 5 is pronounced "ha"), *jajaja* (Spanish), or *MDR* (French for *mort de rire*—"dying of laughter").

May 1 is **FREE COMIC BOOK DAY!** On the first Saturday in May, participating comics stores around the world give away at least one FREE book to anyone who visits.

The longest-running newspaper comic in history is *The Katzenjammer Kids.* The main characters, Hans and Fritz, have been getting into cartoon trouble since 1897.

May 25
NATIONAL
TAP DANCE DAY

The record for most taps in one minute— **1,163!**—was set in 2011.

Tap is a purely American dance style. It's a blend of African tribal dances and Scottish, Irish, and English clog dances, hornpipes, and jigs. Shuffle and stomp to honor the birth date of legendary tap dancer Bill "Bojangles" Robinson, born in 1878.

Find the names of tap-dance steps in this word grid.

```
      R S L X
     O I Q L G K
   P V F G O U U L
    K E F A R H R K
  Y C L F G P C D P A
  Z A D E L M W I N G
  C B D L S A S F D K
  M L A D H R P W I C
  D L P D I C I O H U
  P U S I M C U L M B
  R P H D S V T A Z I
   A U A H K T F C
   N F R A W G F L
   P F A M V I U
   L L P H V D B
    E C O H Y W
```

```
    Z Z D P R U
   H Y T M O P L
   E O T O R K R
   L S W T N W N
   O T S F T
     M I R
```

WORD LIST

BUCK
BUFFALO
CHUG
CRAMP ROLL
FLAP
PADDLE
PARADIDDLE
PULLBACK
RIFF
SHIM SHAM
SHUFFLE
SLURP
STOMP
TOE
WING

In 2001, David Meenan tap-danced **32 MILES IN 7½ HOURS** around a track in Red Bank, New Jersey.

In 1992, **6,000 DANCERS** tapped through the streets of New York City in the Macy's Thanksgiving Day Parade.

STEPPING OUT

A life-size statue of Bill "Bojangles" Robinson stands at the corner of Adams and Leigh Streets in Richmond, Virginia. It's where Robinson donated a traffic light, in 1933, for the safety of the high school students trying to cross the busy intersection.

The statue shows him dancing on stair steps, one of his famous moves.

NATIONAL HOAGIE DAY

That's what Philadelphians call a submarine, or sub. Elsewhere, this supersandwich goes by *hero* (New York City), *grinder* (New England), *spuckie* (South Boston), and *po' boy* (New Orleans). But whatever you call it, **never** put mayo on it!

Which two hoagies are exactly the same?

The name may have started as "hoggie," for the lunch brought by Italian shipyard workers in the Philadelphia area known as Hog Island. Or, some say, you "had to be a hog to eat a sandwich that big."

May 13

INTERNATIONAL HUMMUS DAY

Hummus means "chickpea" in Arabic. Nobody knows where it originated, but the earliest mention of hummus is from thirteenth-century Egypt. Chickpea and garbanzo beans are actually the same thing—and whatever you call them, they're one of the most widely consumed legumes in the world.

The largest serving of hummus was **23,042 POUNDS** in Beirut, Lebanon, on May 8, 2010.

1. Cut 1 **lemon** in half and squeeze the juice into a food processor or blender.

2. Rinse and drain a 15-ounce can of **chickpeas**. Add the beans to the food processor or blender along with ½ cup **tahini**, ¼ cup **water**, ⅓ cup **olive oil**, and ½ teaspoon **salt**. Blend until the mixture is smooth and creamy.

Shake up your hummus with these variations!

For olive hummus: Add 15 pitted **Kalamata olives** after step 2.

For pesto hummus: Add 3–4 tablespoons prepared **pesto** after step 2.

For feta-spinach hummus: Add 2 tablespoons **feta cheese** and a ½ cup **baby spinach** with stems removed.

May 28
NATIONAL HAMBURGER DAY

Ground-beef-and-onion patties cooked up by immigrants in the U.S. were named after the German city of Hamburg. "Hamburg steak" was served in New York restaurants as early as 1837. Build your own ~~buns~~ puns by using the picture code to fill in the letters and finish these three jokes.

Can't get enough beef on a bun? May is also National Hamburger Month!

Americans eat about **13 BILLION BURGERS** each year—enough to circle the Earth 32 times!

A	B	C	E	I	K	L	M	P	T	Y

What did Mr. and Mrs. Hamburger name their daughter?

__ __ __ __ __

The record for the largest hamburger weighs in at more than **2,566 POUNDS**, set in Pilsting, Germany, in 2017.

How do you make a hamburger laugh?

__ __ __ __ __ __ __ __!

What kind of dance does a hamburger go to?

__ __ __ __ __ __ __ __ __

TOP THIS!
A food-ordering app reports America's top burger toppings in this order:

Condiments
1. Mayo
2. Ketchup
3. Mustard

Cheeses
1. American
2. Cheddar
3. Swiss
4. Provolone
5. Pepper Jack

Add-ons
1. Pickles
2. Tomatoes
3. Lettuce
4. Onions
5. Bacon

What do you like on your burger?

THE FRIED ONION BURGER DAY FESTIVAL is held every year on the first Friday and Saturday in May in El Reno, Oklahoma. Chefs cook up the world's largest hamburger topped with fried onions. The current record holder is an 850-pound burger—complete with a massive bun and heaps of onions—measuring 8½ feet across.

May 5

CINCO DE MAYO

Today marks Mexico's victory over an invading French army in the Battle of Puebla in 1862. In the U.S., Cinco de Mayo (*Fifth of May*) spotlights Mexican heritage and culture with parties, parades, piñatas, and plenty of *deliciosa* food. Although it's a pretty minor holiday in Mexico, it became an official U.S. holiday in 2005, to celebrate Mexican culture and heritage.

MOLE POBLANO, a sauce containing chili pepper, chocolate, and spices, is the official dish of Cinco de Mayo.

Cinco de Mayo is NOT Mexico's Independence Day. That's September 16.

Match these Spanish words with their English translations.

1. La familia
2. El amigo
3. La fiesta
4. El país
5. El desfile
6. La comida

A. Friend
B. Country
C. Food
D. Family
E. Parade
F. Party

MINI PIÑATAS

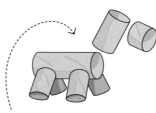

1. For each piñata, collect **four short paper tubes**. For legs, cut two of the tubes in half. Tape the legs to a full-sized tube. If you like, fill the tubes with **wrapped candy** (or leave them empty and use the mini piñata as a table decoration). Tape over the ends.

2. For the head, cut off the end of the fourth tube and tape it back on sideways, as shown. Tape the head to the body.

3. Wrap the piñata with **masking tape**. Shape ears from the tape.

4. Cover the piñata with **crepe-paper strips**. Add **wiggle eyes**.

Although piñatas are most commonly associated with Mexico, they may be Chinese in origin. In the 14th century, the tradition of smashing clay pots came to Europe. The Italians called it *pignatta*, meaning "earthenware cooking pot." In the 16th century, Europeans brought the tradition to Mexico, although Mayans and Aztecs had previously decorated clay pots with feathers to be broken. Today, piñatas are made from paper and cardboard rather than clay pots, for safety.

MOTHER'S DAY

In 1868, Ann Jarvis tried to establish "Mother's Friendship Day" between mothers on both sides of the Civil War. But it was her daughter, Anna Jarvis, who was able to convince President Woodrow Wilson to sign a bill in 1914 recognizing Mother's Day as a national holiday, celebrated on the second Sunday in May.

CUPCAKE CARD

1. Fold a piece of **cardstock** in half. Cut it to form the bottom of a cupcake.

2. Cut a piece of **thin cardboard** for support. **Glue** it to the back of the cardstock.

3. Glue **cotton-ball** "frosting" to the top of the cardboard. Add **glitter-glue** "sprinkles."

4. Decorate the card with **markers** and cardstock. Write a message on the front and inside.

You're Sweet, Mom!

Mother's Day is celebrated in nearly 50 countries, though some on different days. The United States, Italy, Australia, Belgium, Denmark, Finland, and Turkey all celebrate it on the second Sunday of May.

Anna Jarvis hated how commercialized Mother's Day had become by the 1920s, and she tried to get people to stop buying flowers, cards, and other gifts.

MOM MATCH

Every year about 113 million Mother's Day cards are sent. Match each card to the animal baby that sent it.

I really look up to you, Mama!

Mommy, you really bring me out of my shell!

To my mother, who makes our den such a cozy place!

Ewe really raise the baaaa, Maaaa!

Even though I'm in a great school now, I'll always be your small fry, Mom!

113

May 12-13, 2021
EID AL-FITR

During the month of Ramadan, Muslims do not eat or drink from dawn to sunset. When Ramadan ends, Muslims everywhere celebrate Eid al-Fitr, the festival of fast-breaking.

They prepare special foods for friends and family. One dish common in India and Pakistan is a sweet noodle pudding called *sheer khurma*, which simply means "milk with dates." In some countries, this joyous holiday goes on for three days!

SWEET NOODLE PUDDING

1. With a parent's help, heat 3 cups **milk**, 1 cup **whipping cream,** and ½ cup **sugar** in a pan on the stove. Stir it until the mixture starts to foam.
2. Add 1 cup **uncooked vermicelli or angel-hair pasta** (broken into 3-inch pieces) and lower the heat. Stir for 15 minutes, or until the milk and cream thicken. Add ¼ cup **chopped dates**.
3. If serving warm, stir in ½ cup **nuts**, such as almonds or pistachios, and ¼ cup **raisins**.
4. If serving cold, add 1 small can **fruit cocktail**, drained, and ⅓ cup **shredded coconut**. Chill the pudding in the refrigerator.

On the Islamic calendar, a new month starts with a new moon. Every year, Eid al-Fitr falls about 11 days earlier than the previous year.

Eid al-Fitr begins when local "moon sighters" report seeing the new moon. The Judicial High Court then decides if Eid has arrived. When the sighting has been verified, Eid is declared on televisions, radio stations, and at mosques.

Children honor elderly relatives or neighbors by kissing their right hand and placing it on their forehead while greeting them.

During Eid al-Fitr, Muslim children in Egypt dance in the streets, swinging *fanous* of all sizes. Below are some countries that celebrate Eid. Read the letters in **red** from top to bottom to find out what a *fanous* is.

MALAYSIA

THAILAND

JORDAN

KUWAIT

INDONESIA

QATAR

BAHRAIN

MEMORIAL DAY

Originally called Decoration Day, Memorial Day is a day to remember soldiers and their sacrifices. The first national celebration took place in 1868 at Arlington National Cemetery. Today, many towns celebrate with a parade to honor and remember soldiers.

PARADE PATH

Help Connor find his way through the crowd to meet his friends at the Memorial Day parade.

START

FINISH

POPPY POWER

*In Flanders fields the **poppies** blow*

Between the crosses, row on row,

That mark our place; and in the sky

The larks, still bravely singing, fly

Scarce heard amid the guns below.

—FROM "IN FLANDERS FIELDS"

Lieutenant Colonel John McCrae, a Canadian doctor, wrote the poem quoted above on May 3, 1915, while treating soldiers on the battlefields of Flanders in Belgium during World War I. His poem inspired a Georgia schoolteacher, Moina Belle Michael, in 1919 to wear and hand out red silk poppies in soldiers' honor. Today, American Legion volunteers distribute more than 2.5 million red crepe-paper poppies each year, with donations used to assist veterans and military families.

MAKE A POPPY BOUQUET

Cut a flower from **red craft foam**. Hold a **black button** to the flower's center. Poke a **green chenille stick** through the back of the flower and thread it through the buttonholes. Poke it back through the flower. Twist the end around the stem. Fill a vase with your poppies.

SPACE DAY

The first Friday in May is all about future astronomers, astronauts, and out-of-this-world explorers. This day encourages kids to study science, technology, engineering, and math, so you can reach for the stars—and the planets!

ASTRONOMY is the study of space, the universe, and all the objects in them. Which three celestial objects can you spell from the letters in ASTRONOMY? What other words can you find?

See how stellar your knowledge of space is with this quiz.

1. Pluto is known as this.
   a. A dwarf planet
   b. A baby planet
   c. A puppy planet

2. Which planet is closest to the sun?
   a. Earth
   b. Venus
   c. Mercury

3. How much bigger is the sun's diameter than that of Earth's?
   a. 19 times bigger
   b. 109 times bigger
   c. 19 million times bigger

4. What are Saturn's rings made up of?
   a. Fiery gas
   b. Gold and diamonds
   c. Ice, dust, and rocks

5. What is a common nickname for Mars?
   a. The Red Planet
   b. The Green Planet
   c. E.T.'s Home Planet

6. What year did astronauts first walk on the moon?
   a. 1949
   b. 1969
   c. 1999

KIDS' SCIENCE QUESTIONS

How do astronomers discover other galaxies?

Astronomer Dr. Ken Croswell says the trick is to find the galaxies among the many objects in the sky. If an object shows as a point of light, it's probably a star, not a galaxy. If the object looks like a pinwheel, it's a galaxy. Each galaxy is made up of many stars swirling around, so only a galaxy can take this swirly shape. If the object is a fuzzy patch whose light is moving faster than 500 kilometers per second, then it's probably a galaxy. It can't be part of our galaxy because it's moving too fast for our galaxy to hold it. So, if it's that far away and still bright enough to see, it's probably another galaxy. But astronomers still make mistakes. If the galaxy is compact, they may think, at first, that it's a star!

Halley's Comet passes by Earth only every 75 to 76 years. The last time was 35 years ago. So, get ready for the next sighting—in **2062!**

NATIONAL LEARN ABOUT COMPOSTING DAY

Food scraps and yard trimmings together make up about 30 percent of what we throw away. Instead, compost that waste! This keeps it out of landfills, where it takes up space and releases methane, a gas linked to global warming. Then use the compost to get things growing.

No backyard? No problem! City dwellers can create an indoor compost.

Worms can turn waste into compost quicker. They wriggle through, breaking up chunks. As they eat dead plants and leaves, their poop adds important nutrients to the mix. Worm tunnels also leave spaces for water and air to reach the deep parts of the pile. Help these worms compost the soil by finding your way from START to FINISH.

Organisms release heat as they break down. The center of a compost pile can reach 140 degrees or more!

International Compost Awareness Week is **MAY 2–8, 2021.**

May 1
MAY DAY AND LEI DAY

For thousands of years, people celebrated May 1 by giving bouquets of wildflowers (often anonymously) and dancing around a maypole decorated with streamers. Since 1928, Hawaiians have celebrated Lei Day. Why not combine the two holidays and leave a flower garland on a friend's doorstep? Thread wildflowers on floral wire or make a daisy chain.

Leis made of flowers are given to visitors as a traditional Hawaiian welcome. Which two of these leis are exactly alike?

Since the 1880s, May Day has also been International Workers' Day—equal to America's Labor Day in some countries. It began as a protest to fight for an eight-hour workday.

Mayday, an airplane distress signal, has nothing to do with the first of May. It comes from the French *m'aider,* meaning "help me."

May 2, 2021
NATIONAL LEMONADE DAY

On the first Sunday in May, be a boss and open your own lemonade stand!

Lydia's bowl of lemons tipped over and the lemons have rolled away! How many can you find?

Lydia is selling her lemonade for 50 cents a cup. She spent $20 on supplies to make 50 cups of lemonade. How many cups of lemonade does she need to sell before she makes a profit? How much money will she make if she sells all 50 cups?

Lemonade is an ancient drink. *Qatarzimat,* lemon juice mixed with sugar, was sold in Egyptian marketplaces at least 900 years ago.

May 8
NO SOCKS DAY

Can't decide on a pair to wear? Free up your toes and your laundry load by going without socks. But first help Henry find a match for each of the socks numbered 1 through 7.
P.S. Henry: May 10 is Clean Up Your Room Day.

Why don't grizzlies wear socks?

They prefer to go bear-foot

May 13
NATIONAL FROG JUMPING DAY

Mark Twain's famous short story "The Celebrated Jumping Frog of Calaveras County," published in 1865, inspired this special day.

Three friends have entered their frogs in the annual Calaveras jumping contest. Using the clues provided, can you figure out whose frog is whose and what place each frog took in the contest?

Use the chart to keep track of your answers. Put an **X** in each box that can't be true and an **O** in boxes that match.

	Tad	Pollie	Hoppy	1st	2nd	3rd
Jordan						
Skyler						
Riley						

1. Jordan's frog finished after Hoppy.
2. Skyler's frog finished before Riley's frog and Pollie.
3. Tad finished second.

119

Take a spin around the globe to see how

May 3, 2021

SHAM EL-NESSIM

Sham El-Nessim, Egypt's oldest celebration, means "inhaling the breeze." So, during this spring festival, families head outdoors to parks, gardens, and zoos. They often picnic with traditional foods, such as salted fish, onions, and eggs. Sham El-Nessim is now a national holiday in Egypt with both Christians and Muslims celebrating.

Ancient Egyptians determined the beginning of the spring equinox by measuring the sun's position over the Great Pyramid in Giza.

May 5

KODOMO NO HI

In Japan, *Kodomo no Hi,* or Children's Day, is all about wishing kids health and happiness. Carp streamers made from brightly colored paper or cloth, called *koinobori*, are hung from the rooftops and public buildings as a symbol of children's determination and strength.

Japanese Carp Kite

1. For the body, cut a vase shape from a **paper bag**. Tape a **chenille stick** to the body's widest part. Leave 1 inch of the chenille stick hanging off each edge.

2. For scales, cut up **cupcake liners** and glue them to the narrow part of the body. Use pieces of **coffee filters** for the tail and fins.

3. Decorate the head with **colored paper**.

4. Punch two holes in the head and tie **yarn** through them for a hanger. Twist the ends of the chenille stick together.

Carp, or koi fish, are thought to be strong and spirited, overcoming all obstacles to swim upstream.

THE WORLD

people around the world celebrate in May.

May 9
📍 VICTORY DAY

This Russian holiday marks Nazi Germany's surrender to the Soviet Union in 1945. It honors the millions of people who lost their lives in World War II, known in Russia as the Great Patriotic War. Military parades are held in major cities, with the largest one in Moscow's Red Square. It ends with fireworks displays set off in 15 parks around the city. **Can you find where the 3 jigsaw pieces fit into this photo of the Red Square fireworks?**

May 17
📍 CONSTITUTION DAY

Norway's celebration of its independence in 1814 is known as *syttende mai* (seventeenth of May). But kids know it as a day when they can have as many *pølser med lompe* (hot dogs in a potato tortilla) and as much *is krem* (ice cream) as they like!

Norwegians eat as much as 10 times more ice cream on May 17 than on any other spring day.

121

SUNDAY	MONDAY	TUESDAY	WEDNESDAY
ZODIAC SIGNS GEMINI: MAY 21–JUNE 20  CANCER: JUNE 21–JULY 22		**National Say Something Nice Day** Say something nice to five different people today. **1**	**National Rotisserie Chicken Day** Drumstick or white meat? **2**
National Day (Sweden) Swedes celebrate this day with special ceremonies welcoming new Swedish citizens. **6**	**National Oklahoma Day** Oklahoma is OK! **7**	**WORLD OCEANS DAY** **8**	*Oh boy, oh boy, oh boy.* On this day in 1934, Donald Duck appeared for the first time. **9**
National Sewing Machine Day A stitch in time . . . **13**	**FLAG DAY** **14**	*Fasten your seatbelts!* In 1921, Bessie Coleman was the first African American to receive a pilot's license. **15**	*Wheeeeee!* In 1884, the first roller coaster in America opened. **16**
FATHER'S DAY **FIRST DAY OF SUMMER** **20**	**National Selfie Day** Say cheese! **21**	**Teacher's Day (El Salvador)** Give *una manzana* to your teacher today. **22**	**National Pink Flamingo Day** Try standing on one leg today. **23**
NATIONAL ICE-CREAM CAKE DAY **27**	**National Alaska Day** *Juneau* the capital of Alaska? **28**	**International Mud Day** Make some mud pies to celebrate. **29**	*A novel of love and war.* On this day in 1936, *Gone with the Wind* was published. **30**

THURSDAY	FRIDAY	SATURDAY

JUNE

He really was walking on air. In 1965, Edward Higgins White II became the first American astronaut to walk in space.

3

NATIONAL HUG YOUR CAT DAY

4

Hot-Air Balloon Day

The highest hot-air balloon flight reached 68,986 feet.

5

National Herbs and Spices Day

They spice things up.

10

National Flip-Flop Day

Give your shoes the day off.

11

NATIONAL RED ROSE DAY

12

Goal! The 2021 FIFA Club World Cup starts today in China and goes until July 4.

17

Constitution Day (Seychelles)

The current constitution of the group of 115 islands was adopted on this day in 1993.

18

World Juggling Day

Keep your eye on the ball today.

19

Swim a Lap Day

Dive in!

24

Was it called New Dominion *back then?* In 1788, Virginia became a state.

25

National Canoe Day

Grab a paddle.

26

BIRTHSTONES
PEARL, ALEXANDRITE, AND MOONSTONE

FLOWERS
ROSE AND HONEYSUCKLE

NATIONAL OCEAN MONTH

How many pairs of matching sea creatures can you find?

HOOKS DINER

LANDFOOD SEAFOOD

TRUE or FALSE?

Which of these ocean facts are true and which are all wet? Circle T or F.

T F The ocean is home to most of Earth's plants and animals.

T F Whales have belly buttons.

T F The world's most active volcanoes are found beneath the Pacific Ocean.

T F A jellyfish's body is made up of water, sugar, and grape flavoring.

T F The seafloor of the Southern Ocean is lined with ceramic bathroom tile.

Why do seahorses like only salt water?

AHCHOoo!

Because pepper water makes them sneeze

Where did the whale play his musical instrument?

In the orca-stra

What kind of fish goes well with peanut butter?

Jellyfish

AFRICAN AMERICAN MUSIC APPRECIATION MONTH

African American musicians have created some of the most innovative music styles, such as jazz. Unscramble the names of musical instruments used in a New Orleans jazz band. Then copy the circled letters in order onto the blanks at the bottom of the page to answer the riddle.

1. JOBAN: ___ ___ ___ ___○
2. BOMTRONE: ___ ___ ___ ___ ___ ○___ ___
3. BUTA: ○___ ___ ___
4. XOOPHENSA: ___ ___ ___ ___ ___ ○___ ___ ___
5. TUPTREM: ___ ___ ___ ___ ○___ ___
6. CARLNITE: ___ ___ ___ ___ ___ ○___ ___
7. IPNOA: ___ ○___ ___ ___
8. SURMD: ___ ○___ ___ ___
9. SABS: ___ ___ ___○
10. ATGUIR: ___ ___ ___ ___ ___ ___

Why do farmers play soft jazz for their corn stalks?

It's easy ___ ___ ___ ___ ___ ___ ___ ___.

NATIONAL CANDY MONTH

Cotton candy was called fairy floss until 1920.

It takes at least seven days to make a jelly bean.

Everyone knows candy is made with sugar. But did you know it can contain acid or oil, too? Try these two simple experiments to unlock the secrets inside your favorite candy.

ACID: Candy that tastes sour contains acid. Most fruit-flavored candy contains citric acid, the sour chemical in lemons. To test a sour candy for acid, try this:

• Dissolve the **candy** in a half-cup of **water**. (WARHEADS and SweeTARTS work well.)

• Sprinkle in a spoonful of **baking soda**.

• If you see bubbles, the candy water contains acid.

What's happening? Baking soda reacts with acid to form the gas, carbon dioxide. The gas makes bubbles in the water.

shiny puddles

bubbles

OIL: Many kinds of chewy candy, like taffy, are made with oil. The oil helps keep the candy smooth, soft, and chewy. To test a chewy candy for oil, try this:

• Dissolve the **candy** in a cup of hot tap **water**. (Try Starburst candy.)

• Look for shiny puddles floating on the surface.

• When the water cools, you may see a white, waxy layer on top.

What's happening? The kinds of oils used in these candies melt in hot water, forming the shiny puddles. In colder water, the oil can cool into a white, waxy solid. Since oil is lighter than water, it floats.

NATIONAL FRESH FRUIT AND VEGETABLE MONTH

Can you spot a fruit or vegetable hiding in each sentence? **Example:** The shi**p eas**ed into port.

1. In the showroom, a car rotated on a platform.

2. Maya looked up each book Liam recommended.

3. The dog's bark alerted the cat.

4. "I'm getting a new bicycle Monday," said Darnell.

5. Adrianna gets up early every morning.

6. I bought a teapot at Oscar's sale.

7. Pete and his mom baked his teacher rye bread.

8. That clown can spin a chair on his hand.

GREAT OUTDOORS MONTH

Without showing this page to anyone, ask friends or family members for the words in parentheses. Then read the story out loud.

Today I went camping. I filled my backpack with _____ (PLURAL NOUN) and headed out. I

enjoyed seeing nature, like the _____ (PLURAL NOUN) growing on a tree. Then I suddenly

heard a noise! It sounded like an angry _____ (WILD ANIMAL) . Or was it a _____ (TYPE OF MONSTER)

from _____ (NEARBY TOWN) ? I got my answer soon enough when I came face to face with

a terrifying _____ (INSECT) . Thinking quickly, I threw it some _____ (FOOD)

and was lucky to escape with my life! I was feeling hungry, so I started roasting some

_____ (PLURAL NOUN) on a stick when I heard another noise. Was it a herd of _____ (ADJECTIVE)

_____ (PLURAL NOUN) ? No, it was Mom on the back deck, calling my name. I happily ended

my scary, _____ (ADJECTIVE) camping trip in the backyard and went in for dinner.

FISHING FOR HIDDEN WORDS

Celebrate by finding these six words (not pictures) in the scene. Can you find BOY, FISH, HOT, NICE, TREE, and WAVE?

TONGUE TWISTERS

The wretched runner ran around the rough and rugged rock.

A flabby flounder fouled Flanders's fishing feast.

The harried hiker helped heat the honeyed ham.

Floyd found a fish before Fran found a fish.

127

June 4, 1896

125 YEARS AGO, HENRY FORD TEST-DROVE HIS FIRST AUTOMOBILE.

A Highlights Classic Puzzle

He called it the Quadricycle. When he tried to drive out of the shed where he had built the car, he discovered the automobile didn't fit through the door. Fortunately, he was able to take his history-making ride after chopping the wall open with an ax! **Can you find 16 objects in this Hidden Pictures puzzle of Ford's first ride?**

Henry Ford didn't invent the automobile. He is famous for figuring out how to build cars cheaply so that most people could buy one.

Ford's car had bicycle wheels for tires.

Ford's assistant had to bike ahead and shoo people and horses out of the way.

A brand-new Ford Model T car cost $300 in 1925. That's over $4,300 dollars in 2021!

The car had no brakes and couldn't go in reverse.

At the beginning of 2019, there were 276 million vehicles on the road in the U.S.

June 6, 1946
75 YEARS AGO, THE NATIONAL BASKETBALL ASSOCIATION WAS FOUNDED.

Watch the NBA Finals this month!

At first, the league was called the Basketball Association of America. It was renamed the NBA three years later, after merging with another league.

Lebron James, of the Los Angeles Lakers, has been the NBA's most valuable player (MVP) 4 times during his career.

Eleven teams played in the league's first year. Only three of them are still around today, although one team is now in a different city and another team shortened its name. **How many team names can you match up?**

Boston	Bombers
Chicago	Capitols
Cleveland	Celtics
Detroit	Falcons
New York	Huskies
Philadelphia	Ironmen
Pittsburgh	Knickerbockers
Providence	Rebels
St. Louis	Stags
Toronto	Steamrollers
Washington	Warriors

NONSENSE NAMES

Many team names are related to the team's home city. But when a team moves, the name usually goes with it— even when it doesn't make sense anymore.

UTAH JAZZ Utah isn't a hotspot for jazz music. The team got its name from its original city: New Orleans, Louisiana, the birthplace of jazz.

MEMPHIS GRIZZLIES You won't find any grizzly bears in the forests of Tennessee. The team started out as the Vancouver (Canada) Grizzlies. Grizzly bears make their home in that part of Canada.

LOS ANGELES LAKERS This team used to be the Minneapolis Lakers. Minneapolis is a city in Minnesota, a state whose nickname is "Land of 10,000 Lakes."

GO SKATEBOARDING DAY

Can you help this skateboarder meet up with his friend
at the skate park?

JUNE IS ALSO NATIONAL SAFETY MONTH!

Follow these safety tips for skateboarding.

- Always wear protective gear that fits well, including a helmet and pads. Wear closed-toe shoes with non-slip soles.

- Choose safe places to skateboard. Never ride in the street, during wet weather, or through crowded areas.

- Find smooth surfaces to ride on. Check for cracks and debris before skateboarding.

- Don't wear headphones while riding.

- Never hold onto a moving vehicle while skateboarding.

- Learn how to fall properly by practicing a fall on a soft surface, such as grass.

SKATEBOARDING TRICKS OR FAKES?

Each pair of words has one skateboarding trick and one phony. **Circle the tricks.**

airwalk or spacewalk?

pluto foot or goofy foot?

kickflip or kiteflip?

McTwist or McNugget?

olive or ollie?

NATIONAL HOCKEY LEAGUE
STANLEY CUP FINAL

The Stanley Cup is named after Lord Stanley of Preston, the governor general of Canada in 1892. He bought the first cup for the league.

Take a shot at the correct answer and score a point for each one you get right.

1. When ice hockey first began, what did players use for a puck?
   a. A frozen hamburger patty
   b. A frozen patty of cow manure
   c. A crushed soda can

2. What was the first hockey mask made of?
   a. Leather
   b. Wood
   c. A carved pumpkin

3. On September 23, 1992, how did goalie Manon Rhéaume make sports history?
   a. Manon caught a puck blindfolded.
   b. Manon performed a figure skating routine during a game.
   c. Manon became the first woman to play in the NHL in a preseason game.

4. What is written on the Stanley Cup?
   a. Famous quotes by people named Stanley
   b. The names of the teams and players who have won the NHL championship
   c. The recipe for Stanley's Cup of Noodles soup

5. When a hockey player scores three goals in a game, what do fans throw on the ice?
   a. Hats
   b. Frozen fish sticks
   c. Hockey pucks

FINAL SCORE:

You scored _____ times!

A new Stanley Cup isn't made every year. The same cup is given to the championship's winning team for 100 days during the off-season.

CHAMPIONSHIP CHAMPS

These teams have won the Stanley Cup the most times since the NHL took over the championship in 1927:

1. Montreal Canadiens

2. Toronto Maple Leafs

3. Detroit Red Wings

4. Boston Bruins

5. Chicago Blackhawks

Why did the hockey rink melt after the game?

Because all the fans left

Why do hockey players make the best birthday cakes?

Because they know all about icing

What did the hockey goalie say to the puck?

"Catch you later."

NATURE PHOTOGRAPHY DAY

Focus in on the 18 hidden objects in and under this tree.

 ghost

 fish

 hanger

candy corn

artist's brush

slice of pizza

 umbrella

bell

 bowling ball

 necktie

bat

 shuttlecock

tooth

 ice-cream cone

heart

 cane

crown

pointy hat

PICTURE THIS!

Here are some tips for taking photos of animals.

- **Wait It Out:** Animals won't follow directions. You'll have to wait patiently to get a good shot.

- **Focus on the Eyes:** Humans often connect with others through eye contact, so focus on the animal's eyes or head.

- **Get Low:** Instead of pointing your camera downwards, kneel or lie down (from a safe distance) so you're on the animal's level.

- **Zoom In:** Close-up photos show a lot of detail about an animal's face, eyes, or fur. Use the camera's zoom feature to get a detailed photo.

- **Snap, Snap, Snap:** Don't expect every photo to be perfect. Photographers often take 100 pictures to end up with one they really like.

- **Practice!** To practice your skills, take plenty of pictures of pets, birds, or insects, or visit a zoo or aquarium.

National Camera Day is June 29!

June 21
WORLD MUSIC DAY

Melody's Music Shop is having a sale! Name the eight instruments on the sale wall, then unscramble their first letters to solve the riddle. We've placed the *A* for *acoustic guitar* in the correct spot to get you started.

Tongue Twisters for Singers

Singers often warm up their mouths, lips, and tongues with tongue twisters. How fast can you say these tricky phrases?

If Stu chews shoes, should Stu choose the shoes he chews?

Wayne went to Wales to watch walruses.

Four furious friends fought for the phone.

Six sleek swans swam swiftly southwards.

Five frantic frogs fled from fifty fierce fishes.

NATIONAL CHEESE DAY

Search for the names of 22 types of cheeses that are hidden in this word search.

WORD LIST

AMERICAN
ASIAGO
BLUE
BRIE
CHEDDAR
COLBY
COTTAGE
EDAM
FETA
GOAT
GORGONZOLA
GOUDA
LIMBURGER
MONTEREY JACK
MOZZARELLA
MUENSTER
PANEER
PARMESAN
PROVOLONE
RICOTTA
ROQUEFORT
SWISS

```
M M A Z C F Y A S P K N U K
R O N A E O S B R A A K C L
E A Z T J I T O L S L A H I
T D A Z A K V T E O J H S M
S U K G A O N M A Y C S G B
N O O X L R R A E G I S O U
E G T O V A E R C W E Z P R
U G N R P X E L S I B C M G
M E H I B T H D L Q R R B E
J D H C N R E E N A P E I R
H J G O R G O N Z O L A M E
V E M T R O F E U Q O R Z A
E D L T P W C H E D D A R O
W A T A B L U E K P G C F I
Q M N V A F S R T A O G B X
```

What do you get when you cross a dragon and a cheese sandwich?

A grilled-cheese sandwich

Celebrate more delicious foods with these four holidays.

June 11

NATIONAL CORN ON THE COB DAY

A typical ear of corn has about 800 kernels.

June 20

NATIONAL SMOOTHIE DAY

Mashed beans will make a smoothie thicker without adding any bean flavor.

June 22

NATIONAL ONION RING DAY

Americans eat an average of 22 pounds of onions per person per year.

June 26

NATIONAL CHOCOLATE PUDDING DAY

The first known recipe for chocolate pudding appears in a cookbook from 1730.

FATHER'S DAY

Make a card for your father or someone you'd like to celebrate on Father's Day.

GOLF BAG

1. For the golf bag, cover a **short cardboard tube** with **paper**. Add a handle.

2. For golf clubs, bend one end of three **chenille sticks** and cover each with **foil**. Glue the clubs into the golf bag.

3. Fold **cardstock** in half to make a card. Glue on the golf bag. Add a paper flag and a message.

LAWN MOWER

1. Fold **cardstock** in half to make a card.

2. Use **paper** to cover a **small box** (such as a raisin box). Add a message. Glue it to the front of the card.

3. Tape on paper wheels, a strip of paper "grass," and a **chenille-stick** handle.

4. Add a message on the "grass" inside.

BARBECUE

1. Fold **cardstock** in half to make a card.

2. For the grate, glue **chenille sticks** across the front.

3. Add **paper** food and handles.

4. Write a message on paper inside.

FLAG DAY

Flag Day celebrates the official adoption of the stars and stripes by the Second Continental Congress on June 14, 1777. Flag Day was first celebrated in 1885 at the Stony Hill School, a one-room school in Waubeka, Wisconsin.

MAKE RED, WHITE, AND BLUE NACHOS

Before you begin, ask an adult to set the oven to broil.

1. Open and spread a 6-ounce bag of **blue tortilla chips** evenly on a 9-by-13-inch pan.

2. Spoon 1 cup of **salsa** over the chips.

3. Sprinkle 1 cup of shredded **white cheddar cheese** on top. Add toppings, such as chopped tomatoes, sliced olives, and black beans, if you'd like.

4. Ask an adult to broil the nachos for 3 minutes. Let stand for 3 minutes before eating.

ON JUNE 14, 1777, Congress decided the U.S. flag would have 13 stripes, alternating in red and white, plus 13 white stars in a blue field. The number 13 was chosen because there were 13 colonies.

After Vermont and Kentucky became the 14th and 15th states, the flag was changed to 15 stars and 15 stripes in 1795.

As new states joined the country, there wasn't enough room to keep adding stripes. So in 1818, Congress decided the flag would go back to 13 stripes and have one star for every state.

The arrangement of the 50 stars on today's flag was created by a high school student. Robert Heft of Ohio created the flag for a class project when Alaska and Hawaii were about to become states. He also sent his design to the White House. Heft got a B- on the project, but the teacher changed it to an A after President Eisenhower chose Heft's design as our new flag.

FIRST DAY

Kick off summer with these fun activities!

3 SUNNY-DAY CRAFTS

- **Create a suncatcher** using colored paper, yarn, and tissue paper.
- **Build a sculpture** using objects from nature.
- **Make your own bubble wands** from chenille sticks. Dip them in some bubble solution, and blow!

3 WAYS TO USE SIDEWALK CHALK

- **Create a story** just by drawing pictures.
- **Create a life-sized board game,** drawing the game spaces with chalk.
- **Write funny jokes** or cheerful messages on your sidewalk.

3 WATER BALLOON GAMES

- **Yard Toss.** Place four rulers (or other markers) at varying distances. See who can toss a water balloon the farthest without bursting it.
- **Exploding Tag.** Fill a few water balloons and set them aside. Instead of tagging another player, *It* lightly tosses a water balloon at that person (below the neck). If it doesn't pop, that person becomes *It*!
- **Balloon Bowling.** Use empty cans and plastic bottles as pins and a water balloon as the ball. Set the pins on a flat surface outdoors and see how many you can knock down.

For people in Australia, Argentina, and the rest of the Southern Hemisphere, today is the first day of winter.

The first day of summer is also called the summer solstice. It's the day with the most daylight hours in the Northern Hemisphere.

In northern Alaska, the sun never fully sets today, and in 1906, locals began celebrating by playing baseball in the midnight sun. The Alaska Goldpanners baseball team took over the tradition in 1960. Their annual summer solstice game starts at 10:30 p.m. and finishes by 2 a.m.—in the sunlight.

Be sure to throw away the pieces after the balloons pop!

OF SUMMER

These kids are having a field day on the first day of summer. Which things in this picture are silly? It's up to you!

FIELD DAY

CHIPS

COACH

WORLD GIRAFFE DAY

Can you find 11 differences between these two pictures?

Giraffes are the tallest living land animals on Earth.

Giraffes have dark purple tongues.

An adult male giraffe can grow to be 18 feet tall.

No two giraffes have the same pattern on their coat.

Giraffes eat at least 75 pounds of leaves and twigs a day.

Giraffes usually run from danger, but a kick from their powerful legs could kill a lion.

A giraffe's foot is the size of a dinner plate.

GIRAFFE
CORD KEEPER

1. On thin **cardboard**, draw a giraffe's head and neck. Cut out the shape.

2. Glue the shape onto **felt**. Cut it out.

3. Decorate the giraffe with felt, **puffy paint**, and **wiggle eyes**.

4. Cut a slit on one side of the neck. Stick one end of your headphones in the slit and wrap the headphones around the giraffe.

June 30
ASTEROID DAY

Asteroid Day marks the anniversary of the 1908 Tunguska impact, in which an asteroid hit the Earth in Siberia, destroying 800 square miles of forest. The goal of Asteroid Day is education and awareness.

ORBITING A SPACE POTATO

Planets aren't the only bodies in space that can have moons orbiting them. The potato-shaped asteroid shown here, which is named **Ida** (EYE-duh), is just one of many asteroids massive enough to have their own moons. Gravity keeps Ida's moon, Dactyl (DACK-tull), going around the asteroid, just as Earth's gravity keeps our Moon in orbit around us.

Dactyl is just 1 mile wide. Our Moon is 2,160 miles wide!

Dactyl orbits Ida the long way.

Like most asteroids, Ida isn't round. It contains so little material that its gravity isn't strong enough to pull it into a sphere shape.

Craters on Ida and Dactyl were caused by smaller asteroids that hit their surfaces over time.

Ida and Dactyl are in the asteroid belt, between the orbits of Mars and Jupiter.

KIDS' SCIENCE QUESTIONS
What is the difference between an asteroid and a meteor?

Asteroids are sometimes called *minor planets*. They are fairly small, rocky worlds. Like Earth and the other planets, asteroids move in orbits around the Sun. Most asteroids are in a "belt"—a group of orbiting paths that lie between Mars and Jupiter.

A *meteor* is a streak of light we see in the sky when a much smaller bit of rock enters Earth's atmosphere and burns from the heat of friction as it falls through the air.

Two other important terms are *meteoroid* and *meteorite*. A meteoroid is a bit of rock that could burn up to create a meteor—before it enters the atmosphere. Meteorites are much more unusual. A meteorite is any part of a meteoroid that hits Earth's surface because it has not been completely burned up during its fall.

Meteorite

NATIONAL YO-YO DAY

Learn even more yo-yo tricks from books at the library or from videos.

GRAB A YO-YO AND DO THESE TRICKS.

THROWDOWN

1. Curl your arm as if you're making a muscle.

2. Bring your elbow down with a snap and release the yo-yo as it goes over the ends of your fingers.

3. Then turn your hand over to catch the yo-yo upon its return.

SLEEPER

1. Start with a Throwdown. Leave the yo-yo spinning at the bottom of the string.

2. Before it slows down too much, turn your hand over (palm down) and give the string a slight upward jerk to return the yo-yo to your hand.

WALK THE DOG

1. Throw a fast Sleeper. Gently lower the yo-yo to the floor so that it barely touches.

2. Don't bounce your hand. The yo-yo will begin to move along the floor.

June 8

NATIONAL BEST FRIENDS DAY

How well do you know your best friend? Fill in the blanks, then ask your friend how you did.

Your best friend's name: _____ Birthday: _____

Favorite food: _____ Favorite game: _____

Phrase they say all the time: _____

Thing they are afraid of: _____

On Saturday mornings, your best friend is usually doing this: _____

Favorite thing you both like to do together: _____

A goal they have for the future: _____

_____

JUNETEENTH

On this day in 1865, a Union general announced to the people of Galveston, Texas, that slavery had been abolished in the United States, more than two-and-a-half years after the Emancipation Proclamation. The newly freed slaves in Texas erupted in a joyous celebration, and the event became known as Juneteenth.

Today people around the country celebrate this anniversary of the freedom from slavery with parades, festivals, and barbecues.

STRAWBERRY BUBBLE LEMONADE

Put 1 cup of **strawberries** into a blender. Blend until thick and smooth. Add 3 cups of **lemonade** and 2 cups of **seltzer.** Blend together and chill. Pour ¼ cup of **maple syrup** onto one plate and 2 packs of **Pop Rocks** onto another. Dip the rims of 6 glasses into the maple syrup and then into the Pop Rocks. Add a few **ice cubes** to each glass and pour in the strawberry lemonade.

The color red is an important part of Juneteenth, and people eat and drink red foods, such as strawberry soda, hot sauce on barbecue, and red velvet cake.

June 27
NATIONAL SUNGLASSES DAY

Find the two columns with the same five pairs of sunglasses.

Reports suggest that someone in the U.S. loses, breaks, or sits on a pair of sunglasses every 14 minutes!

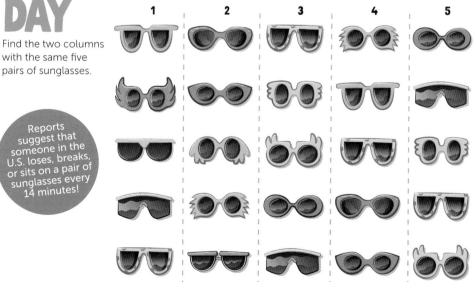

1 2 3 4 5

June 12
◉ DIA DOS NAMORADOS

Valentine's Day falls in February, but in Brazil the holiday honoring love is in June. *Dia dos Namorados* means "Boyfriend and Girlfriend's Day." Couples celebrate with cards, candy, and dinner.

These kids tangled up their balloon strings. Can you figure out whose is whose?

June 16
◉ YOUTH DAY

South Africa's flag is unique in that it uses six main colors in the design.

Youth Day commemorates a protest by black students in South Africa in 1976.
At the time, the government discriminated against people who weren't white, and the students were peacefully protesting an unfair law. The police fired on the protesters and many students lost their lives. This terrible event eventually led to a change in the government. Today, South Africans honor those students on Youth Day by visiting museums, attending events about history, and by helping their communities.

THE WORLD

June 17
⦿ NATIONAL DAY

National Day in Iceland celebrates the country's independence from Denmark in 1944. In every town, a woman is chosen to read a poem or give a speech. She wears the national costume of Iceland, and many other people do, too. The whole country celebrates with parades, marching bands, carnivals, and concerts.

June 20
⦿ FLAG DAY

Día de la Bandera Nacional honors the flag of Argentina and the man who created it, Manuel Belgrano, a military leader who helped the country become independent from Spain. Every June 20, Argentina's president gives a speech and a big parade is held in the town where the flag was first flown.

The "Sun of May" was added to the flag in 1818, inspired by the sun on the first Argentine coin. It also honors an Incan sun deity, Inti.

The blue stripes are known as *celeste,* which means "sky blue."

Although Belgrano first raised the flag in 1812, it went through many variations until this official version was approved in 1861.

145

SUNDAY	MONDAY	TUESDAY	WEDNESDAY

ZODIAC SIGNS
CANCER:
JUNE 21–JULY 22

LEO:
JULY 23–AUGUST 22

BIRTHSTONE
RUBY

FLOWERS
LARKSPUR AND
WATER LILY

INDEPENDENCE DAY

4

National Hawaii Day

Aloha!

5

Play ball! In 1933, the first Major League Baseball All-Star Game was played.

6

NATIONAL MACARONI DAY

7

World Population Day

The U.S. Census Bureau estimates there are 7.7 billion people on Earth.

11

National Paper Bag Day

Time to make some crafts!

12

International Rock Day

Don't take today for granite.

13

Far out! In 2015, NASA's New Horizons probe became the first spacecraft to fly near Pluto.

1

NATIONAL SOUR CANDY DAY

18

EID AL-ADHA

begins at sunset.

19

International Chess Day

A day that's fit for a king . . . and a queen.

20

Liberation Day (Guam)

People celebrate with a carnival and parade with giant floats.

21

NATIONAL HOT FUDGE SUNDAE DAY

25

It happened in a New York minute. In 1788, New York became the 11th state.

26

National Walk on Stilts Day

How's the view up there?

27

National Soccer Day

28

JULY

THURSDAY	FRIDAY	SATURDAY
National Postal Worker Day Deliver your thanks to your mail carrier. **1**	**World UFO Day** Keep your eyes on the skies. **2**	*"We are the keepers of the flame of liberty."* In 1986, after a two-year restoration, President Reagan lit the Statue of Liberty's torch in honor of its 100th anniversary. **3**
National Video Game Day Get your thumbs in shape. **8**	**National Sugar Cookie Day** Sweet! **9**	**Don't Step on a Bee Day** **10**
National Give Something Away Day Give something to someone less fortunate. **15**	**World Snake Day** *Yessssss.* **16**	*There's a mouse in the house.* In 1955, Disneyland opened in Anaheim, California. **17**	**Your favorite meal, made by** _____ (PERSON OR PLACE) **on July 24, 2021, is** _____ .
NATIONAL HAMMOCK DAY **22**	**National Children's Day (Indonesia)** Indonesians dedicate this day to focusing on improving the lives of children. **23**	**National Drive-Thru Day** Please drive up to the window and celebrate. **24**
Global Tiger Day Wear stripes today! **29**	**Paperback Book Day** Find a shady spot outside and dive into a good story. **30**	**NATIONAL MUTT DAY** Sit, stay, and celebrate. **31**

ICE CREAM MONTH

America's top 10 favorite ice-cream flavors are listed here. Can you crack the code and fill in their names? Each number stands for a different letter. Once you know one number's letter, you can fill in that letter in all the words.

We'll give you a hint—vanilla and chocolate take the first two spots!

1. ___ ___ ___ ___ ___ ___ ___
3   2   7   12 10 10 2

2. ___ ___ ___ ___ ___ ___ ___ ___ ___
8   1   11 8   11 10 2   19 6

3. ___ ___ ___ ___ ___ ___
8   11 11 17 12 6   18

___ ___ ___   ___ ___ ___ ___ ___
2   7   13   8   4   6   2   14

4. ___ ___ ___ ___
14 12 7   19

___ ___ ___ ___ ___ ___ ___ ___
8   1   11 8   11 10 2   19 6

___ ___ ___ ___
8   1   12 9

5. ___ ___ ___ ___ ___ ___ ___ ___ ___
8   1   11 8   11 10 2   19 6

___ ___ ___ ___   ___ ___ ___ ___ ___ ___
8   1   12 9   8   11 11 17 12 6

___ ___ ___ ___ ___
21 11 20 22 1

6. ___ ___ ___ ___ ___ ___   ___ ___ ___ ___ ___
5   20 19 19 6   4   9   6   8   2   7

7. ___ ___ ___ ___ ___ ___   ___ ___ ___ ___ ___
8   11 11 17 12 6   21 11 20 22 1

8. ___ ___ ___ ___ ___ ___ ___ ___ ___ ___
18 19 4   2   16 5   6   4   4   15

9. ___ ___ ___ ___ ___   ___ ___ ___ ___ ___ ___
14 11 11 18 6   19 4   2   8   17 18

10. ___ ___ ___ ___ ___ ___ ___ ___ ___ ___
7   6   2   9   11 10 12 19 2   7

This flavor is made up of #1, #2, and #8!

The average American eats more than
23 pounds
of ice cream per year.

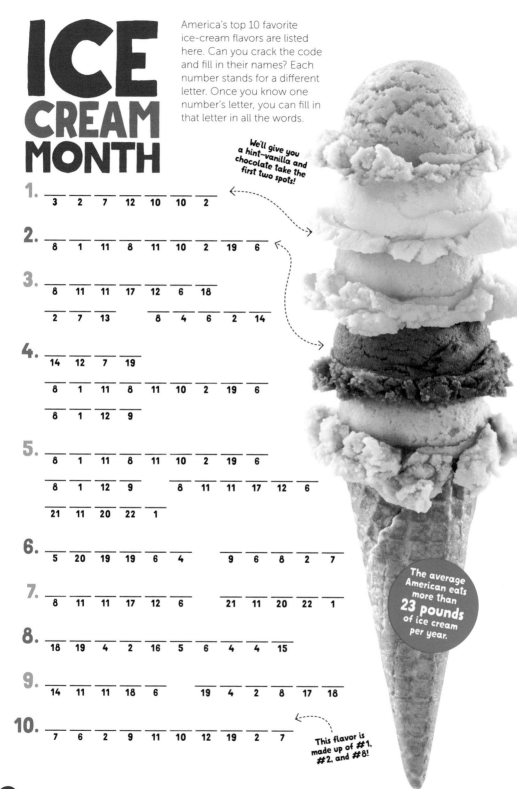

NATIONAL BERRY MONTH

The bumps on blackberries and raspberries are called drupelets.

July is also National Blueberry Month, National Blackberry Month, and National Raspberry Month. But you'll have to turn the calendar back to May for National Strawberry Month. Which things are silly in this berry-picking picture? It's up to you!

TONGUE TWISTERS

Some berries will color your tongue, but these berry fun sentences will twist your tongue. Try saying each five times, fast!

Bumblebees pick black blueberries.

Barry's blueberry baklava beat Bob's blackberry bake at the bake-off.

Bridget's blueberry bucket is bigger than Brock's blueberry bucket.

NATIONAL BISON MONTH

July is also Wild About Wildlife Month! What animal would you like to learn more about?

Buffalo and *bison* are often used interchangeably, but only bison live in North America. Buffalo mostly live in Africa and Asia. Bison have a large shoulder hump, a huge head, and lots of hair, including a beard! Buffalo have rounded horns, but no hump or thick hair.

Use these fun facts to solve the code below. Each coded space has two numbers. The first number tells you what fun fact to look at; the second number tells you which letter to use.

Bison . . .

1. are the largest mammals in North America.
2. grow up to six feet tall and weigh more than two thousand pounds!
3. have lived in Yellowstone National Park since prehistoric times.
4. raise their tails straight up when they're about to charge.
5. run at speeds up to 35 miles per hour.
6. live to be 10 to 20 years old.
7. have excellent hearing and sense of smell but are nearsighted.

Bison trails were later used for

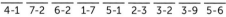

‾‾ ‾‾ ‾‾ ‾‾ ‾‾ ‾‾ ‾‾ ‾‾ ‾‾ .
4-1 7-2 6-2 1-7 5-1 2-3 3-2 3-9 5-6

MAKE A MATCH

Can you find 6 pairs of bison?

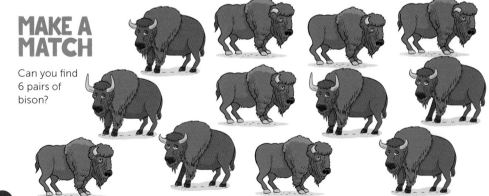

NATIONAL PARK AND RECREATION MONTH

This month was first celebrated in 1985!

There's lots of recreation going on at this park. Can you help Malik fly his toy plane from START to FINISH?

PLASTIC FREE JULY

Water bottles, grocery bags, straws—too many plastic items are used only once and then thrown away. Plastic garbage is polluting the ground and turning up in rivers and oceans, where it's harming birds and fish.

Give the environment a break this month and stick with reusable water bottles, cloth tote bags, and paper straws. Try making it a habit that lasts past July.

Paper, cloth, and glass are reusable materials that are also reusable in this puzzle. Combine each word with one from the Word List to form a new word.

WORD LIST
back
dish
eye
hour
table
weight

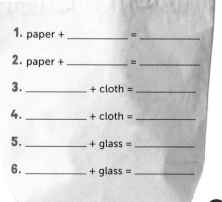

1. paper + _____ = _____

2. paper + _____ = _____

3. _____ + cloth = _____

4. _____ + cloth = _____

5. _____ + glass = _____

6. _____ + glass = _____

July 1, 1971

50 YEARS AGO, CONGRESS RATIFIED THE 26th AMENDMENT TO THE U.S. CONSTITUTION, GIVING 18-YEAR-OLDS THE RIGHT TO VOTE.

Before this amendment, you had to be 21 to vote. But many 18- to 20-year-olds were being drafted to fight in the Vietnam War. They thought it wasn't fair that they couldn't vote. So they used the slogan "Old Enough to Fight, Old Enough to Vote" for their cause. Most of the country agreed, and the law was passed quickly.

THE YOUTH VOTE

Elected officials make laws and solve problems in our communities and throughout the nation. They make decisions about everything from schools, to the environment, to sending soldiers to war. Their decisions affect all Americans, which is why voting is so important.

Although young adults were excited to vote in 1971, only 44 percent of 18- to 30-year-olds voted in the 2016 presidential election.

ELECTION SELECTION

Tanya, Liz, Tadashi, and Ray were recently elected to their student council. Use the clues below to figure out which candidate was voted to each position.

- One of the students' names starts with the same letter as the position they hold.
- Secretary was won by a candidate with eyeglasses.
- Vice President was won by the candidate with a patterned suit.
- Treasurer was won by a candidate with a collared shirt.

STUDENT COUNCIL POSITIONS

President _____

Vice President _____

Treasurer _____

Secretary _____

TANYA   LIZ   TADASHI   RAY

July 9, 1981

40 YEARS AGO, THE CHARACTER MARIO APPEARED IN A VIDEO GAME FOR THE FIRST TIME.

The arcade game *Donkey Kong* was released on this day, and Mario was a character called Jumpman. He was later renamed Mario and became the star of his own games.

Jumpman, now known as Mario, hops over a rolling barrel that was thrown by Donkey Kong, the gorilla star of the game.

- -

To find the *purr*-fect answer to the riddle below, first cross out all the pairs of matching letters. Then write the remaining letters in order in the spaces beneath the riddle.

AA	TT	II	TH	SS	QQ	EY
HH	OO	BB	RR	AL	EE	VV
LH	NN	ZZ	YY	CC	AV	AA
II	QQ	EE	EN	DD	PP	WW
IN	GG	LL	TT	VV	EL	ZZ
XX	HH	IV	II	BB	OO	SS
TT	UU	NN	EE	SS	ES	MM

Why are cats good at video games?

☐☐☐☐ ☐☐☐ ☐☐ ☐☐☐☐ ☐☐☐
☐☐☐☐ ☐☐☐☐☐.

153

SPORT CLIMBING

Similar to basketball, but the basket is higher, and it doesn't have a backboard

KORFBALL

MUAYTHAI

Similar to volleyball, but players can only use a fist or arm to hit the ball, never an open hand

FISTBALL

THE WORLD GAMES 2021

This Thai martial art is also known as *The Art of the Eight Limbs* because fighters frequently use their elbows and knees.

The World Games are held every four years in the year following the Summer Olympic Games. The world's best athletes compete in sports and events that are not part of the Olympic Games. In 2021, more than 3,600 athletes from around the world will compete at the 40th anniversary games in Birmingham, Alabama.

WORD LIST

AIR SPORTS
ARCHERY
BILLIARDS
BOULES SPORTS
BOWLING
CANOE / KAYAK
DANCESPORT
DUATHLON
FINSWIMMING
FISTBALL
FLOORBALL

FLYING DISC
GYMNASTICS
HANDBALL
JU-JITSU
KARATE
KICKBOXING
KORFBALL
LACROSSE
LIFESAVING
MUAYTHAI
ORIENTEERING

POWERLIFTING
RACQUETBALL
ROLLER SPORTS
SOFTBALL
SPORT CLIMBING
SQUASH
SUMO
TUG OF WAR
WATER SKI AND
   WAKEBOARD
WHEELCHAIR RUGBY

WATER SKI AND WAKEBOARD

Includes breaking, Latin, rock 'n' roll, and standard

DANCESPORT

Includes acrobatic gymnastics, aerobic gymnastics, parkour, rhythmic gymnastics, trampoline, and tumbling

GYMNASTICS

Swimmers use a mask, snorkel, and fins.

FINSWIMMING

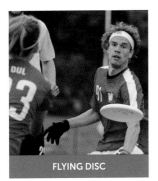

FLYING DISC

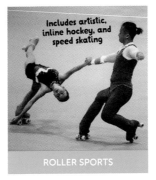

Includes artistic, inline hockey, and speed skating

ROLLER SPORTS

DUATHLON

You'll find these 32 sports played at the 2021 World Games in this grid. Search up, down, across, backwards, and diagonally to find the name of each game.

This event was part of the Olympic Games from 1900 to 1920.

TUG OF WAR

```
L D E G T A M D H L L F F B M I Y L
L R F C N K I S A L L L N U A B E L
A A L B B I A R A N O A A G G W Q A
B O Y G O U M B S O C Y B U P P K B
T B I V Q W F M R P T E R T O J G D
E E N S Y R L B I H O R S W S N M N
U K G H O B A I A W I R E P I I A A
Q A D K U L O I N A S R T X O Z F H
C W I N L S W U H G L N O S L R S O
A D S P O R T C L I M B I N G A T R
R N C V S U L I F E K Z F F L W L I
B A F C Y E J T J C S U M O P F L E
I I X U E A I Z I U X S P E E O A N
L K Y H U N T K U P J A P A T G B T
L S W G G N O L H T A U D O A U T E
I R C A N O E K A Y A K H V R T F E
A E S T R O P S R E L L O R A T O R
R T A S C I T S A N M Y G E K E S I
D A O F B M V L I F E S A V I N G N
S W L A C R O S S E A R C H E R Y G
```

This sport originated in the 6th century BCE in Ancient Greece.

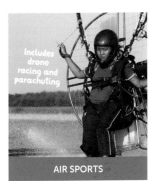

Includes drone racing and parachuting

AIR SPORTS

BOULES SPORTS

KICKBOXING

Runners use a map to figure out the route to the finish.

ORIENTEERING

July 25

NATIONAL
MERRY-GO-ROUND DAY

The first carousels were simple machines boys used for training to become knights in Europe in the Middle Ages. In the 1800s, the carousel became popular again as a carnival ride. There are at least 13 differences in these pictures. How many can you find?

July 31

UNCOMMON
MUSICAL INSTRUMENT
AWARENESS DAY

Check out how each of these three one-of-a-kind instruments makes its unique sound.

The Singing Ringing Tree in Burnley, England, is a swirling, 9.8-foot-tall sculpture made out of more than three hundred steel pipes. As the wind blows on the hill, the pipes make a beautiful and eerie sound.

The Great Stalacpipe Organ at Luray Caverns in Virginia is the world's largest musical instrument. It produces sound by gently tapping stalactites that hang from the ceiling of the caves.

The Sea Organ in Zadar, Croatia, is a series of 35 pipes of different sizes and lengths that are hidden in a series of stairs. The Adriatic Sea produces sound as the tide pushes water and air into the echoing chambers under the steps.

July 31, 2021
NATIONAL DANCE DAY
A HIGHLIGHTS CLASSIC PUZZLE

These flamingos are cha-cha-cha-ing their way to a win!
Can you find 16 objects in this Hidden Pictures puzzle?

adhesive bandage · heart · wedge of lemon · crown · butterfly · doughnut · clock · domino · plunger · fish · scissors · magnet · toothbrush · rope · hot dog · cane

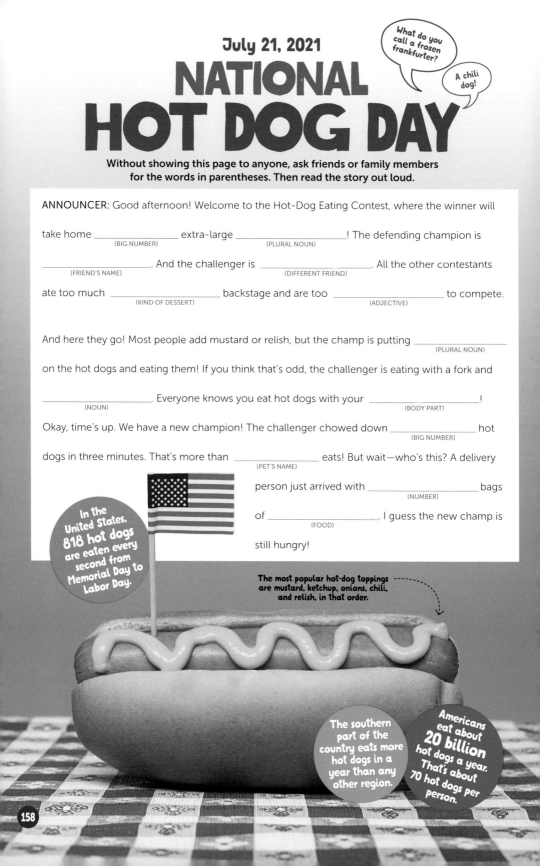

July 21, 2021

NATIONAL HOT DOG DAY

What do you call a frozen frankfurter?

A chili dog!

Without showing this page to anyone, ask friends or family members for the words in parentheses. Then read the story out loud.

ANNOUNCER: Good afternoon! Welcome to the Hot-Dog Eating Contest, where the winner will

take home _____ extra-large _____! The defending champion is
　　　　　　(BIG NUMBER)　　　　　　　　　　(PLURAL NOUN)

_____. And the challenger is _____. All the other contestants
(FRIEND'S NAME)　　　　　　　　　　　　　(DIFFERENT FRIEND)

ate too much _____ backstage and are too _____ to compete.
　　　　　　(KIND OF DESSERT)　　　　　　　　　　　　(ADJECTIVE)

And here they go! Most people add mustard or relish, but the champ is putting _____
　　　　　　　　　　　　　　　　　　　　　　　　　　　　　　(PLURAL NOUN)

on the hot dogs and eating them! If you think that's odd, the challenger is eating with a fork and

_____. Everyone knows you eat hot dogs with your _____!
(NOUN)　　　　　　　　　　　　　　　　　　　　　　　　(BODY PART)

Okay, time's up. We have a new champion! The challenger chowed down _____ hot
　　　　　　　　　　　　　　　　　　　　　　　　　　　　　(BIG NUMBER)

dogs in three minutes. That's more than _____ eats! But wait—who's this? A delivery
　　　　　　　　　　　　　　　　　(PET'S NAME)

person just arrived with _____ bags
　　　　　　　　　　　　(NUMBER)

of _____. I guess the new champ is
　　　(FOOD)

still hungry!

In the United States, 818 hot dogs are eaten every second from Memorial Day to Labor Day.

The most popular hot-dog toppings are mustard, ketchup, onions, chili, and relish, in that order.

The southern part of the country eats more hot dogs in a year than any other region.

Americans eat about 20 billion hot dogs a year. That's about 70 hot dogs per person.

July 31
NATIONAL AVOCADO DAY

Celebrate the day with these delicious avocado boats.

1. Ask an adult to help you cut 1 ripe **avocado** in half and remove the pit. Then scoop out the avocado into a bowl. Set the empty shells aside.

2. Combine ¼ cup finely chopped **celery**, 1 cup shredded or cubed cooked **chicken**, and 2 tablespoons **mayonnaise** in a bowl. Mix well.

3. Lightly mash the avocado with a potato masher or fork. Add it to the chicken mixture.

4. Fill each avocado "boat" with the mixture. Sprinkle **paprika** on top and dig in!

These four holidays give you a chance to celebrate even more delicious foods.

July 12	July 13	July 15	July 22

NATIONAL PECAN PIE DAY

NATIONAL FRENCH FRY DAY

NATIONAL GUMMY WORM DAY

NATIONAL MANGO DAY

The pecans float to the top of the pie by themselves while the pie is baking.

Belgium is the world's top french-fry eater. Belgians eat about 165 pounds of fries per person in a year.

Gummy worms were invented as a way to get kids' attention and gross out their parents.

Mangoes, cashews, and pistachios are all part of the Anacardiaceae family, which also includes poison ivy!

INDEPENDENCE

GET THE FACTS BEHIND THIS STAR-SPANGLED CELEBRATION.

EPIC FIREWORKS

There are over

16,000

fireworks displays around the country to celebrate the Fourth of July.

THE FIRST THIRTEEN

WHICH OF THESE WAS **NOT** ONE OF THE 13 ORIGINAL COLONIES?

- Delaware
- Georgia
- New York
- South Carolina
- New Hampshire
- Massachusetts
- North Carolina
- Rhode Island
- New Jersey
- Virginia
- Pennsylvania
- Maryland
- Vermont
- Connecticut

PATRIOTIC TOWN NAMES

EAGLE COLORADO

Patriot INDIANA

Equality ILLINOIS

Liberty Kentucky

FREEDOM CALIFORNIA

INDEPENDENCE MISSOURI

DAY

Life, liberty, and what else?

The pursuit of happiness!

PICNIC PREP

TOP SELLERS FOR JULY 4

MEAT	PRODUCE	SAUCE
Beef	**Berries**	**Barbecue**

WHAT'S IT ALL ABOUT?

The Revolutionary War (1775–1783) was the 13 American colonies' fight for independence from England.

On July 4, 1776, the Second Continental Congress adopted the Declaration of Independence, officially cutting ties with the British.

STILL GOING!

OLDEST FOURTH OF JULY FESTIVITIES
Bristol, Rhode Island

Bristol had its first celebration in 1785. (July 4 wasn't a holiday until 1870!)

How come there's no knock-knock joke about America?

Because freedom rings

HISTORIC FLAG

A Revolutionary War battle flag from 1776 sold for

$12,336,000

at an auction in 2006.

HOW MANY PEOPLE?

ESTIMATED U.S. POPULATION

JULY 1776

2.5
MILLION

JULY 2020

335
MILLION

July 14
SHARK AWARENESS DAY

This day celebrates these fascinating and diverse creatures and their important role in keeping oceans healthy. Started by the Shark Trust, Shark Awareness Day seeks to create positive attitudes toward sharks. **Celebrate by making this shark treasure box!**

1. Cut six fins and two tails from **thin cardboard.** Bend a ½-inch flap on the bottom of each piece.

2. Glue the pieces together in pairs, leaving the flaps unglued. Glue the fin and tail flaps to an empty **tissue box.** Hold them in place with **masking tape** while the glue dries.

3. **Paint** the shark or cover it with **paper.** Let it dry.

4. Cut teeth, eyes, and a mouth from **felt.** Glue them on.

5. Store treasures inside. To retrieve them, stick your hand in the shark's mouth!

What sharks would you find at a construction site?

Hammerhead sharks

Sharks existed about **450 million** years ago, well before the dinosaurs.

Sharks don't have bones. Their skeletons are made of cartilage, the same stuff that makes up your ears or the tip of your nose.

Shark skin feels like sandpaper. It's covered with tiny teeth-like scales.

When you flip a shark over on its back, it goes into a trancelike state. Scientists use this trick to study or help sharks.

July 29
RAIN DAY

In the late 1800s in Waynesburg, Pennsylvania, a local farmer mentioned that it always seemed to rain on his birthday, July 29, which inspired his pharmacist to start an annual record of rainfall on that day. According to the official Rain Day Record Chart, it has rained in Waynesburg 115 times on July 29 between 1874 and 2019. Since 1979, the town of Waynesburg has celebrated Rain Day with a street fair, which includes an umbrella decorating contest!

Wayne Drop is the official Rain Day mascot!

KIDS' SCIENCE QUESTIONS

Why doesn't water that evaporates in your house form clouds and rain?

To form clouds and rain, water vapor (water that has evaporated into the air) needs both cool temperatures and a surface on which to condense (turn back into a liquid).

As warm, moist air rises outdoors, it carries water vapor high into the atmosphere where there is less air pressure. The air expands, causing it to cool. Its water vapor condenses on atmospheric dust and may form a cloud.

Indoors, warm, moist air can't rise high because of ceilings. It can cool by meeting up with cold surfaces like windows. But any drops that form on airborne dust don't get large enough to fall as rain.

CREATE RAIN!

1. Pour a few inches of very warm **tap water** into a clear **drinking glass**.
2. Cover the glass with **plastic wrap.** Use a **rubber band** to hold it in place.
3. Set a few **ice cubes** on top. Over the next few minutes, watch as water vapor condenses beneath the plastic wrap. It may even "rain"—watch for drops!

163

WORLD EMOJI DAY

The term *emoji* comes from the Japanese words for *picture* (絵/e) and *character* (文字/moji).
Two of these columns have all the same emojis. Can you find which 2 columns?

BONUS: Which emoji appears in every column?

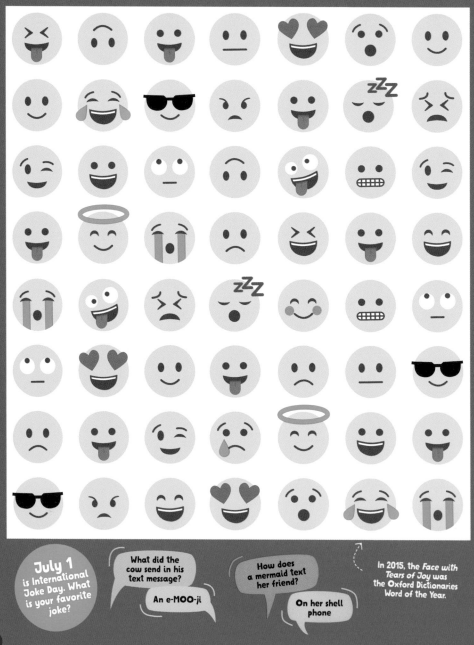

July 1 is International Joke Day. What is your favorite joke?

What did the cow send in his text message?

An e-MOO-ji

How does a mermaid text her friend?

On her shell phone

In 2015, the *Face with Tears of Joy* was the Oxford Dictionaries Word of the Year.

July 28
NATIONAL WATERPARK DAY

Today is a *grrrr*-8 day to visit the water park! Figure out which path gets you from START to FINISH.

BONUS: See how many 8's you can find in the scene.

How many other words can you make out of the letters in **WATERPARK?** We found a fruit, a martial art, and warm jacket.

BACKYARD WATERPARK

Even if you can't celebrate at a waterpark, have a splashing good time at home playing these water games.

With a parent's permission, set up plastic chairs in a circle around a sprinkler. Play **"musical" chairs** with water instead of music! Have someone in charge of turning the **sprinkler** on and off. Walk around the chairs when the water is on, and try to take a seat as soon as the water turns off.

Play **spray-bottle freeze tag**. To "freeze" the other players, *It* must squirt them using a small plastic spray bottle filled with water.

Instead of Duck, Duck, Goose, play **Duck, Duck, Drench**. Fill a cup with water. Walk around your friends in a circle. Choose your "goose," and dump the water on him or her.

July 1
CANADA DAY

This holiday celebrates the anniversary of July 1, 1867, on which the British government combined three North American colonies into one area called Canada. People celebrate with parades, barbecues, and fireworks.

Take a spin around the globe to see how

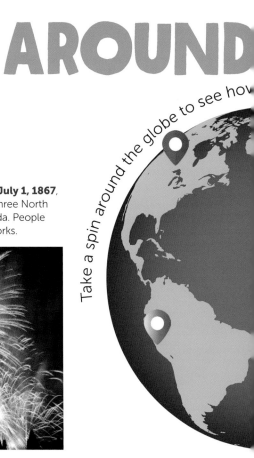

July 14
LA FÊTE NATIONALE

Known as Bastille Day outside of France, this celebration commemorates the beginning of the French Revolution. On July 14, 1789, an angry group of Parisians stormed a prison called the Bastille. The French Revolution sparked the abolishment of the French monarchy. French people spend the day with family and friends and watch fireworks at night.

Can you find at least 15 differences between these two pictures?

THE WORLD

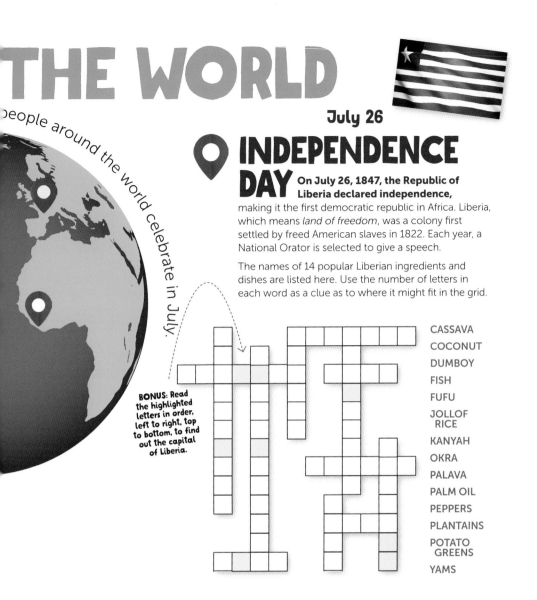

people around the world celebrate in July.

July 26

◉ INDEPENDENCE DAY

On July 26, 1847, the Republic of Liberia declared independence, making it the first democratic republic in Africa. Liberia, which means *land of freedom*, was a colony first settled by freed American slaves in 1822. Each year, a National Orator is selected to give a speech.

The names of 14 popular Liberian ingredients and dishes are listed here. Use the number of letters in each word as a clue as to where it might fit in the grid.

BONUS: Read the highlighted letters in order, left to right, top to bottom, to find out the capital of Liberia.

CASSAVA
COCONUT
DUMBOY
FISH
FUFU
JOLLOF RICE
KANYAH
OKRA
PALAVA
PALM OIL
PEPPERS
PLANTAINS
POTATO GREENS
YAMS

July 28-29

◉ FIESTAS PATRIAS

Peru's biggest holiday spans two days. July 28 marks the date Peru declared its independence from Spain in 1821. And on July 29 people honor Peru's armed forces and police. Peruvians around the country celebrate with parades, concerts, food fairs, and fireworks.

SUNDAY	MONDAY	TUESDAY	WEDNESDAY

National Alpaca Day (Peru)

This day celebrates the important Andean animal and the hard work of alpaca breeders.

1

NATIONAL ICE-CREAM SANDWICH DAY

2

Go for the gold!
In 1936, Jesse Owens won his first of four gold medals at the Berlin Olympics.

3

International Owl Awareness Day

4

Melon Day (Turkmenistan)

On this day, festivities celebrate the country's muskmelon, in particular the Turkmenbashi melon.

8

National Book Lovers' Day

Curl up with your favorite book.

9

You go, girl!
In 1993, Ruth Bader Ginsberg became the second woman to be sworn in as a Supreme Court justice.

10

Home run!
In 1929, Babe Ruth became the first baseball player to hit 500 home runs.

11

National Relaxation Day

What do you think is the best way to relax?

15

Game on!
In 1954, the first issue of *Sports Illustrated* was released.

16

BLACK CAT APPRECIATION DAY

17

Going up.
In 1868, helium was discovered by French astronomer Pierre Janssen.

18

NATIONAL EAT A PEACH DAY

22

National Sponge Cake Day

Do you prefer chocolate or vanilla sponge cake?

23

Fly high!
In 1932, Amelia Earhart began the flight that made her the first woman to fly across the U.S. nonstop, from LA to Newark.

24

La Tomatina (Spain)

During this festival in Buñol, Valencia, participants throw tomatoes at each other.

25

Movie time!
In 1997, Netflix was founded, initially as an online DVD rental service.

29

Doing good.
In 1967, Thurgood Marshall became the first African American Supreme Court justice.

30

National Trail Mix Day

What are your favorite trail mix ingredients?

31

FLOWERS
GLADIOLUS AND POPPY

THURSDAY	FRIDAY	SATURDAY

THURSDAY

Abracadabra!
In 1926, Houdini spent 91 minutes underwater in a sealed tank before escaping.

5

FRIDAY

Far out!
In 2012, NASA's Curiosity rover landed on Mars.

6

SATURDAY

National Sandcastle and Sculpture Day

What would your sandcastle look like?

7

NATIONAL MIDDLE CHILD DAY

12

Oh, deer!
In 1942, *Bambi* premiered at Radio City Music Hall.

13

Qixi Festival (China)

Also known as Chinese Valentine's Day, this festival celebrates the romantic legend of the cowherd and the weaver girl.

14

World Photography Day

Say *cheese!*

19

World Mosquito Day

This day commemorates the 1897 discovery that misquitoes transmit malaria.

20

Aloha!
In 1959, Hawaii became the 50th state.

21

WOMEN'S EQUALITY DAY

This day celebrates the adoption of the Nineteenth Amendment in 1920, which gave women the right to vote.

26

National Banana Lovers' Day

What an a-peel-ing day!

27

Cheers!
In 1898, Caleb Bradham named his carbonated soft drink Pepsi-Cola. He had invented the drink five years earlier in 1893.

28

BIRTHSTONES
PERIDOT AND PINEL

ZODIAC SIGNS

♌ LEO:
JULY 23—
AUGUST 22

♍ VIRGO:
AUGUST 23—
SEPTEMBER 22

AUGUST

NATIONAL CRAYON COLLECTION MONTH

Encourage friends, family, and restaurants to save their used crayons! Collect the crayons and donate them to classrooms in need of these colorful supplies.

Can you find the jigsaw pieces in this photo of crayons?

FAMILY FUN MONTH

What fun things will you do with your family this month? Get some ideas by unscrambling the activities below!

kihe   ___ ___ ___ ___

somevi   ___ ___ ___ ___ ___ ___

mage ignht   ___ ___ ___ ___   ___ ___ ___ ___

baek   ___ ___ ___ ___

becaberu   ___ ___ ___ ___ ___ ___ ___ ___

cmpa   ___ ___ ___ ___

birofne   ___ ___ ___ ___ ___ ___ ___

fhsi   ___ ___ ___ ___

ikbe   ___ ___ ___ ___

aftrc   ___ ___ ___ ___ ___

NATIONAL SANDWICH MONTH

A picnic is the perfect time to pack your favorite sandwich—along with some other tasty treats. Use the clues to figure out these 13 classic picnic foods and fill in the answers.

What silly things could you put in a sandwich? Pick a filling for each letter of your name.

ACROSS

3. Refreshing citrus drink
4. Hard-boiled appetizer
6. Pastry filled with fruit
8. Square chocolate baked good
9. Two slices of bread with a filling
10. Beef patty on a bun
11. Side dish with spuds and sauce
12. Poultry cooked in hot oil

DOWN

1. Also known as a Frankfurter
2. Shredded cabbage salad
5. Crispy potato snack
6. Side dish with macaroni and mayo
7. A mixture of apples, grapes, and other sweet treats

People in the U.S. used to eat sandwiches mainly as a **light snack** or at a picnic.

Pre-sliced bread was invented in the late 1920s. It helped make the sandwich popular, especially with kids.

Even though the sandwich didn't get its name until the 1760s, **people have eaten meat inside sliced bread for thousands of years**.

171

August 12, 1851
170 YEARS AGO, SINGER PATENTED HIS SEWING MACHINE

On August 12, 1851, Issac Singer's patent led to his brand becoming one of the most widely distributed sewing machines in the U.S. Can you find 15 objects in this Hidden Pictures puzzle?

A Highlights Classic Puzzle

needle · ice-cream cone · paper clip · 2 crowns · egg · worm · shovel · slice of pie · flower pot · paper airplane · ring · hatchet · sailboat · flag

August 12, 1981

The BASIC IBM MODEL 5150

HAD ONLY 16 KILOBYTES OF MEMORY

ON AUGUST 12, 1981, the IBM PERSONAL COMPUTER was RELEASED.

TODAY'S SMARTPHONES HAVE UP TO 8 GIGABYTES of memory

That's 500,000 TIMES MORE MEMORY

IBM released its first personal computer on August 12, 1981.
Use its keyboard to decode the answers to these computer riddles.
Change each letter to the one found on the **LEFT** or **RIGHT** of it on the keyboard.

1. What do you call a computer superhero? Look 1 key **LEFT** on the keyboard.

___ ___ ___ ___ ___ ___   ___ ___ ___ ___ ___

S   D   V   T   R   R   M   D   S   B   R   T

2. Where do computers go to dance? Look 1 key **RIGHT** on the keyboard.

___ ___ ___   ___ ___ ___ ___ – ___

R   G   W   S   U   A   X   I

3. Why did the computer cross the road? Look 1 key **LEFT** on the keyboard.

___ ___   ___ ___ ___ ___   ___ ___ ___ ___   ___ ___ ___ ___

Y   P   H   R   Y   S   N   U   Y   R   Y   P   R   S   Y

173

NATIONAL GOLF

Ready to take a swing on this one? Which things are silly in this What's Wrong? puzzle? It's up to you!

2. The dimples on a golf ball help with the control, lift, and smoothness of the ball's flight. How many dimples are typically on a golf ball?

a. 100–300 **b.** 300–500 **c.** 500–700

1. Where did the modern game of golf originate in the 1400s?

a. Germany **b.** England **c.** Scotland

3. Which astronaut took this sport to space?

a. Alan Shepard   **b.** Neil Armstrong
c. Buzz Aldrin

August 9–15, 2021
U.S. AMATEUR CHAMPIONSHIP

The U.S. Amateur Championship, created in 1895, **is the oldest United States Golf Association (USGA) championship**. This year, it will be held at Oakmont Country Club in Oakmont, Pennsylvania.

August 13
LEFT-HANDERS DAY

Here are the left-handed champions of the USGA Amateurs:

Erica Shepherd
2017 Girls' Junior

Julia Potter
2013, 2016 Women's Mid-Amateur

Brad Benjamin
2009 Amateur Public Links

Cory Whitsett
2007 Junior Amateur

Brian Harman
2003 Junior Amateur

Phil Mickelson
1990 Amateur

Ralph Howe III
1988 Amateur Public Links

NATIONAL CLOWN WEEK!

Can you tell what's alike in each row of clowns, across, down, and diagonally?

"Bump a nose!" is how clowns wish each other good luck before a show.

CIRCUS LINGO

Step right up and try to match each of these slang terms for circus workers to their meaning.

1. candy butcher
2. funambulist
3. icarist
4. joey
5. mitt reader
6. roustabout
7. rubberman
8. slanger

A. acrobat who juggles another acrobat with their feet
B. balloon vendor
C. big cat trainer
D. circus laborer
E. clown
F. concession vendor
G. fortune teller
H. tightrope walker

NATIONAL TELL-A-JOKE DAY

Telling a good joke can be a nice way to break the ice with a new friend or help people relax and have fun. Here are some top tips for joke telling.

Know your joke well. You don't want to forget the punch line, so practice first.

Don't begin by telling your audience how funny your joke is. Let them find out for themselves.

Try to deliver your joke with a straight face. If you laugh yourself, you'll interrupt the flow.

Don't tell jokes that make fun of people.

To uncover these elephant joke punch lines, use the fractions of the words below. We did the first one for you.

What do elephants wear on their legs?

Why do elephants have trunks?

First ¹/₄ of **E**XIT
Last ²/₅ of WHALE
First ²/₃ of PARENT
Last ¹/₂ of RENT
First ¹/₅ of SMILE

First ¹/₂ of THEMES
Last ²/₅ of VINYL
First ³/₄ of OVEN
Last ¹/₃ of POTATO
First ³/₅ of TRAIN
First ¹/₂ of VELVET

E __ __ __ __ __ __

__ __ __ __ __ __ __ __ __ __ __ __ __ __ __ .

August 7, 2021
CAMPFIRE DAY AND NIGHT

Solve the riddle, then celebrate Campfire Day and Night (the first Saturday in August) and Toasted Marshmallow Day (August 30) by finding 12 differences between these two pictures.

I'm squishy and sweet and airy and light.
I'm brown when I'm roasted. Inside, I'm still white.
Need s'more hints? This might do the trick:
I'll be at the campfire stuck on your stick.

August 10
NATIONAL S'MORES DAY

Don't forget about National S'mores Day on August 10! Try these tasty twists on the classic treat!

Stuffed Apple

With a spoon, scoop out the core of a small **apple**. (Leave some apple at the bottom.) Combine **melted butter**, crushed **graham crackers**, **brown sugar**, **mini marshmallows**, **chocolate chips**, and **butterscotch chips**. Fill the center of the apple. Bake in a small baking dish until the apple is soft.

Banana Sandwich

Graham cracker

Marshmallow creme

Chocolate syrup and peanut butter

Banana

EAT OUTSIDE DAY

Celebrate Eat Outside Day by finding things that rhyme with **grill** or **eat** in this scene.

BONUS! Find 10 grill spatulas in the scene.

The largest hamburger ever made weighed 2,566 lb 9 oz!

What's the best side of the house to put the grill on?

The outside

August 3

NATIONAL WATERMELON DAY

Find 8 pairs of matching watermelon slices.

WATERMELON PUNCH

In a blender, puree chunks of **watermelon**. Blend in some **honey**. Pour the puree into a punch bowl or a hollowed-out watermelon. (Make sure it's not wobbly!) Stir in cold **seltzer**. Garnish with **basil leaves**.

Did you know that the whole fruit is edible? Rinds can be pickled, stir-fried, or stewed. In some places, the seeds are dried and roasted like pumpkin seeds.

180

NAME THAT WATERMELON

More than 1,200 varieties of watermelon are grown in more than 96 countries around the world. Check out some of the fun names of each of the four main types.

Seedless Watermelons	Picnic Watermelons	Icebox Watermelons	Yellow or Orange Watermelons
Queen of Hearts	Charleston Gray	Sugar Baby	Desert King
King of Hearts	Jubilee	Tiger Baby	Tendergold
Millionaire	Crimson Sweet	Minilee	Honeyheart
Nova	Black Diamond	Rainbow Sherbet	Chiffon

A watermelon is both a fruit and a vegetable! It grows from a seed like a fruit, but it's part of the same family as squash.

WATERMELON FAN

When do you go on red and stop on green?

When you are eating watermelon

1. Arrange three **large craft sticks** in a fan shape. Glue them together at the bottom. Let the glue dry.

2. Trace around the sticks on **red craft foam**. Cut a "rind" from **green** and **white craft foam**. Glue on the rind.

3. Cut a "bite" from the watermelon. Draw seeds with a **black marker**.

4. Glue the foam fan onto the craft sticks.

KIDS' SCIENCE QUESTIONS

How do seedless watermelons grow when the watermelons come from the seeds?

To understand how this is done, you first have to know some basic ideas about how a normal seed works. Each seed contains a complete set of coding—a blueprint—for making a new plant. That coding is in a set of long, chain-like molecules. All together, that set of molecules is called the plant's DNA.

When one watermelon flower is fertilized by pollen from a different watermelon plant, that flower makes new seeds. In each seed, half of the blueprint comes from one plant, and the other half comes from the other plant. That's what happens in most plants.

To make seedless watermelons, scientists use a trick. They use a special chemical to give each seed twice as much DNA as a normal seed has. These seeds can grow into watermelon vines and make watermelons that contain seeds.

But after one of these double-DNA seeds grows into a vine and that vine is fertilized by a normal plant, the new seeds will grow into an unusual vine. The vine is healthy, but because it has one and one-half sets of DNA, seeds will not form. So the vine gives seedless watermelons.

Scientists have grown watermelon vines that produce watermelons with no seeds.

Watermelons are 92% water! No wonder they're so refreshing.

HURRICANE

Hurricane season starts to peak in mid-August, although the official season for tropical cyclones and hurricanes in the Atlantic Basin is from June 1 to November 30. Hurricane Katrina hit the Gulf Coast on August 29, 2005, and Hurricane Irene struck the East Coast on August 27, 2011.

Be a storm tracker and search for the 21 hurricane names for 2021 hiding in this grid. Look for them up, down, across, backward, and diagonally. How many can you spot?

```
O  B  W  Q  P  V  T  Y  N  N  A  D  B  E
P  D  E  J  I  T  E  W  V  Z  U  I  S  T
B  E  E  C  F  Y  R  A  O  A  L  O  A  T
U  H  T  T  U  V  E  N  D  L  R  C  M  E
C  O  E  E  T  P  S  D  O  Q  D  D  P  D
R  J  M  A  R  E  A  A  U  N  X  E  H  U
A  S  L  E  I  M  Z  G  F  Q  B  R  F  A
U  H  E  K  O  D  H  S  I  G  F  H  T  L
D  E  Z  Y  K  Z  A  I  R  H  E  F  D  C
S  U  C  D  M  L  M  I  N  D  Y  R  G  W
B  D  X  A  O  A  M  S  E  P  B  E  J  J
X  I  E  H  R  X  Z  W  H  O  Y  T  I  W
E  B  C  R  V  G  J  P  C  R  C  A  N  A
S  I  M  E  F  U  W  M  R  Y  N  K  D  Q
N  W  X  P  N  S  D  A  X  W  V  J  N  I
J  U  L  I  A  N  L  Y  W  V  K  B  Y  W
```

2021 HURRICANE NAMES

ANA	GRACE	MINDY	TERESA
BILL	HENRI	NICHOLAS	VICTOR
CLAUDETTE	IDA	ODETTE	WANDA
DANNY	JULIAN	PETER	
ELSA	KATE	ROSE	
FRED	LARRY	SAM	

The World Meteorological Organization has six lists of names that are used on a rotating basis. The list of names from 2021 will be used again in 2027.

SEASON

If a storm is so deadly that using the name again would be insensitive, that name is replaced.

This list of names is for the Atlantic Basin, which includes the **Atlantic Ocean**, the **Caribbean Sea**, and the **Gulf of Mexico**. There are different lists of names for storms in different parts of the world.

Wind speed is the difference between a hurricane and a tropical storm. Hurricane wind speeds are at least 74 miles per hour.

Hurricanes rotate around the eye in a counter-clockwise direction. The eyewall, created by the rotating storm clouds, is the most destructive part of a hurricane.

NATIONAL ROLLER COASTER DAY

Take this stomach-dropping coaster all the way from **START** to **FINISH**.

START

Formula Rossa in Abu Dhabi, the fastest roller coaster in the world, reaches a top speed of 149 miles per hour!

Kingda Ka in New Jersey, the tallest roller coaster in the world, soars to 456 feet high!

Leap-The-Dips in Pennsylvania, the oldest roller coaster in the world, opened to the public in 1902!

The Steel Dragon in Japan, the longest roller coaster in the world, is 8,133 feet long!

FINISH

Take a spin around the globe to see how

August 15
THE DAY THE LIGHT RETURNED

On August 15, South Koreans celebrate the National Liberation Day of Korea, or _Gwangbokjeol_, which literally means "the day the light returned." The holiday commemorates when Korea was liberated from Japanese occupation in 1945. Koreans take the day off from work and school to attend parades and celebrations. The national flag, called _Taegukgi_, is proudly displayed everywhere.

ROYAL EDINBURGH MILITARY TATTOO

Every August at Edinburgh Castle, more than 1,200 performers from around the world put on a spectacular show of music, dance, and military marches called a tattoo. Since the first Edinburgh Tattoo in 1950, more than 14 million people have attended. Each year, around 100 million people in 30 countries also watch on television.

Can you find 16 differences between these two pictures?

THE WORLD

people around the world celebrate in August.

HAPPY 1,021st BIRTHDAY, HUNGARY!

Known as both Az államalapítás ünnepe (State Foundation Day) and Szent István ünnepe (Saint Stephen's Day), there are lots of reasons for celebration on August 20. Hungarians celebrate the foundation of the Kingdom of Hungary in the year 1000; the name day of the first king of Hungary, Stephen I; and the Day of the New Bread, which marks the traditional end of the grain harvest. Throughout the country on this national holiday, there are festivals, parades, and fireworks. The largest fireworks display is in the capital city, Budapest, over the Danube River in front of Parliament. Since 2007, there has also been a competition to find "The Birthday Cake of Hungary," with the winning cake announced (and eaten) on August 20.

A rakhi is a bracelet made of red and gold thread, like these here.

August 21, 2021

RAKSHA BANDHAN

Raksha Bandhan is an Indian festival that celebrates the loving and caring bond between sisters and brothers. This year, it falls on August 21. A sister ties a *rakhi* to her brother's wrist, and her brother responds with a gift. It is a special day when sisters and brothers think fondly of each other and pray for each others' blessings.

SUNDAY	MONDAY	TUESDAY	WEDNESDAY

BIRTHSTONE
SAPPHIRE

ZODIAC SIGNS
VIRGO: AUGUST 23–SEPTEMBER 22

LIBRA: SEPTEMBER 23–OCTOBER 22

FLOWERS
ASTER AND MORNING GLORY

No Rhyme or Reason Day
This day celebrates words that don't rhyme and silly idioms.

1

International Day of Charity
Offer to help someone today.

5

LABOR DAY

ROSH HASHANAH
begins at sunset.

6

National Salami Day
It's a good day, any way you slice it.

7

International Literacy Day
You read it here first!

8

National Day of Encouragement
You can do it!

12

On your mark, get set, GO! In 1970, the first New York City Marathon was held.

13

National Cream-Filled Doughnut Day
Doughnut make you smile?

14

YOM KIPPUR
begins at sunset.

15

:-)
In 1982, the first emoticon—a typed, sideways smiley face—was created.

19

SUKKOT
begins at sunset.

20

National Miniature Golf Day
FORE!

21

FIRST DAY OF FALL

22

National Lumberjack Day
What's a lumberjack's favorite month? Sep-TIMBER!

26

NATIONAL SCARF DAY

27

National Good Neighbor Day
Be a good neighbor today and every day.

28

She was on top of the world! In 1988, Stacy Allison of Portland, Oregon, became the first American woman to climb Mount Everest.

29

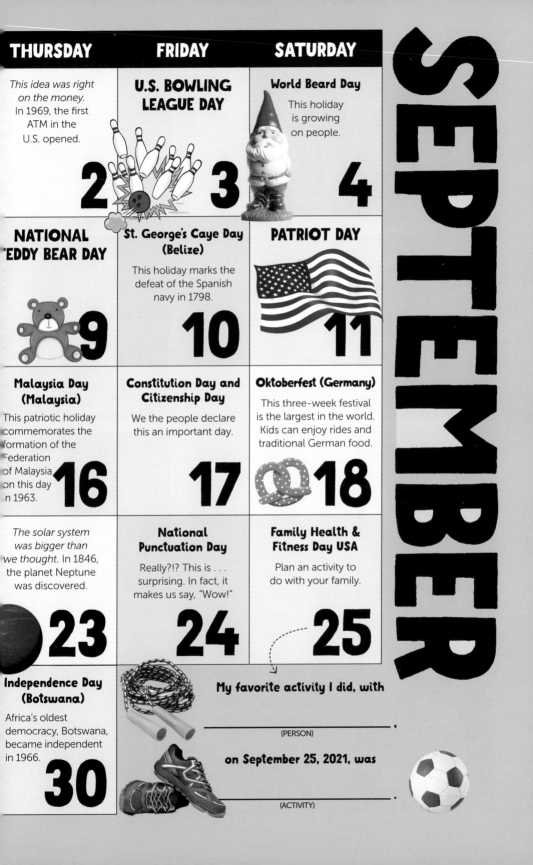

SEPTEMBER

THURSDAY	FRIDAY	SATURDAY

THURSDAY | **FRIDAY** | **SATURDAY**

This idea was right on the money. In 1969, the first ATM in the U.S. opened.
2

U.S. BOWLING LEAGUE DAY
3

World Beard Day
This holiday is growing on people.
4

NATIONAL TEDDY BEAR DAY
9

St. George's Caye Day (Belize)
This holiday marks the defeat of the Spanish navy in 1798.
10

PATRIOT DAY
11

Malaysia Day (Malaysia)
This patriotic holiday commemorates the formation of the Federation of Malaysia on this day in 1963.
16

Constitution Day and Citizenship Day
We the people declare this an important day.
17

Oktoberfest (Germany)
This three-week festival is the largest in the world. Kids can enjoy rides and traditional German food.
18

The solar system was bigger than we thought. In 1846, the planet Neptune was discovered.
23

National Punctuation Day
Really?!? This is . . . surprising. In fact, it makes us say, "Wow!"
24

Family Health & Fitness Day USA
Plan an activity to do with your family.
25

Independence Day (Botswana)
Africa's oldest democracy, Botswana, became independent in 1966.
30

My favorite activity I did, with

_____,
(PERSON)

on September 25, 2021, was

_____.
(ACTIVITY)

Franklin Chang-Díaz

NATIONAL HISPANIC HERITAGE MONTH

Sonia Sotomayor

This month-long celebration (September 15–October 15) recognizes the contributions of Hispanic Americans and honors their history and culture. Match each pioneering Hispanic American with his or her historic achievement.

Octaviano Ambrosio Larrazolo

1. Who was the first Hispanic American to serve in the U.S. Senate (1928)?

2. Who was the first Hispanic American MLB Hall of Fame inductee (1973)?

3. Who was the first Hispanic American to earn an EGOT, winning an Emmy, Grammy, Oscar, and Tony award (1977)?

4. Who was the first Hispanic American astronaut (1980)?

5. Who was the first Hispanic American doctor—and the first woman—to become U.S. surgeon general (1990)?

6. Who was the first Hispanic American activist inducted into the National Women's Hall of Fame (1993)?

7. Who was the first Hispanic American musician inducted into the Rock & Roll Hall of Fame (1998)?

8. Who was the first Hispanic American U.S. Supreme Court justice (2009)?

Rita Moreno

Carlos Santana

Dr. Antonia Novello

Roberto Clemente

Hispanic and **Latinx** don't mean the same thing. **Latinx** means that someone is from Latin America (nearly every country south of the U.S., including the Caribbean). **Hispanic** means from a Spanish-speaking country, and not all Latin American countries speak Spanish.

Dolores Huerta

NATIONAL CHICKEN MONTH

These chickens are cracking up! To join the fun, read each riddle,
then unscramble the letters on the eggs for the answer.

BETTER BREAKFAST MONTH

SUNNYSIDEUP

Use the clues below to fill in the boxes of this spiral—but there's a twist! The last letter of each word is also the first letter of the next word. Use the linking letters to help you spin all the way to the center.

1. One way to serve fried eggs

11. People eat these by the stack

18. Fresh-_____ orange juice

25. Small, sweet fried cake, usually with a hole in the center

32. Machine used to heat slices of bread

38. Dried fruit topping for oatmeal

44. Popular flavor of jam

53. Color of butter

58. Type of dark-colored bread, heated up

67. This pouch sits in a mug of hot water to make a common breakfast drink

72. What you pour over biscuits

76. Yellow parts of eggs

80. What you pour over waffles

84. Containers of yogurt are made of this

90. _____ cheese is typically spread on a bagel

94. Liquid poured over cereal

97. Utensil used to spread butter or jelly

According to a 2019 survey, America's top 5 breakfast foods are eggs, sausage, bacon, pancakes, and toast. What's your favorite way to start the day?

HAPPY HEALTHY CAT MONTH

Each of these cats has something in common with the other two cats in the same row—across, down, and diagonally. For example, in the top row, all 3 cats are sleeping. Can you tell what's alike in each row?

PET-SITTER EDUCATION MONTH

Pet sitters don't have it easy! Nicole is watching four fussy cats who are waiting to be fed. They each get a different flavor of cat food: chicken, tuna, beef, or liver. Use the clues to figure out which flavor Nicole should give each cat.

chicken

tuna

beef

liver

Lucy will not eat chicken or beef.

Bailey will not eat tuna or liver.

Luna will not eat liver or beef.

Peanut will only eat chicken.

Lucy

Bailey

Peanut

Luna

Ten cats were on a boat. One jumped off. How many were left?

None. They were all copycats.

September 4, 1781
240 YEARS AGO, LOS ANGELES, CALIFORNIA, WAS FOUNDED.

Forty-four settlers established the original farming community in 1781. Today, there are around four million people in Los Angeles, making it the second-largest city in the U.S.

All those people make for a lot of traffic. Can you help Carl drive the freeways around Los Angeles to get home in time for dinner?

FINISH

START

This travel brochure from the 1950s encourages tourism to Los Angeles. In 2018, an estimated **50 million people** visited Los Angeles County.

Los Angeles International Airport (LAX) is the fourth busiest airport in the world. In 2019, more than **87.5 million passengers** flew through it!

September 11, 2001

20 YEARS AGO, al-Qaeda terrorists hijacked four airplanes, intentionally crashing two of them into the North and South Towers of the World Trade Center, and one of them into the Pentagon in Virginia. The fourth plane crashed in an empty field in Pennsylvania after passengers on the plane fought back. These horrific attacks were the deadliest terrorist attacks on American soil in U.S. history.

The 9/11 Memorial honors the 2,977 people killed on September 11, 2001. It features two reflecting pools that sit where the Twin Towers once stood, and is surrounded by bronze panels inscribed with the names of the victims.

. . . .

September 23, 1986
35 YEARS AGO,

Congress voted the rose as the official flower of the United States.
To celebrate, find the two columns with the same six roses.

1 **2** **3** **4** **5**

Yellow roses signify friendship.

White roses stand for innocence.

Pink roses represent gratitude.

Red roses symbolize love.

NATIONAL GYMNASTICS

Get ready to flip. There are some strange sights at this gymnastics competition. Which things in this picture are silly? It's up to you!

INSIDER GYMNASTICS TERMS

FLICFLAC: a back handspring, also called a flip-flop

RIP: a blister a gymnast gets on the hands or wrists from training on the horizontal, parallel, or uneven bars

SALTO: a somersault, or flip

SKILLS: elements of a routine, such as a cartwheel or handstand

STICK A LANDING: when a gymnast lands and his or her feet don't move, as if they stuck to the ground

DAY

The predecessor to the U.S. Open was first held in 1881. It was a men's only tournament for members of the U.S. National Lawn Tennis Association.

August 30– September 12, 2021

U.S. OPEN TENNIS FINALS

The U.S. Open Tennis tournament is held every year at the USTA Billie Jean King National Tennis Center in New York. **Each tennis ball has an exact match. Can you find all 20 pairs?**

Around 70,000 tennis balls are used in each two-week tournament.

In 1973, the U.S. Open became the first Grand Slam tournament to offer equal prize money to male and female winners. In 2019, more than $57 million in prize money was awarded.

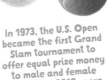

Since 2005, all U.S. Open in-bounds courts have been painted a trademarked shade of blue to contrast against yellow tennis balls and make them easier to see.

The U.S. Open is one of four games that make up the Grand Slam. The other three are the Australian Open, the French Open, and Wimbledon.

NATIONAL COLORING DAY

A HIGHLIGHTS CLASSIC PUZZLE

In this picture, find the handbag, carrot, dog bone, ladder, candle, banana, feather, frying pan, arrow, loaf of bread, hot dog, fried egg, toothbrush, belt, pear, bell, cane, boot, tennis racket, envelope, and screwdriver. Then celebrate the day by coloring in the picture!

MOST POPULAR CRAYOLA CRAYON COLORS

Aquamarine	Caribbean Green	Cerulean	Periwinkle
Blizzard Blue	Cerise	Denim	Purple Heart
Blue		Midnight Blue	

7 out of the top 10 colors are shades of blue!

INTERNATIONAL
COUNTRY MUSIC DAY

International Country Music Day is celebrated on September 17, the birthday of Hank Williams, one of the most influential singer-songwriters in 20th century America. Williams was rejected by the *Grand Ole Opry* show after his first audition in 1946, but he didn't give up and finally made his debut in 1949.

Take a trip to the Opry House in Nashville and find at least 20 differences between these two pictures.

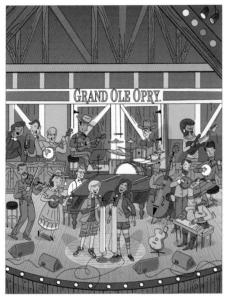

The Grand Ole Opry is a live country music concert and radio show held a few times a week in Nashville, Tennessee. The show has been broadcast since 1925, making it one of the world's longest-running radio shows.

The best-selling country music artists of all time are Garth Brooks, George Strait, and Shania Twain.

The birthplace of country music is Bristol, Tennessee.

Nashville, Tennessee, is called the Music City because it's the home of the country music industry.

This photo of Hank Williams is a publicity photo from 1951. Radio stations used photos like this one to make listeners familiar with the voices they heard on the radio.

September 5
NATIONAL CHEESE PIZZA DAY

Is a day not long enough? October is National Pizza MONTH.

Can you find 21 slices of pizza at this restaurant?

National Pepperoni Pizza Day is September 20.

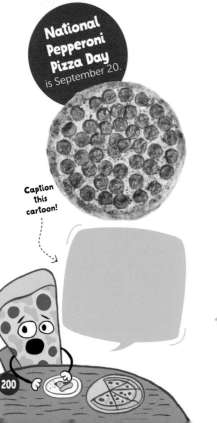

Caption this cartoon!

TOP 10 MOST POPULAR TOPPINGS

Thirty-seven percent of people typically order plain cheese pizza. But if you want a little something extra on your pizza, unscramble the letters to reveal the top 10 choices.

1. NOPEPPIER _____

2. HOURSMOMS _____

3. SNOION _____

4. GASASUE _____

5. CABNO _____

6. TAXER SECHEE _____

7. KALCB IVOLES _____

8. REGEN REPSEPP_____

9. ALPINEPEP _____

10. CANSHIP _____

What do you use to fix a broken pizza? Tomato paste

INTERNATIONAL CHOCOLATE DAY

How does your knowledge of this tasty treat stack up? Fill in each cocoa fact with the correct number.

1. It takes _____ cocoa beans to make one pound of chocolate.

2. Chocolate melts around _____ °F, just below the temperature of the human body. That's why it melts easily on your tongue.

3. A cacao tree doesn't produce its first beans for up to _____ years.

4. Up to _____ people around the world depend on cocoa for a living.

5. There are approximately _____ cocoa farms in West Africa.

6. Côte d'Ivoire provides about _____ percent of the world's cocoa supply.

7. Most dark chocolate bars contain at least _____ percent chocolate liquor.

5 **50 million** **1.5 million** **35** **400** **40** **90**

September 18, 2021

Celebrate by making these three apple snacks.

INTERNATIONAL EAT AN APPLE DAY

About **2,500 types** of apples grow in the United States.

Apples are a member of the rose family.

APPLE SANDWICHES
Core and slice an apple. Use two slices for "bread." Possible fillings: cheese, peanut butter, or chocolate spread.

SWEET APPLE YOGURT
Chop up an apple. Put it in a bowl. Stir in honey and yogurt. Sprinkle cinnamon on top.

CARAMEL APPLE ON A STICK
Soften caramel dip in a microwave. Skewer an apple chunk and dip it in the caramel. Sprinkle it with chopped nuts, mini chocolate chips, or sprinkles. Let it set in the fridge.

Ask an adult to help with anything sharp or hot!

A "shear" pleasure.

I'm drawn to it.

It's a piece of cake!

Out of this world!

I get a kick out of it!

Moving right along.

An apple a day couldn't keep me away!

September 6, 2021

LABOR DAY

DOCTOR

BAKER

Labor Day honors the contributions of American workers. The first U.S. Labor Day was celebrated in 1882 as part of the labor union movement. Today, it's unofficially seen as the last weekend of summer. **"How's your job?"** Match each silly answer above to the worker.

SOCCER PLAYER

ASTRONAUT

ARTIST

HAIRDRESSER

TRAFFIC OFFICER

Think of other jobs, and create your own answers!

THE EIGHT-HOUR WORK DAY was established by the Adamson Act, which was passed on September 3, 1916. In the 19th century, Americans worked 12 hours a day, seven days a week!

At least **20,000 PEOPLE** showed support for unions by attending the first Labor Day parade in New York City in 1882.

Women ride on a float in the 1909 Labor Day parade in New York City.

WOMEN'S AUXILIARY TYPOGRAPHICAL UNION

Grover Cleveland signed an act in 1894 to make **LABOR DAY** a national holiday.

202

NATIONAL GRANDPARENTS DAY

SEPTEMBER 16 is National Stepfamily Day! Nearly 1.4 million households in the U.S. are made up of stepfamilies.

This holiday to honor grandparents is celebrated on the second Sunday in September. The 24 grandparent names below are hidden in this word search. Search up, down, across, backwards, and diagonally to find them all. Only the words in CAPITAL LETTERS are hidden.

GRANDMOTHER WORD LIST

ABUELA (Spanish)
BABCIA (Polish)
BIBI (Swahili)
GRAMMY
GRANDMA
HALMONI (Korean)
LOLA (Filipino)
MAWMAW
NANA
NONNA (Italian)
OMA (German)
YIAYIA (Greek)

GRANDFATHER WORD LIST

ABUELO (Spanish)
BABU (Swahili)
DZIADZIU (Polish)
GRAMPS
GRANDPA
HALABEOJI (Korean)
LOLO (Filipino)
NONNO (Italian)
OPA (German)
PAPPOÚS (Greek)
PAWPAW
POP

The number of grandparents you have doubles with each generation: 4 grandparents, 8 great-grandparents, and 16 great-great-grandparents. How many grandparents do you have 10 generations back?

What do you call your grandparents?

```
M A Y S I W U A G N F P K I
F M U O A B P I O B V L N N
G D F M P D I N Z P W G O N
X N W S N A N B B D K G N R
W A W A X O P A W P A W N K
M R R R V P C P T I F I A E
P G B X L K Y Q O H A A Z B
I J O E B A L A H Ú Q B L D
U B A B O K Y N J A S U S O
Z H A L M O N I B F C E P P
T Q O T P C Y U A Q B L M A
O L N A N A E M C Y R A A L
V M R R W L B T M T I B R O
Z A A U O K T O P A W A G L
N X G G B M J V Z D R C V T
P O P O Ú A I C B A B G N W
```

5 WAYS TO HAVE FUN WITH YOUR GRANDPARENTS

1. Have a picnic together.
2. Build a zany sculpture.
3. Send each other postcards.
4. Play a board game or a video game.
5. Read stories aloud to each other.

HIGH HOLY DAYS

In Judaism, the High Holy Days are the holidays of Rosh Hashanah and Yom Kippur.

Rosh Hashanah marks the start of a new year in the Hebrew calendar. Jewish people often celebrate by eating apples and honey to symbolize a sweet new year. This year, Rosh Hashanah begins at sunset on **September 6** and ends at nightfall on **September 8**. It begins the ten days when Jews think about their actions from the previous year.

Yom Kippur means "Day of Atonement," and many Jews fast on this day and spend the day praying in a synagogue. This year, Yom Kippur begins at sunset on **September 15** and ends at nightfall on **September 16**.

SHOFAR

1. From **cardstock**, cut out two horns.

2. Glue the sides together to make a pocket. Use a **marker** to add decorations.

3. Punch two holes at the top. Tie on a **ribbon** hanger.

4. Write notes on **paper**. Place them inside the horn.

A shofar is a ram's horn that is blown like a trumpet on the Jewish High Holy Days. Most scholars and rabbis agree that it is meant as a wake-up call. The blast of the shofar reminds people to take time to think about what they can do to make the world a better place.

APPLES-AND-HONEY PLATE

1. From **tissue paper**, cut out apples, leaves, and a beehive.

2. Use a **sealer** (such as Mod Podge) to glue the shapes to the back of a **clear plastic plate**. Use as many layers of tissue paper as needed to get the color you want.

3. Cover the shapes with two or three coats of sealer, letting it dry between coats.

Be sure to keep the sealer on the back of the plate, away from any food!

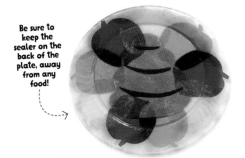

Apples and honey symbolize a sweet new year!

Pomegranate seeds symbolize mitzvahs, or good deeds, and are often eaten on Rosh Hashanah.

GOOD DEED POMEGRANATE

1. From **cardstock**, cut out a pomegranate-shaped card, two circles, and pomegranate seeds.

2. Glue the circles inside the card. Glue the seeds on the circles.

3. On each seed, write a good deed you plan to do in the coming year.

THE FIRST DAY OF ~~FALL~~ ~~AUTUMN~~ FALL

Wait a minute, is it *fall* or *autumn*? Why do the other three seasons only have one name? A long time ago, this season was called *harvest* because farmers gathered their crops between August and November for winter storage; however, as more and more people moved to cities in the 16th century, new names popped up.

Autumn comes from *autumnus*, a Latin word that means "drying-up season." Fall comes from *fiaell*, an Old English word that means "falls from a height," like the leaves that fall . . . in fall. Today, *autumn* is used more commonly in British English and *fall* is used more commonly in American English, but they're interchangeable.

So, whatever you call it, here are some ways to celebrate the season!

AUTUMN

Weaving Through Autumn Leaves

Help these kids find a clear path to the hot cider.

4 Ways to Have Fun with Autumn Leaves

1. Cut out a bird shape from **poster board**. Glue on colorful leaves as feathers.

2. Write a message on two small pieces of **brown paper**. Fill two buckets with leaves, and hide a message in each. Give the buckets to two friends. Whoever finds the message first wins!

3. Make a mobile! Use **string** to hang leaves from a **stick**.

4. Cut out the inside circle from a **paper plate**. Glue leaves around the outer rim to make a festive wreath.

FALL

Leafy Fall Maze

Help these kids find a clear path to their house.

4 Ways to Celebrate Fall

1. Make leaf-creature place mats! Use colorful **leaves**, clear **self-adhesive paper**, and **construction paper**.

2. Sip a warm autumn drink. Heat up some **apple juice**, stir it with a **cinnamon stick**, and toss in a few **cranberries**.

3. Pumpkin greetings! Instead of making a card, paint a small **pumpkin** for someone special.

4. In a nearby park, your backyard, or on a hike with your family, collect **leaves** and match them to the tree they fell from. For an added challenge, identify the tree.

September 11, 2021

NATIONAL IGUANA AWARENESS DAY

The green iguana is one of the world's best-known plant-eating reptiles. This lizard makes its home in the trees of the forests in Mexico, South America, and on some Caribbean islands.

A thin layer of skin covers the ears.

Males have taller spines than females do.

The subtympanic ("below the ear") plate is a big scale. Its use is unknown.

The whiplike tail can be used for balance and to defend against predators like hawks.

The dewlap is a flap of skin the lizard can open to look bigger when defending itself or its territory.

Its long toes and claws help it climb trees to eat leaves, flowers, and fruits and can also be used in defense.

September 19–25, 2021

SEA OTTER AWARENESS WEEK

The last full week in September recognizes the important role that sea otters play in the ecosystem where they live.

Where do otters go to watch movies?

What is an otter's favorite book series?

What did the otter say to the rock star?

An otter-torium

Harry Otter

"Can I have your otter-graph?"

Otters have the **thickest fur** of any mammal. They don't have blubber like other sea mammals, so the fur helps keep them warm.

Otters are one of the few mammals to use **tools** They use rocks to break open clams and other shellfish.

September 22
WORLD RHINO DAY

Can you find the 12 hidden objects among these rhinos?

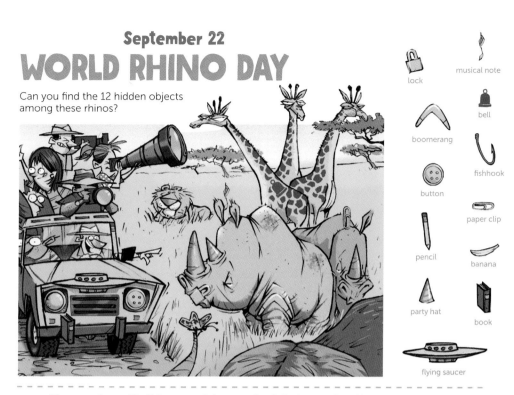

lock

musical note

boomerang

bell

button

fishhook

pencil

paper clip

party hat

banana

book

flying saucer

There are lots of holidays to celebrate animals in September. Here are just a few:

September 18, 2021
INTERNATIONAL RED PANDA DAY

Red pandas like to munch on bamboo, but they are not related to pandas. They are related to raccoons, weasels, and skunks.

September 25, 2021
INTERNATIONAL RABBIT DAY

Rabbits can turn their ears 180 degrees to listen for predators.

September 25
NATIONAL LOBSTER DAY

In the wild, most lobsters are greenish blue to blackish brown, but about one out of every two million lobsters is blue!

September 3
NATIONAL SKYSCRAPER DAY

Soar to the top with this skyscraper quiz.

1. Completed in 1885, the world's first skyscraper was the Home Insurance Building in Chicago, Illinois. How tall was it?
   a. 10 stories
   b. 20 stories
   c. 30 stories

2. Where is the Jeddah Tower, which started construction in 2013, located?
   a. Antarctica
   b. Batuu
   c. Saudi Arabia

3. When it was completed in 2010, the Burj Khalifa in Dubai, United Arab Emirates, was the world's tallest building. How many floors does it have?
   a. 16 floors with really high ceilings
   b. 163
   c. 1,630

4. Which New York City skyscraper was the tallest building in the world from 1931 to 1972?
   a. Chrysler Building
   b. Empire State Building
   c. Woolworth Building

5. The tallest building in the U.S. is the One World Trade Center in New York City. How tall is it?
   a. 1,001 feet
   b. 1,555 feet
   c. 1,776 feet

6. The Shanghai Tower in China has the world's tallest elevator, at 2,074 feet tall. How fast can it travel?
   a. 45.8 mph
   b. Mach 5
   c. warp speed

September 8
NATIONAL AMPERSAND DAY

The ampersand symbol (&) means "and." September 8 was chosen for this celebration because *9/8* looks sort of like the ampersand symbol. Can you fill in the missing word in these famous pairs?

1. Peanut butter & _____

2. Thunder & _____

3. Shoes & _____

4. Bacon & _____

5. Rock & _____

6. Beauty & _____

7. Macaroni & _____

8. Arts & _____

9. Salt & _____

In the late 1800s, the ampersand was considered the **LAST LETTER OF THE ALPHABET**.

The ampersand symbol came from Latin, the language of ancient Rome. In Latin, the word *et* means "and." A writer joined the letters *et* into one symbol and created the &.

INTERNATIONAL SUDOKU DAY

September 9 is the perfect day to celebrate Sudoku. This logic number puzzle challenges puzzle lovers to fill a 9 x 9 grid with numbers from 1 to 9. The name is Japanese for "single number," but the first modern appearance of the puzzle, called "Number Place," was in an American magazine in 1979.

This Riddle Sudoku puzzle uses letters instead of numbers. Fill in the squares so that the six letters appear once in each row, column, and 2 x 3 box. Then read the yellow squares to find out the answer to the riddle.

Riddle: Where do bugs go on vacation?

—— —— —— —— —— ——

Letters: A F N R S T

	S			R	
		T		F	
N	F				
				A	F
S	N	F	A		
	A				

INTERNATIONAL TALK LIKE A PIRATE DAY

Ahoy, maties! Aaaaarrr you ready to get into the spirit of this silly holiday, which was created in 1995? Celebrate by helping these pirates find each sock's match on the ship. Then write the letter on each match to spell out the answer to the riddle.

What kind of socks does a pirate wear?

—— —— —— —— —— —— ——

The lotus flower is a symbol of hope and purity.

September 2

⊙ NATIONAL DAY

On September 2, 1945, Ho Chi Minh declared Vietnam's independence from France. Today, Vietnamese people commemorate this holiday by decorating streets and buildings with the country's flag to display patriotism.

Make a lotus, the national flower of Vietnam.

1. Cut a lily-pad shape from **green cardstock**.

2. For petals, cut out ten 4-inch raindrop shapes from **pink cardstock**. Cut a 1-inch slit in the rounded end of each petal to create two flaps. Glue one flap over the other so the petal creates a cupped shape. Repeat this with the remaining nine petals.

3. Glue the cupped ends of five petals in a circle on the lily pad. Glue a second circle inside the first with the remaining petals.

4. Cut two squares from **yellow cardstock**. Crumple one into a ball. Wrap the other around the ball. Flatten the wrapped ball and glue it to the center of the flower.

September 11

⊙ ENKUTATASH

These flowers are also known as adey abeba.

Happy Ethiopian New Year! Enkutatash marks the first day of the first month of the Ethiopian calendar. People celebrate Enkutatash by eating a traditional meal with their families and giving gifts to children. Children sing, dance, pick flowers, and paint pictures to give to their families and neighbors.

Children pick yellow daisies called meskel flowers, which only bloom during this season. Can you find the three puzzle pieces in this photo?

THE WORLD

people around the world celebrate in September.

September 18
FIESTAS PATRIAS

On this day in 1810, Chile decided to establish a Congress, a step which eventually led to the country becoming independent from Spain. Today, the September 18 anniversary is celebrated with "patriotic parties." Every town throws a large party with live music, dancing, and barbecues.

The national dance of Chile is called the *cueca*. During independence day celebrations, dancers will wear traditional clothing to perform the dance. Unscramble the names of five musical instruments that are traditionally used to accompany the cueca.

ARTIGU _____

PRAH _____

ANOPI _____

COCODRAIN _____

MEANITURBO _____

September 23
SAUDI NATIONAL DAY

On this day in 1932, two kingdoms were unified by King Abdulaziz ibn Saud, who changed the name to the Kingdom of Saudi Arabia to honor his family, the House of Saud. Today, people commemorate this occasion with all kinds of cultural events and celebrations. The people wear green, and everywhere they go, the country is decorated with Saudi Arabia's green flag.

Green represents Islam, as it is believed to be the prophet Muhammad's favorite color.

The Arabic inscription is the *shahāda*, the Islamic declaration of faith. The words are written in an artistic form of Islamic calligraphy called *Thuluth*.

The sword symbolizes how strictly the nation will uphold justice.

SUNDAY	MONDAY	TUESDAY	WEDNESDAY
BIRTHSTONES OPAL — TOURMALINE	**ZODIAC SIGNS** LIBRA: SEPTEMBER 23– OCTOBER 22	CAPRICORN: OCTOBER 23– NOVEMBER 21	**FLOWERS** MARIGOLD
Soldiers' Day (Honduras) This holiday takes place on the birthday of Francisco Morazán, a famous Honduran military leader. **3**	*Charlie Brown's best friend.* Snoopy appeared in the comic strip *Peanuts* for the first time in 1950. **4**	**NATIONAL DO SOMETHING NICE DAY** **5**	**National Walk to School Day** If you live close enough, ask an adult to walk with you to school today! **6**
NATIONAL CAKE DECORATING DAY **10**	**INDIGENOUS PEOPLES' DAY** **COLUMBUS DAY** **11**	*Table for six billion?* On this day in 1999, the six billionth living human was born. **12**	**NATIONAL M&M DAY** **13**
Dessalines Day (Haiti) This national holiday celebrates the founding father of Haiti, Jean-Jacques Dessalines, who was killed on this day in 1806. **17**	**Alaska Day** In 1867, the U.S. purchased Alaska, our biggest state. **18**	**NATIONAL NEW FRIENDS DAY** Make new friends, but keep the old! **19**	**NATIONAL SUSPENDERS DAY** **20**
24 **UNITED NATIONS DAY** **31** **HALLOWEEN**	**WORLD PASTA DAY** **25**	**National Mule Day** A mule is a hybrid cross between a male donkey and a female horse. **26**	*City of Brotherly Love.* In 1682, Philadelphia was founded. **27**

THURSDAY	FRIDAY	SATURDAY

THURSDAY | **FRIDAY** | **SATURDAY**

COSMOS

National Hair Day
What unique hairstyles can you come up with?

1

Gandhi Jayanti (India)
This national holiday honors Mahatma Gandhi's birthday with ceremonies and tributes.
It is also the International Day of Nonviolence.

2

NATIONAL LED LIGHT DAY

7

National Fluffernutter Day
Peanut butter and marshmallow: sticky, but satisfying.

8

NATIONAL CHESS DAY
Checkmate!

9

Elementary, my dear Watson. The first installment of *The Adventures of Sherlock Holmes* was published in 1892.

14

National I Love Lucy Day
The show premiered on CBS on this day in 1951.

15

Talk about a wordsmith. Today is Noah Webster's birthday, the author of the first American dictionary.

DICTIONARY A-Z

16

NATIONAL REPTILE AWARENESS DAY

21

International Caps Lock Day
IT'S LIKE YELLING BUT ON PAPER.

22

National iPod Day
The iPod was released 20 years ago today, and listening to music has never been the same.

23

National First Responders Day
Celebrate the helpers who take immediate action in emergency situations

28

INTERNET DAY

29

NATIONAL PIT BULL AWARENESS DAY

30

OCTOBER

What's your favorite way to listen to music?

EAT BETTER, EAT TOGETHER MONTH

A HIGHLIGHTS CLASSIC PUZZLE

To celebrate this month, make a goal to eat with your family every night. Get involved in helping pick a healthy menu filled with protein, fruits, and veggies!

There are 15 objects hidden in this dinnertime scene. Can you find them all?

banana

golf club

clothespin

snail

candle

crescent moon

needle

drinking straw

tack

glove

mug

pencil

envelope

slice of pie

binoculars

NATIONAL
BULLYING PREVENTION
MONTH

If you've ever wondered if you have been a bully, this quiz could help you find out.

The sad truth is, bullying is pretty common. Without realizing it, even you could have been a bully to someone in your life. This month, make an extra effort to be kind to everyone you meet. The bullying can stop with you!

1. You hear your best friend teasing a kid about being overweight. You:

   a. Laugh. Your friend said it in a funny way.

   b. Leave. You don't want any part of your friend's behavior.

   c. Quietly urge your friend to leave the kid alone.

2. A really embarrassing picture of a kid you know is being sent around. You:

   a. Show it to everyone around you and then forward it to someone else.

   b. Refuse to accept it, or if it's electronic, delete it from your phone or e-mail.

   c. Tell an adult you trust and ask him or her what to do.

3. When your teacher tells you to form groups, you notice that the same kids are excluded every time. This time, you:

   a. Hurry to form your group so that you won't get stuck with those kids.

   b. Don't worry about those kids. Someone else will choose them.

   c. Invite them into your group. No one wants to be left out.

4. A popular group of kids you really want to be friends with asks you to help play a mean trick on someone. You:

   a. Play along. They are going to do it with or without you, and this might make you friends with the popular kids.

   b. Pretend you are not going to be in school the day of the trick so you can't be part of it.

   c. Tell them you think it sounds mean and they shouldn't do it.

5. You see your friend pushing around a kid at recess. You:

   a. Watch. The kid probably had it coming, and no one else who's watching is stopping the fight.

   b. Leave. It isn't your fight.

   c. Get a teacher. Your friend may not like it, but at least no one will get hurt.

Results

If you answered mostly a:
Careful! You could be a bit of a bully. Before you act, think about how your actions might make others feel.

If you answered mostly b:
You don't bully others, but you don't stick up for kids who are being bullied, either. Ask yourself, "How can I help?"

If you answered mostly c:
You stick up for kids who are being bullied. Good for you! Soon, others may follow your lead.

GLOBAL DIVERSITY
AWARENESS MONTH

The world is full of many different cultures, and this month we get to celebrate them! You probably have friends who have different traditions than you. Many of these traditions have come from other cultures.

The diversity we can find in the United States is one of the things that make it such a great country. We celebrate our differences and learn from each other.

What goes around the world but doesn't move?

The equator

Birthday Traditions Around the World

On birthdays in **MEXICO**, it's traditional for someone to shove the birthday boy or girl's face into their cake after they take their first bite.

AUSTRALIANS celebrate their birthday by eating fairy bread—buttered bread with rainbow sprinkles.

In **THE NETHERLANDS**, everyone in the family gets birthday wishes, not just the birthday person.

JAMAICAN birthday boys or girls get flour thrown at them!

In **VIETNAM**, everyone celebrates their birthday on the same day of the year, called Tet, which is also the beginning of the new year. Children get red envelopes filled with money as presents.

Can you match the cultural tradition with the country that practices it?

China   Greece   Norway

Indonesia   Japan

1. In the most populated country in Asia, it isn't rude to slurp noodles—it just means you're enjoying the food!

2. It's rude to point with your pointer finger in this country. Instead, use your thumb!

3. In homes in this large island country, you always remove your shoes before entering.

4. Even when eating a sandwich, this country is big on using silverware. Table manners are very important to them.

5. Instead of putting their baby teeth under a pillow, kids in this country throw their teeth onto their roofs.

ITALIAN AMERICAN
HERITAGE MONTH

Calling all readers with Italian ancestors—this month is for you! Take time this month to learn about your family that came from Italy, and learn a little bit more about Italy, too.

There are over **17 million** Italian Americans living in the U.S., about 5% of the population.

October is also **German American** and **Polish American** Heritage Month. Where are your ancestors from?

We've collected 35 words that have to do with Italy. There are cities, foods, historic sites, famous Italians, and more. To find them, look up, down, across, backwards, and diagonally.

G	A	L	I	L	E	O	O	T	T	O	S	I	R	P
G	R	E	E	N	C	O	L	O	S	S	E	U	M	A
N	A	L	I	M	G	E	L	A	T	O	L	V	I	N
F	L	O	R	E	N	C	E	L	D	R	P	A	Q	T
W	P	E	S	T	O	Y	E	O	A	L	A	T	T	H
H	S	I	M	U	N	A	V	S	V	E	N	I	C	E
I	P	I	S	A	H	C	E	D	I	P	B	C	A	O
T	O	I	C	P	B	A	S	M	N	A	R	A	K	N
E	F	S	A	O	C	N	U	A	C	H	L	N	U	I
R	U	R	R	M	A	N	V	Z	I	C	A	J	A	L
T	O	B	E	P	R	O	I	Z	N	E	C	I	A	O
K	O	M	D	E	E	L	U	A	V	N	N	Q	L	I
L	U	R	E	I	P	I	S	I	C	I	L	Y	D	V
F	L	A	G	I	O	O	V	P	D	T	L	Y	Y	A
C	L	A	Z	Z	I	P	N	R	Q	S	Q	L	C	R
M	A	R	I	N	A	R	A	R	T	I	E	A	A	H
E	I	Z	A	R	G	S	X	L	A	S	A	G	N	A
M	I	C	H	E	L	A	N	G	E	L	O	B	G	I

ALPS
ARNO
CAESAR
CANNOLI
CIAO
COLOSSEUM
DA VINCI
FLORENCE
GALILEO
GELATO
GRAZIE
LASAGNA
MARINARA
MICHELANGELO
MILAN
NAPLES
OPERA
PANTHEON
PESTO
PIAZZA
PISA
PIZZA
POMPEII
RAPHAEL
RAVIOLI
RISOTTO
ROME
SARDINIA
SICILY
SISTINE CHAPEL
TUSCANY
VATICAN
VENICE
VESUVIUS
VILLA

ALBUQUERQUE INTERNATIONAL
BALLOON FIESTA

For nine days every October, Albuquerque, New Mexico, holds its International Balloon Fiesta. Balloonists from all over the world come to ride, race, and revel in the hundreds of hot-air balloons in attendance. **Find at least 12 differences between the two pictures.**

October 8, 1871
THE GREAT CHICAGO FIRE BEGINS

No one knows what started the Chicago fire 150 years ago. What we do know is that it began at Catherine O'Leary's barn. For years people blamed her cow, saying that she must have kicked a lantern over, sparking the flames. But witnesses later said they saw men smoking pipes by the barn that night. A spark from a pipe could easily set a barn full of hay on fire! Whatever the cause, the fire burned for two days, spreading toward the city's center, destroying thousands of buildings. The firefighters were finally able to stop the fire with some help from the rain.

Follow the steps to draw a fire truck.

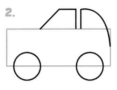

Mrs. O'Leary always denied her cow started the fire, but it wasn't until 126 years later in 1997 that the Chicago City Council officially removed blame from Mrs. O'Leary and her cow.

It's illegal to go over Niagara Falls—not to mention extremely dangerous. Definitely do not try this yourself!

30 MILLION people visit Niagara Falls each year!

October 24, 1901
THE FIRST BARREL RIDE DOWN NIAGARA FALLS

One hundred and twenty years ago, Annie Edson Taylor, a 63-year-old teacher, took the first barrel ride down Niagara Falls. She hoped the trip would make her famous and earn her some money—but unfortunately that didn't quite work out. She did, however, inspire several other thrill-seekers who would follow her over the falls over the next 50 years.

WORLD SERIES

The annual championship series of North American Major League Baseball has been played since 1903. The American League champion team faces off against the National League champion team in a best-of-seven-games series. But why is it called the *World* Series if only North American teams are eligible to play? One legend is that the *New York World* newspaper was the series's original sponsor; however, that's incorrect. When the World Series was first created at the turn of the century, baseball was the quintessential all-American game, and it wasn't played in many other countries around the world. So the organizers claimed that their championship series was showcasing the best baseball players in the world, as a way to draw a bigger crowd. And the name stuck, even as baseball has gained popularity in many countries around the world.

October 5, 1921

One hundred years ago, the first radio broadcast of a World Series game took place as the New York Giants played against the New York Yankees.

A Yankees player, a Giants player, and umpires at the 1921 World Series

This is what a home radio looked like in the 1920s!

RECORD SETTERS

Which player holds each of these career records?

511 WINS
Cy Young
or Sandy Koufax?

5,714 STRIKEOUTS
Nolan Ryan
or Randy Johnson?

1,406 STOLEN BASES
Willie Mays
or Rickey Henderson?

4,256 HITS
Ty Cobb
or Pete Rose?

14 WORLD SERIES APPEARANCES
Yogi Berra
or Babe Ruth?

How do baseball players stay cool?

By sitting next to the fans

Why are baseball players so rich?

Because they play on diamonds

How is a baseball team similar to a pancake?

They both need a good batter

CHAMPIONSHIP

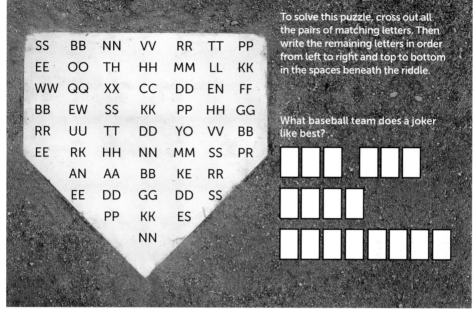

SS	BB	NN	VV	RR	TT	PP
EE	OO	TH	HH	MM	LL	KK
WW	QQ	XX	CC	DD	EN	FF
BB	EW	SS	KK	PP	HH	GG
RR	UU	TT	DD	YO	VV	BB
EE	RK	HH	NN	MM	SS	PR
	AN	AA	BB	KE	RR	
	EE	DD	GG	DD	SS	
		PP	KK	ES		
			NN			

To solve this puzzle, cross out all the pairs of matching letters. Then write the remaining letters in order from left to right and top to bottom in the spaces beneath the riddle.

What baseball team does a joker like best?

☐☐☐ ☐☐☐

☐☐☐☐

☐☐☐☐☐☐☐☐☐

TIC TAC ROW

What do the baseball cards in each row—horizontally, vertically, and diagonally—have in common?

FLY CATCHER

Can you help this outfielder catch the fly ball before it hits the ground?

START

FINISH

October 2, 2021
WORLD CARD MAKING DAY

Celebrate the day by making these Halloween-inspired cards to give to a friend!

Spooky Eyeball Card

1. Fold a piece of **cardstock** in half.

2. On the front, use a **white paint pen** to write: *"Eye" hope you have a "ball" this Halloween!*

3. For eyes, glue **cotton balls** onto the card. Cut out irises from cardstock and draw pupils on them with a black **marker**. Glue the irises to the cotton balls.

4. Write a message inside.

Drizzle Art Card

1. Drizzle **gel glue** in a fun design onto **craft foam**. Let the glue dry overnight.

2. Paint over the craft foam and dried glue using no more than two coats of **acrylic paint**. Let it dry.

3. Carefully peel off the glue. Glue the drizzle art to a folded piece of **cardstock** to make a card.

70% of people include their pet's name when signing greeting cards.

October 6, 2021
RANDOM ACTS OF POETRY DAY

What kind of tree has poems on it?

A poetry

4 Random Ways to Celebrate Poetry

1. Make up a tune and turn your favorite poem into a song. Perform it for your family.

2. Write a poem from an interesting point of view. For example, imagine what a fork would say about being in the dishwasher.

3. Research some poets and read their poems. Try to memorize a poem you like.

4. Challenge yourself to write a short poem and share it with a friend.

What hand is best to write poetry with?

Neither—you should use a pencil!

October 16
DICTIONARY DAY

There are tons of fun words hidden in the dictionary. Take a moment to find a new word to add to your vocabulary. Here are some of our favorites. **What are your favorite words?**

A dictionary's pages contain many words, but so do its letters! Using only letters in the word DICTIONARY, spell:

1. A child's plaything

___ ___ ___

2. An insect in a colony

___ ___ ___

3. A vegetable on a cob

___ ___ ___ ___

4. Dry mud

___ ___ ___ ___

5. Falling drops of water

___ ___ ___ ___

6. Railroad cars and an engine

___ ___ ___ ___ ___

7. A milk container

___ ___ ___ ___ ___ ___

gewgaw: a trinket

splendiferous: magnificent

collywobbles: a stomachache or feeling of nervousness

bumfuzzle: to confuse

widdershins: counterclockwise

flibbertigibbet: someone who is silly and talks a lot

xertz: to greedily eat or drink

The Oxford English Dictionary is one of the most widely used dictionaries in the English language. The first edition took 50 years to complete and was finished in 1928. It included more than 400,000 words and phrases from the 12th century to the present!

October 22
NATIONAL COLOR DAY

Each group of 3 words describes a shade of color. Use your color IQ to figure out which ones.

Where do crayons go on vacation?

Color-ado

1. Crimson	Ruby	Scarlet
2. Azure	Cobalt	Teal
3. Auburn	Mahogany	Sepia
4. Amber	Citron	Canary
5. Sage	Chartreuse	Jade
6. Plum	Mauve	Lavender
7. Tangerine	Marigold	Persimmon
8. Jet	Charcoal	Onyx

October 22 is also **National Smart Is Cool Day.** Get together with your friends and share your favorite trivia!

October 4

NATIONAL TACO DAY

Take-Along Taco Cup

Spoon the following ingredients into a plastic cup, in this order:

- ¼ cup **canned black beans**
- ¼ cup **guacamole**
- ¼ cup **sour cream**
- 2 tablespoons crushed **tortilla chips**
- ¼ cup **salsa**
- 2 tablespoons shredded **cheddar cheese**

Americans love tacos. They love them so much that they eat about **4.5 BILLION TACOS** every year!

shredded cheddar cheese

salsa

crushed tortilla chips

sour cream

guacamole

black beans

October 14

NATIONAL DESSERT DAY

Celebrate by making this tasty s'more fudge!

1. Over low heat, combine 14 ounces of **sweetened condensed milk** and 12 ounces of **chocolate chips**. Stir until melted, then remove from the heat.

2. Gently stir in 1–2 cups of **mini marshmallows** and ½ cup of broken **graham crackers**.

3. Pour into a square pan lined with parchment paper. Chill until firm, then cut.

TOP 10
MOST POPULAR
DESSERTS

1. Fudge
2. Chocolate Cake
3. Chocolate Chip Cookies
4. Brownies
5. Ice Cream
6. Apple Pie
7. Carrot Cake
8. Jell-O
9. Cupcakes
10. Cheesecake

October 16

WORLD FOOD DAY

KIDS' SCIENCE QUESTIONS

Why do some kids like foods that other kids don't?

The foods people like best are often the ones they're used to eating or that they think of positively. A good or bad experience can make a person like or dislike a certain flavor or even a food's texture or appearance. You'd probably rather eat a food you always eat at parties than a food you remember eating just before getting sick!

People can also inherit traits that make them more likely to enjoy or dislike certain foods. For example, if you inherited an ability to detect very small differences in flavors, you might think a food is way too spicy while other kids think it's just right.

But good news! Scientists say that we can learn to like foods. So even if you give a thumbs-down to a food today, in time you might give it a thumbs-up.

World Food Day is celebrated in more than 150 countries. This day promotes awareness of and action for people who suffer from hunger and emphasizes the importance of healthy diets.

October 26

NATIONAL PUMPKIN DAY

Find 18 pairs of matching pumpkins.

October 31
HALLOWEEN

Check out these frightening and fascinating facts!

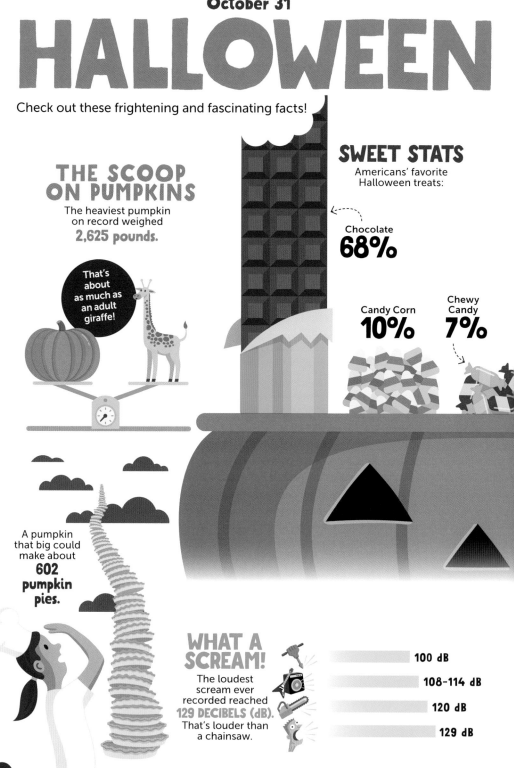

THE SCOOP ON PUMPKINS

The heaviest pumpkin on record weighed
2,625 pounds.

That's about as much as an adult giraffe!

A pumpkin that big could make about
602 pumpkin pies.

SWEET STATS

Americans' favorite Halloween treats:

Chocolate
68%

Candy Corn
10%

Chewy Candy
7%

WHAT A SCREAM!

The loudest scream ever recorded reached
129 DECIBELS (dB).
That's louder than a chainsaw.

	100 dB
	108-114 dB
	120 dB
	129 dB

BY THE NUMBERS

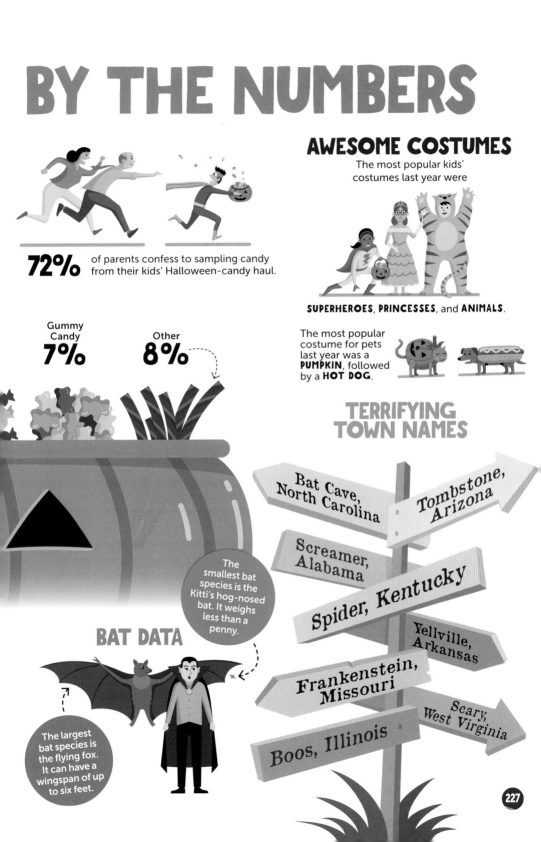

72% of parents confess to sampling candy from their kids' Halloween-candy haul.

AWESOME COSTUMES

The most popular kids' costumes last year were

SUPERHEROES, **PRINCESSES**, and **ANIMALS**.

The most popular costume for pets last year was a **PUMPKIN**, followed by a **HOT DOG**.

Gummy Candy
7%

Other
8%

TERRIFYING TOWN NAMES

Bat Cave, North Carolina

Tombstone, Arizona

Screamer, Alabama

Spider, Kentucky

Yellville, Arkansas

Frankenstein, Missouri

Scary, West Virginia

Boos, Illinois

BAT DATA

The smallest bat species is the Kitti's hog-nosed bat. It weighs less than a penny.

The largest bat species is the flying fox. It can have a wingspan of up to six feet.

October 3

NATIONAL BUTTERFLY AND HUMMINGBIRD DAY

BUTTERFLY

Butterflies are well known for having bright, beautiful colors on their wings. But did you know that when certain butterflies close their wings, the colors are replaced with shades of brown? This camouflage helps these butterflies blend in with their surroundings, like a rock or leaf.

Match the four brightly colored butterflies on the left with their camouflaged selves on the right.

A.

B.

C.

D.

2. American Snout

1. Goatweed Leafwing

4. Pearl Crescent

3. Mourning Cloak

Why didn't the butterfly go to the dance?

Because it was a moth ball

HUMMINGBIRD

A hummingbird's long tongue can reach nectar that is deep within a flower.

Its tongue has a forked tip that grabs more nectar with each lick than an unforked tongue could get.

Each wing moves in a figure 8, beating 70 to 80 times a second. The hummingbird can fly in all directions, as well as backward, upside down, and in a hover.

A hummingbird's iridescent colors can vary, because tiny structures on the feathers reflect light differently at different angles.

Its tiny feet grip branches as it rests, but it doesn't walk much.

INTERNATIONAL SLOTH DAY

The sloths are all celebrating International Sloth Day at Sloth-Land Adventure Park! Snoozanne wants to see a concert, Snorbert can't wait to go on a tube tour, and Dozalita is eager to try the ropes course. But all 3 activities have just started! What time is it?

ROCK-A-BYE CONCERTS
Every 3 hours from 12:00 P.M. to 9:00 P.M.

LAZY RIVER TUBE TOURS
Every 1½ hours from 12:00 P.M. to 9:00 P.M.

TREETOP ROPES COURSE
Every 2 hours from 2:00 P.M. to 8:00 P.M.

Three-toed sloths' fur is home to moths and algae. The moths help the algae grow, and the algae is a form of food and camouflage for the sloths.

Sloths live for a long time—on average about 20 years. The oldest sloth grew up in Australia's Adelaide Zoo and lived to be **43 years old!**

October 29

NATIONAL SEA SLUG DAY

Sea slugs roam the ocean floors and coral reefs. They are known as nudibranchs (NEW-duh-branks), which means "naked gill." This snail-without-a-shell looks as if it would be easy prey, but even without a shell, nudibranchs have ways to avoid predators.

What is the definition of a sea slug?

A sea snail with a housing problem

Rhinophores (RYE-no-fours) detect odors, helping the nudibranch find prey and avoid predators.

These bright colors may warn a predator who takes a toxic taste to stay away next time!

This nudibranch's "naked gills" are on its back.

With a wavelike motion of its long, muscular foot, the nudibranch can crawl with the current. Some species even swim.

It can safely eat toxic prey like anemones and sponges, absorbing the toxins to use for its own defense.

October 4 is World Animal Day! With over 1.2 million species discovered so far, there is a lot to celebrate today.

NATIONAL BATHTUB DAY

Today is a great day to take a bubble bath! While you wait for the water to fill up, see if you can find the objects hidden in this bathroom scene.

banana egg watch

book owl crayon

ring bell teacup

October 12, 2021
ADA LOVELACE DAY

This holiday celebrates the achievements of women in STEM (science, technology, engineering, and math). It is named for Ada Lovelace, who has been called the world's first computer programmer because of her work translating and commenting on Charles Babbage's Analytical Engine. She realized that computers had potential beyond mathematics.

Using the clues below, can you figure out which women in STEM each kid is learning about and how they're presenting their project?

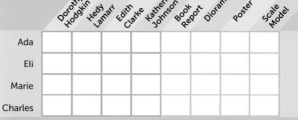

	Dorothy Hodgkin	Hedy Lamarr	Edith Clarke	Katherine Johnson	Book Report	Diorama	Poster	Scale Model
Ada								
Eli								
Marie								
Charles								

1. One of the kids picked a woman whose first name starts with the same letter as his name and who was the first woman to earn an electrical engineering degree from MIT.

2. Marie checked out a biography to write about the 1964 Nobel Prize in Chemistry winner.

3. Ada drew a movie poster to show the inventions of the actress and inventor she selected.

4. Everyone loved the space capsule model Charles did about his subject, whose mathematical calculations for NASA helped send astronauts to the moon.

WORLDWIDE HOWL AT THE MOON NIGHT

Have you heard of a wolf howling at the moon? It's a popular image. But did you know that wolves don't actually howl at the moon? They howl to communicate with other wolves who are far away from them. Since they are nocturnal, the moon is often up when they howl. It's all just a big coincidence!

Even if wolves don't howl at the moon, tonight is the night for you to do it and do it loud. Head outside and give your best howl at that shiny orb in the sky. Maybe you'll hear some howling in return.

How does the man on the moon cut his hair?

Eclipse it

October 31

NATIONAL MAGIC DAY

Celebrate the holiday by wowing your friends with your cool magic tricks! Here's one for you to try.

1. Ask a friend to pick any number without telling you what it is (example: 13).

2. Have him add 5 to it (13 + 5 = 18).

3. Tell him to multiply that new number by 3 (18 x 3 = 54).

4. Have him subtract 9 (54 − 9 = 45).

5. Tell him to divide that number by 3 (45 / 3 = 15).

6. Have him subtract his original number from his new number (15 − 13 = 2). The answer is always 2!

What do you call an owl magician?

Whoo-dini

AROUND

October 10
NATIONAL DAY

National Day in Taiwan, also known as Double Ten Day, celebrates the 1911 Wuchang Uprising, which ultimately led to the collapse of the Qing Dynasty. There is a large parade held at the Presidential Office Building and a huge fireworks display held in the evening.

One of Taiwan's most famous buildings, the Presidential Office Building in Taipei has more than 300 rooms.

October 18
INDEPENDENCE DAY

The blue stripe and the crescent represent Azerbaijan's Turkic origins.

30 years ago, in 1991, Azerbaijan adopted a constitutional act that restored its independence from the Soviet Union. The vote to support the act was unanimous among the citizens of Azerbaijan.

There are over **400 VOLCANOES** in Azerbaijan, but they don't shoot lava—they shoot mud and sometimes oil. When they aren't making a muddy mess, they let out sulfur gases, making the area smell a lot like eggs.

Like most flags, this one is full of symbolism.

The red portion symbolizes developing democracy.

The green is a nod to Islam, the most practiced religion in Azerbaijan.

The eight-point star is a reference to how Azerbaijan was written in the old alphabet, with eight letters.

THE WORLD

people around the world celebrate in October.

The Austrian Parliament building in Vienna was built between 1874 and 1883. The main statue in front of the building is Athena, the Greek goddess of wisdom.

October 26
NATIONAL DAY

This day is a celebration of the Austrian Parliament passing a law in 1955 that Austria would remain a neutral country.

At the time, it was occupied by four countries (the Soviet Union, the United States, Great Britain, and France), post-World War II. By declaring neutrality, the law ended the occupation and allowed Austria to be its own country again. On this day, in addition to several rituals performed by the government, federal museums open their doors for free to Austrian citizens.

October 29
REPUBLIC DAY

This is a day to celebrate in Turkey, as people remember Turkey's victory in the War of Independence in 1923. There are fireworks, art events, concerts, and celebrations throughout the country. Can you find where the 3 jigsaw pieces fit into this photo of a Republic Day celebration?

233

SUNDAY	MONDAY	TUESDAY	WEDNESDAY

National Author's Day

Who's your favorite author? Is there an author whose books you've wanted to read? **1**

ELECTION DAY

2

Representing Illinois. In 1992, Carol Moseley Braun became the first African American woman to be elected to the United States Senate. **3**

Bye-bye Daylight Saving Time! Did you turn back your clock one hour?*

*Not you, Arizona and Hawaii. **7**

National STEM/ STEAM Day

STEM stands for Science, Technology, Engineering, and Math. The *A* in *STEAM* stands for Arts. **8**

Independence Day (Cambodia)

This holiday celebrates independence from France in 1953 with speeches and a torch-lighting ceremony. **9**

Sesame Street Day

"Sunny day, sweepin' the clouds away . . ." In 1969, *Sesame Street* debuted on public television. **10**

In 1989, President H. W. Bush made pardoning a live Thanksgiving turkey a national tradition. **14**

America Recycles Day

Take the pledge to "Keep America Beautiful"! **15**

HAVE A PARTY WITH YOUR BEAR DAY

16

Click this! In 1970, Douglas Engelbart was granted a patent for the "X-Y Position Indicator for a Display System" what we now call a computer mouse. **17**

World Hello Day

Guten Tag! Hola! Konnichiwa! Aim to greet 10 new people today. **21**

Go for a Ride Day

Hop on your bike or board, and get out of the house! **22**

National Cashew Day

Cashews grow out of cashew apples, so they're technically a seed, not a nut. **23**

Celebrate Your Unique Talent Day

What is your unique talent? **24**

HANUKKAH

begins at sunset. **28**

One giant footstep . . . In 2004, movie monster Godzilla was given a star on the Hollywood Walk of Fame. **29**

Saint Andrew's Day (Scotland)

Scots honor the patron saint of Scotland with festivals and celebrations full of music, dance, and food. **30**

BIRTHSTONES

TOPAZ

CITRINE

THURSDAY

4
Westward, ho! The first wagon train arrived in California 180 years ago. The group had left Independence, Missouri, on May 1, 1841.

11
VETERANS DAY

18
World Philosophy Day
What do you think about that?

25
THANKSGIVING DAY

FRIDAY

5
National Love Your Red Hair Day
Don't have red hair? Appreciate someone else's ginger locks!

12
Say cheese, Nessie! In 1933, Hugh Grey snapped the first known photo of Scotland's fabled "Loch Ness Monster."

19
Loy Krathong (Thailand)
Thais celebrate the end of the rainy season by floating small boats down the river.

26
Down the rabbit hole . . . In 1864, Charles Dodgson sent a handwritten story to 10-year-old Alice Liddell. It was later published as *Alice's Adventures in Wonderland* under his pen name, Lewis Carroll.

SATURDAY

6
NATIONAL SAXOPHONE DAY

13
WORLD KINDNESS DAY
You're welcome!

20
NATIONAL PEANUT BUTTER FUDGE DAY
Take a bite of this sweet treat!

27
So many floats! In 1924, Macy's department store sponsored its first Thanksgiving Day Parade. Although held on Thanksgiving, it was actually a Christmas parade.

NOVEMBER

FLOWER
CHRYSANTHEMUM

ZODIAC SIGNS
SCORPIO: OCTOBER 23– NOVEMBER 21

SAGITTARIUS: NOVEMBER 23– DECEMBER 21

NATIONAL NATIVE AMERICAN HERITAGE MONTH

November celebrates the diverse and rich culture, history, and traditions of Native peoples. It's also a time to raise awareness about the struggles Native people have faced in the past as well as in the present.

There are 573 federally recognized Native American Nations in the United States. Two hundred and twenty-nine of these are in Alaska.

More than 5.2 million Americans, or 1.7 percent of the U.S. population, are of Native heritage.

The sport of lacrosse comes from stickball games the Native Americans played as early as the 12th century. It could be a violent sport, which gave the game the reputation of being good for combat training.

A Navajo girl in traditional handwoven blanket looks out over Monument Valley.

The names of the 10 largest Native American tribes are listed here in alphabetical order. Use the number of letters in each word as a clue to where it might fit in the grid.

APACHE   CHOCTAW
BLACKFEET   IROQUOIS
CHEROKEE   MUSCOGEE
CHICKASAW   NAVAJO
CHIPPEWA   PUEBLO

Ask a teacher or librarian to help you learn about the Native history of your area.

NATIONAL MODEL RAILROAD MONTH

Passenger railroads started in the 1820s, and toy trains made of wood and metal arrived in the 1860s. Today, kids and adults enjoy model railroading.

Fill in the letters in the picture code to answer the riddle.

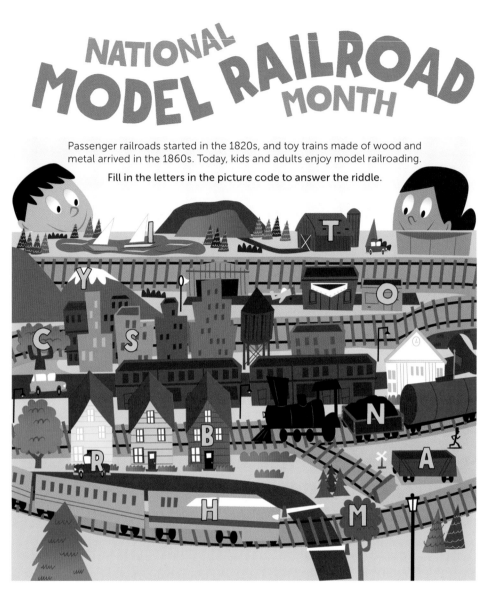

What do you call a locomotive that sneezes?

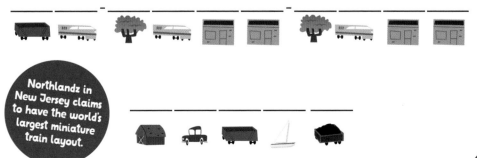

Northlandz in New Jersey claims to have the world's largest miniature train layout.

FAMILY STORIES MONTH

Everyone has a story. Ask your parents, grandparents, or other family members for theirs! Share yours, too.

What's silly in this family photo? Take turns telling a silly (but true!) story about your family.

STORY STARTS

Genealogy is the study of family history and ancestry. Be your family's genealogist! Write down or record your relatives' stories. You might ask these questions:

- What is your earliest memory?
- What was your favorite game growing up?
- Who was your best friend when you were my age?
- What was your first job?
- What was your favorite song, TV show, or movie?
- Where was your favorite place to visit?

Look around your house. An old photo album, school diploma, or favorite knickknack may spark a family member's story.

KIDS' SCIENCE QUESTIONS

Why can't you remember anything from when you were a baby?

Short-term memories last for seconds to hours. Long-term memories last for years.

Babies do form memories as building blocks for their development. Babies remember faces, copy what they see, and learn how to talk. Later on, using words to store memories helps them to recall specific events. We may not remember events from when we were babies because we didn't have the words to attach to the memories. Thank goodness for baby photos and videos!

HISTORIC BRIDGE AWARENESS MONTH

The famous Golden Gate Bridge spans San Francisco Bay in California, but it isn't gold and it has no gate! The bridge is named after the Golden Gate Strait, where the bay meets the Pacific Ocean. (A *strait* is a narrow passageway connecting two large bodies of water.) This month, visit a famous bridge or learn the history of your favorite crossing.

Can you find 17 objects in this Hidden Pictures puzzle of the Golden Gate Bridge?

Why did the goose cross the bridge?

To show he was no chicken

ORANGE YOU GLAD?

The U.S. Navy wanted the bridge painted black with yellow stripes, to be visible in the foggy bay. But the bridge's architect was inspired by the reddish color of the rust-proof paint on the steel beams during construction and created a version of a color called International Orange. He liked the way it blended with the landscape but stood out against the sea and sky. To this day, the color is specially mixed when the bridge needs a touch up of paint. Five to ten thousand gallons are used yearly.

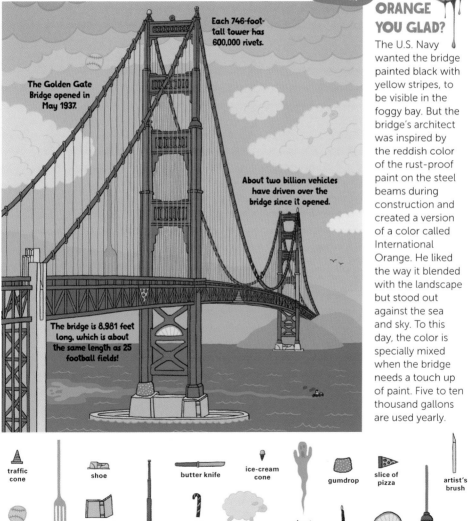

Each 746-foot-tall tower has 600,000 rivets.

The Golden Gate Bridge opened in May 1937.

About two billion vehicles have driven over the bridge since it opened.

The bridge is 8,981 feet long, which is about the same length as 25 football fields!

traffic cone

shoe

butter knife

ice-cream cone

gumdrop

slice of pizza

artist's brush

baseball

fork

open book

telescope

candy cane

sheep

ghost

candle

wedge of lime

plunger

November 11, 1921

100 YEARS AGO, the Tomb of the Unknown Soldier was dedicated at Arlington National Cemetery in Virginia, near Washington, D.C.

Created soon after World War I, this memorial site honors members of the United States Armed Forces who died fighting for their country and whose remains could not be identified. The marble tomb lies above the gravesite of an unknown World War I soldier.

Carved on the tomb are the words:
Here rests in honored glory an American soldier known but to God.

Since 1948, members of the army's Fourth Battalion, Third U.S. Infantry Regiment, also known as The Old Guard, have served as sentinels.

Since 1937, the tomb has been guarded by a sentinel every minute of every day.

Each sentinel "walks the mat," taking 21 precisely timed paces in each direction in front of the tomb. The number is based on the 21-gun salute used to honor soldiers at their burials.

11 AM, NOVEMBER 11

Every year at the 11th hour of the 11th day of the 11th month, a wreath is placed at the Tomb of the Unknown Soldier, as part of the National Veterans Day Observance. To honor a veteran, make your own wreath or a star frame.

ribbon

photo of a service member

craft foam

The Tomb of the Unknown Soldier site also holds three graves marked by white marble slabs. Two hold the remains of military personnel from World War II and the Korean War. The third had held a Vietnam War air force officer who was later identified through DNA testing. That gravesite now remains vacant. Its cover bears the inscription *Honoring and Keeping Faith with America's Missing Servicemen, 1958–1975*.

Then-president Calvin Coolidge paid tribute by placing a wreath on the Tomb of the Unknown Soldier on Armistice Day 1924.

Armistice Day was renamed **Veterans Day** in 1954.

November 14, 1981

40 YEARS AGO, Double Eagle V was the first manned balloon to make a successful crossing of the Pacific Ocean.

Double Eagle V was launched from Nagashima, Japan, on November 10, with four passengers. It landed in Mendocino National Forest in California 84 hours and 31 minutes later. The balloon traveled 5,209 miles, setting a new long-distance record for gas balloons at the time.

The balloon was **26 stories tall** and filled with helium.

Can you find the 4 pairs of identical balloons, the 3 balloons that are exactly alike, and the 1 balloon that has no match?

The hot-air balloon was invented in 1783 by two brothers in France.

NATIONAL TAKE A HIKE DAY

About **35 million** Americans go day hiking.

The Appalachian Trail is the longest hiking-only footpath in the world. It covers about **2,190 miles** from Maine to Georgia, passing through **14 states.** Each year, more than 3 million people walk a bit of it and about 3,000 try to hike it from beginning to end, which takes five to seven months.

As Mike hiked with his family, he wrote about their day. Later, he noticed that each sentence contained an item they took on the hike! Can you find a hiking item hidden in each of the sentences below? Hint: All the items are in the scene.

EXAMPLE: Like all good hikers, we left the trail unchanged. (lunch)

1. Emma planned the route.

2. We stopped to sketch at the bridge.

3. Two squirrels came racing along a log!

4. The whole crew ate raisins for energy.

5. We came upon chopped trees near a beaver dam.

6. Our pace had to slow at challenging, rocky parts of the trail.

BONUS! How many squirrels can you find in the scene?

COMPASS CODE

To answer the riddle below, **start at the North (N) circle.** Then move in the directions listed and write the letters you find in the correct spaces.

Where's the best place to eat while hiking?

Where there's _____   _____ _____ _____ _____   _____ _____

_____ _____ _____   _____ _____ _____ _____ _____

1. S 1 _____	6. NE 3 _____	11. W 3 _____
2. SE 2 _____	7. W 1 _____	12. N 1 _____
3. W 3 _____	8. S 2 _____	13. E 2 _____
4. NW 1 _____	9. N 1 _____	14. NW 2 _____
5. S 3 _____	10. SE 2 _____	

NATIONAL SQUARE DANCE DAY

Swing your partner—do-si-do! In this folk dance, four couples face each other to form a square and follow the steps sung or called out by a "caller."

There are at least 10 differences in these pictures. How many can you find?

BOW TO YOUR PARTNER!

Here's how to do some of the most common square-dance moves.

Allemande Left: Turn to the dancer next to you who is not your partner (also called your *corner*). Then join left hands or link elbows, and circle around until you are back next to your partner.

Do-Si-Do: Face your partner. Step past each other, passing right shoulders. Without turning, step around, back to back, passing left shoulders, until you are in front of your partner again.

Right and Left Grand: Face your partner, join right hands, and walk past each other. Then join left hands with the next person stepping toward you. Circle around, switching hands, until you come back to your partner.

Promenade: Stand side by side with your partner and join hands, right with right, left with left. Walk together counterclockwise in a circle until you reach your starting position.

Swing Your Partner: Link right elbows and step in a clockwise circle, staying in the same spot in the square.

The largest square dance, with **1,632 PARTICIPANTS,** took place at the 66th National Square Dance Convention in 2017.

FROM ALABAMA TO WASHINGTON, as many as 31 states have listed the square dance as their "state dance" or "state folk dance."

NATIONAL COOK FOR YOUR PETS DAY

Make a special meal for your furry or feathered or scaly friend. You won't even need a stove to "cook up" these treats!

Ask an adult for help with anything sharp. Check with your vet before feeding new foods to your pet.

PUP CAKE

1. Mix together 2 tablespoons of **dry dog food**, 1 tablespoon of **peanut butter**, and 1 tablespoon of **mashed banana**.
2. Press the mixture into a muffin-tin cup. Carefully tap the treat out and place it on a dog dish.
3. Add **banana slices**. Top with a **dog treat**.

CAT SNACK

1. Mix together 2 tablespoons of **tuna**, 1 tablespoon of **shredded cheese**, and 1 teaspoon of **oatmeal**.
2. Press the mixture into a muffin-tin cup. Carefully tap the treat out and place it on a cat dish.
3. Top with small **cat treats**.

TOWERING TREAT

1. For other animals, slice up their favorite **fruits** and **vegetables**.
2. Stack the pieces in layers.
3. Top with their favorite **treat**.

NATIONAL SANDWICH DAY

What do the sandwiches in each row—horizontally, vertically, and diagonally—have in common?

MENU MIX-UP

What's between the bread of these sandwiches?
Match each sandwich to its filling.

1. Ham and cheese on French toast

2. Bacon, lettuce, and tomato on toast with mayo

3. Corned beef, sauerkraut, Swiss cheese, with Russian dressing, on rye bread

4. Triple-decker sandwich with sliced turkey or chicken, bacon, tomato, lettuce, and mayo

5. Ham, roasted pork, Swiss cheese, and pickles, with mustard, on a crusty loaf

6. Meats, cheeses, and olive salad on a round Italian bread

A. Cuban

B. Reuben

C. Muffaletta

D. Club

E. BLT

F. Monte Cristo

THANKSGIVING

THANKFUL TURKEY

Cut a head, body, wings, and feet from poster board. Decorate them with cardstock, yarn, and markers.

Buddy, my hamster

hugs!

Ice CReam

wednesdays With Grandma

my Teacher

flute lessons

Birthday parties

My CAT

I AM THANKFUL FOR . . .

Cut 15 feathers from cardstock. Write something you're thankful for on each feather. Glue or tape them onto the turkey.

Adult turkeys have **5,000–6,000** feathers, including 18 large quill feathers on their tails.

Pickles

Save some feathers and have your Thanksgiving guests write what they're thankful for!

WHICH THANKSGIVING FOOD ARE YOU?

1. To cheer up a friend, you . . .
a. Play their favorite game.
b. Talk about what's wrong.
c. Make them a card full of jokes.

2. Your ideal birthday is . . .
a. Playing laser tag.
b. Going to the movies.
c. Visiting an animal shelter.

3. Which do you do for fun?
a. Try out a new activity.
b. Read.
c. Invite friends over to play.

4. What is your favorite part of the school day?
a. Recess.
b. Art class.
c. Talking with friends at lunch.

5. Which do you love most about Thanksgiving?
a. Goofing around with family.
b. Remembering what you're thankful for.
c. Helping to prepare the Thanksgiving feast.

MOSTLY As: You are turkey. You are an outgoing person who likes to be in the middle of the action.
MOSTLY Bs: You are mashed potatoes. Friends and family are drawn to your quiet, warm personality.
MOSTLY Cs: You are pumpkin pie. You go out of your way to do or say sweet things to brighten someone's day.

TURKEY TROT

Help Tara get to the oven to take the turkey out.

FINISH

START

MAKE A MATCH

Find five pairs of matching turkeys.

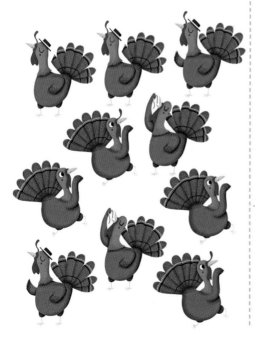

FAVORITE FOODS

Unscramble these top 10 favorite Thanksgiving foods. Which dish is your favorite?

1. IPE
2. GUFFNITS
3. VAGYR
4. EWEST APESTOTO
5. MAH
6. ASHDEM ETTAOOPS
7. CAM NAD ESHEEC
8. ENGER ANEB ACRESOLES
9. NCOR DEBRA
10. KURTYE

The Wampanoag, or Wôpanâak, have lived in what is now New England for about twelve thousand years. Their ancestors met the Pilgrims in 1620. One year later, they and the settlers participated in several days of feasting and games that we now call the first Thanksgiving.

HANUKKAH

Every year, in late November or December, Jewish people enjoy an eight-day celebration that began about two thousand years ago. After a victory over the Syrian-Greek army around 165 BCE, the Jews rededicated the Second Temple of Jerusalem. They found only enough oil to keep the Temple lamp lit for one day. Yet the oil burned until a new supply arrived—eight days later! Today, Jewish people remember this miracle by lighting the Hanukkah menorah—one candle for each day. The traditional potato pancakes called *latkes*, usually fried in oil, are a reminder of that miracle, too.

MAKE A MAGNETIC MENORAH

1. Place a sheet of **blue craft foam** on a protected surface. Cover your palms and fingers with **poster paint**. Overlap your thumbs and spread out your fingers, then press both hands onto the craft foam.

2. Wash and dry your hands. Cover your thumb with gold paint. Make nine thumbprints on **yellow craft foam**.

3. Cut out the "menorah" and the "flames." Glue **magnets** to the back.

4. Put the menorah and flames on a refrigerator. "Light" the candles during Hanukkah.

WHOLE LOTTA LATKES

You're making latkes for two dozen (24) people. You already have oil, salt, pepper, and matzo meal. How much will you spend on the three main ingredients if one potato is 89 cents, one dozen eggs is $2.67, and an onion is 99 cents?

> **POTATO LATKE RECIPE**
> (serves 6)
> 5 large potatoes
> 3 eggs
> 1 onion

SPINNING FUN

During the holiday, Jewish children play games with a dreidel, a four-sided top. On each side is a Hebrew letter. Pronounced *nun, gimmel, hay,* and *shin,* the letters stand for the words *nes gadol hayah sham*, which mean "a great miracle happened there." Make your own simple dreidel.

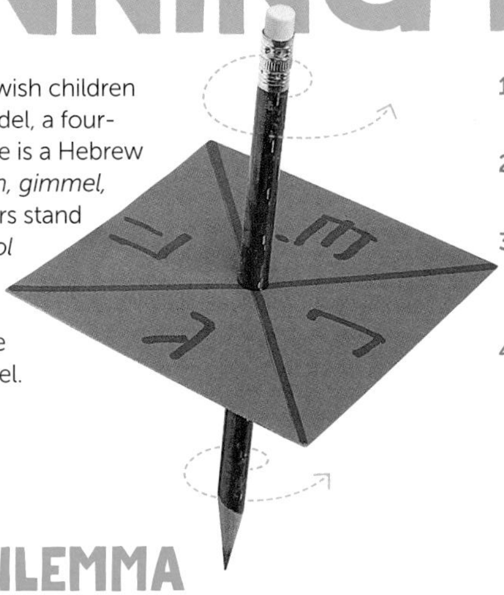

1. Cut a 4-inch square out of **cardboard**.
2. With a **marker**, draw a big X across the square.
3. In the triangles, write the Hebrew letters *Nun* נ, *Gimel* ג, *Hay* ה, and *Shin* ש.
4. Push a **sharpened pencil** through the center of the cardboard. Your dreidel will spin on the pencil point.

DREIDEL DILEMMA

Aaron, Avi, and Ariel love to play dreidel. In their game, each Hebrew letter has a numerical value: *Nun* = 50, *Gimel* = 3, *Hay* = 5, and *Shin* = 300. Each player takes turns spinning the dreidel. Whichever letter faces up when the dreidel falls shows the number of points the player receives for that round. The player who reaches 1,000 first is the winner. Can you figure out who won this game?

	NUN נ	GIMEL ג	HAY ה	SHIN ש
Ariel	0 times	4 times	11 times	3 times
Avi	5 times	6 times	5 times	2 times
Aaron	1 time	10 times	4 times	3 times

Dreidel means "turn."

During Hanukkah, kids are often given *gelt* (money) to share with a charity.

To play, everyone adds on items to the game's pot every round. This can be anything, such as pennies, nickels, nuts, or chocolate coins covered in gold foil—a Hanukkah treat that represents *gelt*.

In a traditional round, if the dreidel lands on *Nun*, do nothing. If *Gimmel*, take the whole pot. If *Hay*, take half of the pot. If *Shin*, give one item back.

WORLD JELLYFISH DAY

Find 22 balloons hiding among the jellyfish.

Test your jellyfish IQ by trying to answer these questions.

1. How do some jellyfish move?
a. They use their tentacles to swim.
b. They suck in water and squirt it out forcefully.
c. They grab onto a shark's tail and hitch a ride.

2. The biggest species of jellyfish is larger than a person. The smallest is the size of a:
a. baseball mitt.
b. clam.
c. pinhead.

3. Some jellyfish glow in the dark, and they've been used to make:
a. light bulbs.
b. glow-in-the-dark ice cream.
c. reflective strips on jackets.

4. Jellyfish don't have bones. They also don't have:
a. eyes.
b. nerves.
c. hearts and brains.

Jellyfish can sting even when they are dead.

5. Why do jellyfish sting?
a. to capture food.
b. to attract a mate.
c. because they're just mean.

6. A jellyfish's body is 95 percent:
a. water.
b. air.
c. slime.

7. A group of jellyfish is called a:
a. blob.
b. smack.
c. school.

8. Jellyfish are important because:
a. They protect small fish from predators.
b. Young crabs ride on them to get around.
c. Sea turtles and other large fish eat them.
d. All of the above.

Most jellyfish live a few days or months. One species of jellyfish may live forever. The tiny **TURRITOPSIS DOHRNII** can turn back into a baby when it is injured or threatened. Then it starts its life cycle all over again and again and . . .

In May 1991, **2,478 JELLYFISH BABIES** were launched into space aboard the shuttle Columbia.

WORLD RADIOGRAPHY DAY

Also known as the International Day of Radiology and National X-Ray Day, this date marks the discovery of the X-ray by Wilhelm Roentgen in 1895.

Follow the correct maze path from START to FINISH. Write down the letters you pick up along the way. Then unscramble them to learn what caused Xavier's tummy ache.

LETTERS: _ _ _ _ _ _ _ _ _ _ _ _

ANSWER: _ _ _ _ _ _ _ _ _ _ _ _ _ _ _ _

BONE UP!

In what part of your body can you find these bones? **Hint:** One letter from each word, in order, spells out the answer.

ULNA

RADIUS

HUMERUS

What has fingers put no bones?

A glove

How do you say "Good morning" to a French skeleton?

"Bone-jour!"

Origami comes from the Japanese words *oru* (to fold) and *kami* (paper).

ORIGAMI DAY

Origami is the art form of folding paper into different shapes. Origami Day began in Japan, where the folded-paper crane has become a symbol of peace.

MAKE AN ORIGAMI DRINKING CUP

1. Fold the paper in half diagonally (corner to corner).

2. Fold the left corner over the right side.

3. Fold the right corner over to the left side.

4. Fold the top front flap down.

5. Flip the cup over. Fold the other top flap down.

6. Open out your cup, fill it up, and take a sip!

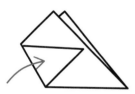

November 13

WORLD KINDNESS DAY

A compliment, a thoughtful gesture, or a helping hand can be all it takes to make someone's day a little brighter. Give it a try! And when you lend a hand, two things often happen: the people you've helped feel good, and you do, too!

Notice the people around you, think about what you can do for them, and take action. Invite a shy classmate to sit with you at lunch. Let someone else go first. Listen carefully when people talk. Here are some other ideas:

"Just four more bags of groceries to go."
"I'll carry these two in."

"I'm not ready for my math test!"
"Want me to help you study?"

"I'm having the worst day."
"I heard the funniest joke. Maybe it'll cheer you up."

INTERNATIONAL
TONGUE TWISTER DAY

Say "It's the second Sunday of the eleventh month" five times fast. That's International Tongue Twister Day. These word workouts have been used to help learn a new language, overcome speech problems, and cure hiccups.

TOUGHEST TWISTERS

Pad kid poured curd pulled cod. This twister was created in a study by speech researchers at the Massachusetts Institute of Technology in 2013. The MIT team said those who tried to say the phrase either could not repeat it or stopped talking altogether.

The sixth sick sheikh's sixth sheep's sick. This was the most difficult tongue twister in the English language as of 1974, the last time the category was listed in *Guinness World Records*.

Iqaqa laziqikaqika kwaze kwaqhawaka uqhoqhoqha. In 1974, *Guinness World Records* also included this as the most difficult tongue twister in the world. It's in the Xhosa language of South Africa and has three clicking sounds in the last word. It means "The skunk rolled down and ruptured its larynx."

TWISTED HISTORY
Peter Piper picked a peck of pickled peppers. This first appeared in 1813 in John Harris's *Peter Piper's Practical Principles of Plain and Perfect Pronunciation*. Some say this phrase refers to a French spice grower named Pierre Poivre, who wrote about his travels in 1769. His name translates to *Peter Pepper*, but *piper* is also a Latin and an Old English word for *pepper*.

November 16
NATIONAL BUTTON DAY

People have been collecting antique and decorative buttons since at least 1938. The National Button Society was founded on this date! This fasten-ating jar holds more than just buttons. Find: 1 letter B, 2 dog bones, 3 rubber balls, 4 pennies, and 5 wrapped candies.

The word button is from the French word **BOUTON**, meaning "bud" or "knob."

The oldest button, carved from a shell, was found in what is now Pakistan. It is about **5,000 YEARS OLD.** But these early buttons were used as decorations on clothing, not as fasteners.

In the 14th century, wearing many buttons—especially those made of gold, silver, or ivory—showed how wealthy you were.

Calacas (skeletons) and calaveras (colorful skulls) appear in parades, as costumes or masks, and even as chocolate or cookie shapes.

Take a spin around the globe to see how people

November 1-2

📍 DÍA DE LOS MUERTOS

Mexicans in Mexico and in other countries celebrate the Day of the Dead (*Día de los Muertos*) as a time to remember family members who have passed away and to encourage their spirits to return for a visit. Many people make the celebration into a party. They have special foods, music, games, stories, and dances.

Can you find **10 hidden objects in this Hidden Pictures puzzle?**

November 4

📍 FLAG DAY

Panama declared independence from Columbia on November 3, 1925. The flag designed by the family of the country's first president, Manuel Amador, was officially adopted the next day.

The flag represents Panama's political parties and values of the time.

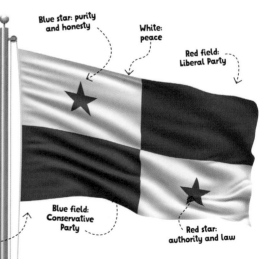

Blue star: purity and honesty

White: peace

Red field: Liberal Party

Blue field: Conservative Party

Red star: authority and law

THE WORLD

around the world celebrate in November.

> *Diwali means "row of lights."*

November 4, 2021
DIWALI

Diwali (dee-WAH-lee) is the Hindu festival of lights. It is celebrated in India, Nepal, Sri Lanka, Singapore, Malaysia, and other places. Clay lamps called *diyas* are lit everywhere! The lamps symbolize the human body and their light is the soul. Here's how to make your own *diya* to celebrate:

1. Shape a candle holder from **air-dry clay**. Wet your finger and press gently to smooth out any cracks. Let it dry.
2. Create decorations, such as flowers, from the clay. Let them dry. Glue them to the candle holder.
3. Glue **craft gems**, **beads**, and other decorations to the holder. Place a **battery-powered candle** into the middle.

November 11
SAINT MARTIN'S DAY

In Germany, this holiday honors St. Martin of Tours, a Roman soldier who was made a bishop and later a saint by the Catholic Church. A kind man, he was said to have cut his cloak in half with his sword to share with a beggar during a snowstorm. Processions are often led by a man on horseback dressed as

St. Martin in his long red cloak. School kids hold paper lanterns as he passes. **Can you find the 3 puzzle pieces in this photo?**

SUNDAY	MONDAY	TUESDAY	WEDNESDAY

BIRTHSTONES
TANZANITE, TURQUOISE, AND ZIRCON

ZODIAC SIGNS
SAGITTARIUS: NOVEMBER 23–DECEMBER 21

CAPRICORN: DECEMBER 22–JANUARY 19

"I was . . . tired of giving in." In 1955, Rosa Parks refused to give up her seat for a white patron on a bus in Montgomery, Alabama, which helped start the civil rights movement.

1

INTERNATIONAL VOLUNTEER DAY

5

With fleece as white as snow. In 1877, Thomas Edison made the first recording of the human voice, a recitation of "Mary Had a Little Lamb."

6

NATIONAL PEARL HARBOR REMEMBRANCE DAY

7

Pretend to be a Time Traveler Day

To what time will you travel?

11:00

8

NATIONAL POINSETTIA DAY

12

Saint Lucia's Day (Scandinavia)
Wearing a crown of candles, the oldest daughter sings a song to wake her family, bringing them saffron buns and gingerbread cookies to eat.

13

INTERNATIONAL MONKEY DAY

14

NATIONAL LEMON CUPCAKE DAY

15

Don't be a Scrooge! In 1843, *A Christmas Carol* by Charles Dickens was published.

19

Go Caroling Day

Warm up your voice with vocal exercises.

20

FIRST DAY OF WINTER

21

Let there be light! In 1882, Edward H. Johnson created the first string of electric Christmas lights.

22

KWANZAA BEGINS

26

National Fruitcake Day

In ancient Roman times, fruitcake was made with pomegranate seeds, raisins, and pine nuts.

27

NATIONAL DOWNLOAD DAY

Seventy-three percent of Americans download apps on this day!

28

It's fun to stay at the YMCA! In 1851, the first American YMCA opened in Boston.

29

DECEMBER

THURSDAY	FRIDAY	SATURDAY
National Fritters Day — Do you prefer sweet or savory? **2**	*Game on.* In 1994, Sony PlayStation was released in Japan at a price of ¥39,800 (about $366). It sold 100,000 consoles on the first day! **3**	**NATIONAL SOCK DAY** **4**
A Charlie Brown Christmas debuted on CBS in 1965. **9**	**Mevlana Festival begins (Turkey)** — This festival features the famous Whirling Dervishes dance, which started as a form of meditation. **10**	**INTERNATIONAL MOUNTAIN DAY** **11**
Fast-spreading flames. In 1835, the Great Fire of New York City destroyed over six hundred buildings. **16**	**NATIONAL UGLY CHRISTMAS SWEATER DAY** **17**	**Answer the Telephone Like Buddy the Elf Day** **18**
Farmer's Day (India) — This holiday that celebrates farmers takes place on the birthday of Choudhary Charan Singh, the fifth prime minister of India. **23**	**Santa GPS** — NORAD tracked Santa for the first time in 1955. **24**	**CHRISTMAS** **25**
We're not alone . . . On this day in 1924, the Hubble telescope helped prove there are other galaxies outside of the Milky Way. **30**	**NEW YEAR'S EVE** — Goodbye, 2021. Hello, 2022! **31**	**FLOWERS** NARCISSUS HOLLY

"HI, NEIGHBOR" MONTH

Get to know your neighbors better this holiday season—it all starts with a smile and a hello! Here are a few other ideas of how you can spread holiday joy.

1. Make a card and write a nice note inside.
2. Bake cookies to share.
3. With permission, shovel snow from a neighbor's sidewalk or driveway.
4. Make a homemade gift to give.
5. Collect food for your local food bank.
6. Tell your neighbors what you admire most about them.

TREE TREATS

Give a "heartwarming" gift.

1. Wash a **plastic ornament** inside and out. Decorate it with **puffy paint**. Let it dry.

2. Make a funnel by rolling and taping a half circle cut from **paper**.

3. Remove the top of the plastic ornament. Use the funnel to fill the ornament with **hot-cocoa powder**, **tea leaves**, or **coffee beans**.

4. Add a **ribbon** hanger and a **cardstock** tag with drink-making instructions.

December 3 is National Make a Gift Day!

NATIONAL WRITE TO A FRIEND MONTH

Four Letter-Writing Twists

Take some time this month to send your friend one of these unique takes on a basic letter!

1. Instead of writing a letter, catch up with a friend by drawing scenes from your life in comic-strip form.

2. Send your friend the first paragraph of a story. Ask him or her to write the next paragraph and send it back. Keep taking turns until the story is finished.

3. Mail your friend a random squiggle on paper. Ask your friend to draw a picture using the squiggle as a starting point and send it back with a new squiggle for you to draw on.

4. Include a secret note. With your friend, decide on a code to use in your letters. For example, perhaps the last letter of each word you write spells out a short hidden message.

PENCIL PATHS

Which* pencil wrote each word?

When is a mailbox like the alphabet?

When it's full of letters

How does a hog write a letter?

With a pigpen

LEARN A FOREIGN LANGUAGE MONTH

To celebrate this month, try your hand at a new language! There are a variety of apps, books, and websites that can help you learn another language. Ask a parent or librarian to help you find the best resource for you to use.

There are many ways to say "hello." Can you match each greeting with the correct language?

1. Hola (OH-lah) — JAPANESE

2. Konnichiwa (co-nee-chee-wah) — CHINESE

3. Hallo (HA-lo) — SPANISH

4. Privet (PREE-viet) — GERMAN

5. Bonjour (bohn-ZHOOR) — RUSSIAN

6. Ciao (chOW) — SWAHILI

7. Jambo (JAM-bo) — FRENCH

8. Ni hao (Nee HaOW) — ITALIAN

Zimbabwe holds the record for the most official languages spoken in one country with a whopping 16 different languages!

UNIVERSAL HUMAN RIGHTS MONTH

Eleanor Roosevelt was the chair of the Human Rights Commission.

On December 10, 1948, the United Nations published a document called the *Universal Declaration of Human Rights*, which states that fundamental human rights must be universally protected. People from all over the world from a variety of backgrounds helped draft the declaration, which was the first of its kind in the history of human rights.

READ A NEW BOOK MONTH

There are six words hidden in this scene. As everyone reads a new book,
can you find the words BOOK, NOVEL, PAGE, READ, STORY, and WORDS?

BOOK SWAP!

One way to find a new book to read is to have
a book swap. With a group of friends, exchange
your favorite books. After you've read them all,
give them awards such as "Coolest Adventure"
or "Favorite Main Character."

You won't find these silly books in your local
library. They're books never written! Try
coming up with your own silly titles.

Zoology by Annie Mals

What to Take on an Airplane by Carrie On

Living with Dinosaurs by Terry Dactel

Help the Environment by Reese Ikel

How to Write a Book by Paige Turner

December 7, 1941

80 YEARS AGO, Pearl Harbor was bombed.

On Sunday, December 7, 1941, Japan's air force attacked the U.S. Naval Base at Pearl Harbor off the island of Oahu in Hawaii. More than two thousand people were killed, 188 airplanes were destroyed, and 18 ships were sunk or crippled. The next day, the United States entered World War II.

On the morning of the attack, there were eight U.S. Navy battleships moored at what was known as Battleship Row. Can you find the names of the ships hidden in these letters? Only the words in italics are hidden.

```
A  U  C  J  M  P  L  T  Q  C
I  X  A  I  L  E  H  E  N  F
N  D  L  N  L  N  Y  N  K  M
I  F  I  T  W  N  D  N  Q  L
G  G  F  Z  N  S  N  E  H  Q
R  Q  O  S  V  Y  A  S  A  A
I  N  R  O  U  L  L  E  A  N
V  E  N  I  M  V  Y  E  W  O
T  V  I  M  B  A  R  B  Y  Z
S  A  A  Y  R  N  A  K  X  I
E  D  S  W  O  I  M  L  J  R
W  A  O  K  L  A  H  O  M  A
```

USS *ARIZONA*

USS *CALIFORNIA*

USS *MARYLAND*

USS *NEVADA*

USS *OKLAHOMA*

USS *PENNSYLVANIA*

USS *TENNESEE*

USS *WEST VIRGINIA*

In a famous speech asking Congress to declare war against Japan, President Franklin D. Roosevelt called December 7, 1941, "a date which will live in infamy." This photo shows him signing the declaration of war.

Opened in 1962, the USS *Arizona* memorial has seven large windows on two walls and the ceiling, to commemorate the date of the attack. There are 21 windows total, which represent a 21-gun salute.

December 21, 1891

130 YEARS AGO,
the first basketball game was played.

James Naismith was a graduate student at what is now Springfield College in Massachusetts. He was asked to create a game that would engage his students, but that wouldn't be as dangerous as football or rugby. After much thinking and planning, Naismith came up with 13 rules to play the game and basketball was born.

The first baskets were literally baskets! James Naismith nailed peach baskets to the wall 10 feet off the floor.

There are at least 15 differences in these pictures. How many can you find?

December 13
NATIONAL VIOLIN DAY

Each violin has an exact match—
except one. Can you find it?

The most expensive violin was built in 1721 by Antonio Stradivari. It was most recently sold in auction for **12 MILLION DOLLARS!**

The oldest existing violin was built by Andre Amati around 1565. Amati is credited as being one of the creators of the instrument.

What did the violin say to the viola when they met?

"Cello"

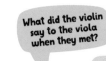

December 21

NATIONAL SHORT STORY DAY

Use one of these story starters to write a story. Or write your own story inspired by the pictures.

IN A LURCH

Chris and Andy were riding the Ferris wheel at the fair. They were having a great time until, suddenly, the ride stopped with a lurch. . . .

CATCHING THE BUS

"I can't be late today, no matter what," Caitlin told herself. But no one told the bus driver. As he drove away without Caitlin, she started to panic. What was she going to do now? . . .

WACKY INVENTIONS

Theo was famous for creating wacky inventions—ones that didn't always work. But he knew his newest invention would change everything. What could possibly go wrong? . . .

December 4
NATIONAL COOKIE DAY

Can't get enough cookies? National Bake Cookies Day is December 18!

We listed 10 kinds of cookies here. It's up to you to crack the code and fill in the names. Each number stands for a different letter. Once you know one number's letter, you can fill in that letter in all of the words. Grab some milk and get started!

M A C A R O O N
7 10 1 10 11 2 2 8

___ ___ ___ ___ ___   ___ ___ ___
6 5 7 2 8   9 10 11

___ ___ ___ ___ ___
13 18 12 10 11

___ ___ ___ ___ ___ ___
19 2 11 16 18 8 5

___ ___ ___ ___ ___ ___ ___ ___ ___
12 4 8 12 5 11 13 8 10 14

___ ___ ___ ___ ___ ___ ___ ___ ___
13 15 2 11 16 9 11 5 10 17

___ ___ ___ ___ ___ ___ ___   ___ ___ ___ ___ ___ ___
2 10 16 7 5 10 6   11 10 4 13 4 8

___ ___ ___ ___ ___ ___   ___ ___ ___ ___ ___ ___
14 5 10 8 18 16   9 18 16 16 5 11

___ ___ ___ ___ ___ ___ ___ ___ ___   ___ ___ ___ ___
1 15 2 1 2 6 10 16 5   1 15 4 14

___ ___ ___ ___ ___ ___ ___ ___ ___ ___ ___ ___
13 8 4 1 3 5 11 17 2 2 17 6 5

The average American eats **18,928** cookies in their lifetime.

BONUS

Did you fill in all the names? Use the same code to answer this riddle.

What did the gingerbread man use to trim his fingernails?

___ ___ ___ ___ ___ ___ ___   ___ ___ ___ ___ ___ ___
10   1 2 2 3 4 5   1 18 16 16 5 11

266

December 16

NATIONAL CHOCOLATE-COVERED ANYTHING DAY

Dunk your favorite treats in this chocolate fondue.

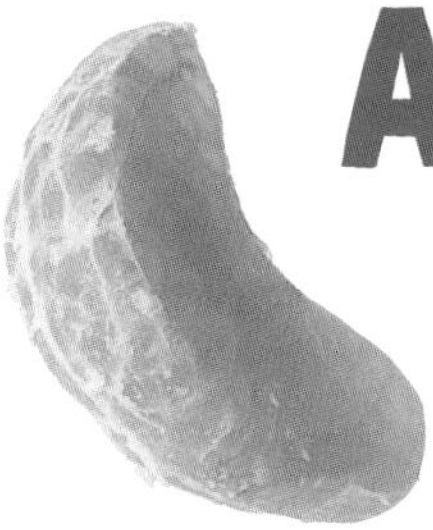

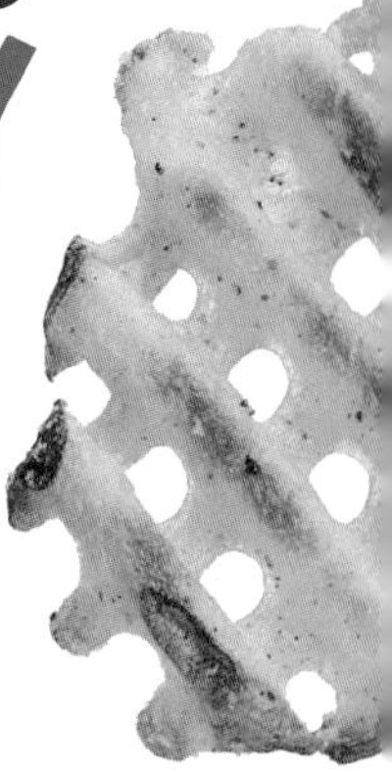

Melt It

1. Put 10 ounces of **semisweet chocolate chips** and ½ cup of **milk** into a microwave-safe bowl. Cover the bowl with a napkin.

2. Heat in a microwave oven for 1–2 minutes on medium power.

3. Stir until smooth. Use skewers, forks, or tongs to dip foods into the fondue.

Dip It

Beef jerky
Grapefruit
Peppers
Strawberries
French fries
Carrots
Nuts
Bananas
Pickles
Nori (edible seaweed)
Cookies
Cheese cubes

Top It

Cocoa powder
Sprinkles
Parmesan cheese
Yogurt
Cinnamon
Sea salt

It takes a whole year for a cocoa tree to produce enough pods to make 10 chocolate bars.

December 21, 2021
The first day of winter
is on the day with the fewest hours of sunlight.

No snow? "Snow" problem! Follow these instructions to create your own wintery fun.

1. Mix ½ cup of school **glue**, 2 teaspoons of **contact-lens solution**, and 2 tablespoons of **glitter** (optional) in a large bowl.

2. Stir 1½ cups of **baking soda** and 1½ cups of **shaving cream** into the mixture.

3. Play and build with the snow. Use **markers** to add details. Store in a sealable **plastic bag**.

DECEMBER 27 is Make Cut-Out Snowflakes Day. You know what to do!

"Gesundheit!"

What do you get when you cross a snowman and a shark?

Frostbite

Why did the elephant stand on the marshmallow?

Because he didn't want to fall into the hot chocolate

What's the best time to look for money on the ground?

When there is some change in the weather

Warm up with these winter jokes!

Which animals are the coldest?

Mice. They're three-fourths ice.

What did the car say when it snowed?

"I'm glad I'm wearing a hood."

KWANZAA

Kwanzaa is a holiday that was created by Dr. Maulana Karenga in 1966. It celebrates family, community, and culture. The holiday stems from the African tradition of giving thanks for the first fruits of the harvest (*Kwanzaa* means "first fruits" in Swahili).

There are seven principles celebrated during this holiday: **unity, self-determination, collective work and responsibility, cooperative economics, purpose, creativity,** and **faith**. A candle is lit each day on a kinara. Each candle represents one of these principles.

"Heri za Kwanzaa!" means "Happy Kwanzaa!"

Wash your hands before you begin.

Makes 12 cornucopias.

Celebrate Kwanzaa by displaying—then eating!— this tasty treat to represent *mazao* ("crops" in Swahili).

1. Peel two small **bananas**, a **mango**, two **pears**, and two **kiwis**. Wash one cup of **berries**.

2. With an adult's help, cut the fruit into small pieces. (Throw away the pear cores and the mango seed.)

3. Gently combine the fruit in a bowl. Then spoon the mixture into **waffle cones**.

4. Arrange the cones on a large plate or serving tray.

5. When it's time to eat them, you can top each cornucopia with a sprinkle of **coconut flakes** or a drizzle of **honey** or **chocolate sauce**. Enjoy!

MAZAO, one of the symbols of Kwanzaa, represents the harvest and the hard work that went into producing it.

Celebrities who have celebrated Kwanzaa include Oprah, Maya Angelou, and Angelina Jolie.

CHRISTMAS

The Christmas holiday celebrates the birth of Jesus Christ. People decorate Christmas trees with lights and ornaments, do good deeds for others, and give gifts to friends and family.

JINGLE-BELL ORNAMENTS

Make these ornaments to hang on your own tree or to give as a gift.

1. Twist one end of a **chenille stick** into a loop. Twist a **jingle bell** onto the other end.

2. Use **colored paper** and **stickers** to create a Nativity scene, a Christmas tree, or a bell. Tape the chenille stick to the back. Add a **yarn** bow.

A TREE FULL OF TREATS

Help the mouse find a clear path to the cheese at the top of the tree!

TRICKY TREES

Each of these trees has the numbers 1 through 6 running along the sides. And in each triangle each side adds up to the number in the middle. Can you place the numbers in each triangle so that everything adds up correctly? Each of the numbers 1 through 6 is only used once in a triangle.

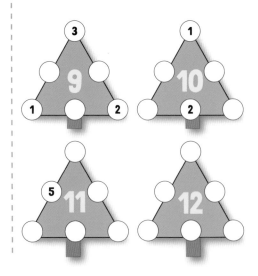

GLEEFUL GIFTS

Amelia and her friends exchanged Christmas gifts. Use the clues below to figure out who received each gift. **Use the chart to keep track of your answers. Put an X in each box that can't be true and an O in boxes that match.**

1. Mason and Bodhi like to play outside.
2. Amelia's gift has multiple pieces.
3. Bodhi's present does not bounce.
4. Charlotte's present does not have pages.

	Video Game	Skateboard	Basketball	Puzzle	Books
Mason					
Javier					
Charlotte					
Bodhi					
Amelia					

SILLY ELVES

How many silly things can you find in this picture?

WORLD WILDLIFE CONSERVATION DAY

This holiday exists to bring awareness to the many wonderful species of wildlife that need our help. Here are a few ideas of how you can help animals in need, not just on this day, but every day.

RECYCLE

Humans make a lot of garbage. Being careless with our garbage is hard on the environment—and some of our favorite animals. Recycling can help control the amount of waste we pile up. Recycling can also protect animal habitats. In fact, the Minnesota Zoo asks that its visitors recycle their phones. The mineral coltan that is used to make phones is mined from lowland gorilla habitats. Recycling phones helps save the gorillas!

STEP-BY-STEP DRAWING

Follow the steps to draw a panda.

1.
2.
3.
4.
5.

There are only **1,800 GIANT PANDAS** living in the wild.

BE SUSTAINABLE

Switching to using metal or other reusable straws can be a huge help. Plastic straws end up in the ocean and hurt animals like sea turtles. If more of us can use reusable straws, then fewer straws will end up as garbage.

TAKE CARE WITH GARBAGE

Remember to always throw garbage away in the proper place to keep it out of animal habitats. And make sure things like plastic soda rings are cut so animals, like this seagull, don't trap their heads inside.

Reusable straws are made from metal or glass, and biodegradable straws are made from paper or bamboo.

COMPUTER SCIENCE EDUCATION WEEK

Computer Science Education Week (CSEdWeek) is dedicated to inspiring students to take an interest in computer science. The date recognizes the December 9 birthday of **Admiral Grace Murray Hopper**, a computer technology pioneer who also helped popularize the term "computer bug" when a moth shorted out her computer. During this week, many schools and organizations participate in the "Hour of Code™" to learn about computer science and computer programming.

Admiral Hopper and colleagues at the UNIVAC keyboard in the 1960s

01001000 01101001
(Hi)

01011001 01101111
(Yo)

KIDS' SCIENCE QUESTIONS
How does binary code work?

Binary code is the special language of ones and zeros that computers read. You can think of it as containing many tiny switches, like switches that turn light bulbs on or off. Think of the number 1 as "on" and 0 as "off." By putting many groups of switches together with some on and some off, programmers can represent big numbers and even pictures and video.

Luckily, people don't have to read and write computer programs in ones and zeros. Computer developers have created programs, called source codes, that are easier for people to work with. Using these source codes, programmers write programs telling a computer what to do. Then another program translates the source-code programs into the binary code that the computer can read.

GOBS OF GIBBLES

Solving puzzles helps develop logical reasoning skills, something computer programmers use frequently.

December 11 is National App Day. What app would you like to create? What would it do? How would it help people?

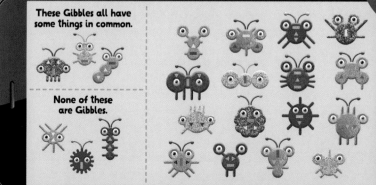

These Gibbles all have some things in common.

None of these are Gibbles.

Can you figure out which of these are Gibbles?

December 9
NATIONAL LLAMA DAY

The Metrollamaten Museum of Art is bustling with fuzzy patrons! As the llamas admire the art, can you find the silly things in this scene?

In South America, llamas are used to carry heavy loads, especially up and down mountains. They can carry **50 TO 75 POUNDS,** but if they think the load is too heavy, they will lay down and refuse to move, or they will spit at their owners until their load is lightened.

December 12
NATIONAL GINGERBREAD HOUSE DAY

Can you tell what's alike in each row of gingerbread houses, across, down, and diagonally?

NATIONAL VISIT THE ZOO DAY

A HIGHLIGHTS CLASSIC PUZZLE

Can you find 21 objects in this Hidden Pictures puzzle?

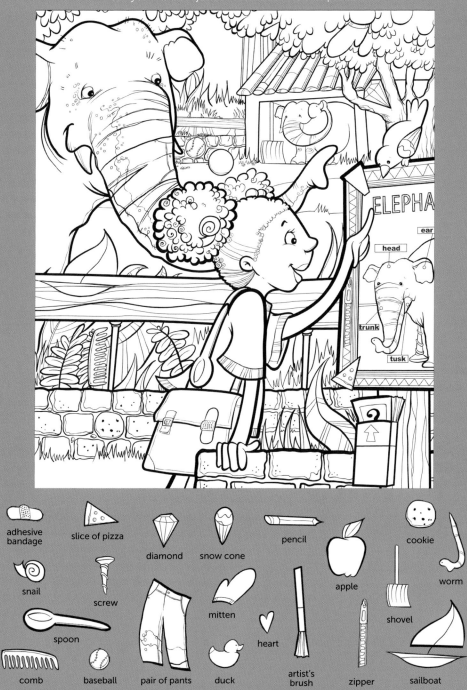

adhesive bandage

slice of pizza

diamond

snow cone

pencil

cookie

snail

screw

mitten

apple

worm

spoon

heart

shovel

comb

baseball

pair of pants

duck

artist's brush

zipper

sailboat

December 6

ST. NICHOLAS DAY

In Belgium, on December 5, children will put out their shoes by the fireplace, along with food and water for St. Nicholas's horse.

The next morning, the shoes will be filled with treats like chocolates, cookies, oranges, and toys.

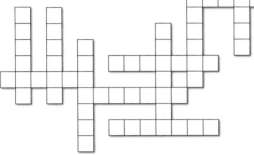

St. Nicholas Day is celebrated in many countries, including the ones listed below. Use the number of letters in each country as a clue to where it might fit in the grid.

AUSTRIA	ENGLAND	ITALY
BELGIUM	FRANCE	MEXICO
CANADA	GERMANY	RUSSIA
CROATIA	ICELAND	TURKEY

December 12

JAMHURI DAY

In Swahili, one of two official languages of Kenya, the word *jamhuri* means "republic." This holiday celebrates Kenya's independence from the United Kingdom on December 12, 1963, as well as Kenya's becoming a republic a year later on December 12, 1964. Kenyans celebrate the holiday with speeches, parades, and feasts to celebrate the country's culture and heritage.

Kenyan dancers perform a traditional dance during Jamhuri Day celebrations.

THE WORLD

December 24
NOCHE BUENA

Filipinos celebrate Christmas Eve with a midnight church mass and a traditional feast called Noche Buena, which means "good night" in Spanish. During the Christmas season in the Philippines, beautiful star-shaped lanterns, known as *parols*, light up the night sky and cast a soft glow on streets and homes. The stars remind Christians of the star of Bethlehem, which they believe guided three wise men to the baby Jesus.

Make a Philippine Parol

1. As shown in the diagram, fold a piece of **cardstock** in half. Mark the center of the side opposite the fold. Draw lines from the center to each lower corner. Cut out the triangle, and unfold it to form a diamond. Repeat with four more pieces of cardstock. Tape the diamonds together to form a star.

2. For a tassel, cut twenty 10-inch pieces of **yarn**. Fold ten of them in half and tie them together at the fold. Tie another piece of yarn below that. Trim the ends of the tassel. Repeat with the other ten pieces of yarn.

3. Punch a hole in the top point of the star and the two lower points. Tie the tassels to the lower holes. Tie a piece of yarn in the top hole for a hanger.

4. Decorate the star with **glitter glue**.

December 26
BOXING DAY

Most of the 53 countries in the Commonwealth—nearly all of which are former territories of the British Empire—celebrate Boxing Day. This holiday is spent with family and friends. People often shop or watch sports, and eat leftover Christmas food.

Deondre, Jada, Ashlyn, and Luke are wrapping presents. Follow the ribbons to figure out who's wrapping each gift.

JANUARY

I celebrated the **start of 2021** by _____
_____
_____

For National Puzzle Day on January 29, I tried

_____
_____
_____

My **favorite January holiday** was

_____
_____

FEBRUARY

On **February 2, 2021**,
the groundhog
☐ **DID**   ☐ **DID NOT**
see his shadow.

I made **valentines** for

_____
_____
_____
_____

My **favorite February holiday** was

_____
_____

MARCH

For National Let's Laugh Day
on **March 19**, these things
made me laugh:

_____
_____
_____
_____
_____

My favorite March holiday was

_____
_____

March 26 was **Make Up Your Own Holiday Day.**
The **holiday I created** was _____
_____
_____

This is how you celebrate it: _____
_____
_____
_____
_____
_____
_____
_____

APRIL

On **April Fools' Day**, I was surprised by _____

_____

_____

_____

I celebrated **Earth Day** by _____

_____

_____

_____

My **favorite April holiday** was

_____

_____

MAY

I spent time with
my **family** in May by

_____

_____

_____

_____

Here is **something new** I tried in May:

_____

_____

_____

_____

My **favorite May holiday** was

_____

_____

JUNE

I celebrated the first
day of summer by

_____

_____

_____

_____

_____

My favorite June
holiday was

_____

_____

_____

Between **Nature Photography Day** on **June 15** and
National Camera Day on **June 29**, I took lots of
photos. Here is **my favorite**:

**PASTE YOUR FAVORITE
PHOTO HERE!**

JULY

I celebrated **Independence Day** by

_____

_____

_____

I played these **sports** or **games** in July:

_____

_____

_____

My **favorite July holiday** was

_____

_____

AUGUST

For **National Book Lovers' Day** on August 8, I read _____

_____

_____

_____

I read _____ books in 2021!

Here are some **foods I ate outside** in August:

_____

_____

_____

_____

My **favorite August holiday** was

_____

SEPTEMBER

I spent time with my friends
this month by

_____

_____

_____

_____

_____

My favorite
September holiday was

_____

_____

_____

September 12 is the National Day of Encouragement.
Here are some things that make me feel encouraged:

_____

_____

_____

_____

_____

_____

_____

_____

_____

OCTOBER

For **National Do Something Nice Day** on **October 5**, I _____

_____

_____

_____

_____

For **Halloween, my costume was**

_____

_____

My **favorite October holiday was**

_____

NOVEMBER

For **Celebrate Your Unique Talent Day** on **November 24**, my talent was

_____

_____

_____

I celebrated **Thanksgiving by**

_____

_____

_____

_____

My **favorite November holiday was**

_____

DECEMBER

For **Pretend to Be a Time Traveler Day** on **December 8**, I would travel to

_____
_____
_____
_____

My favorite December holiday was

_____
_____
_____

I sang or played these songs in December:

_____
_____
_____

_____
_____
_____
_____
_____
_____
_____

285

2021 MEMORIES

I learned these three things about myself in 2021:

1. _____
_____
_____
_____

2. _____
_____
_____
_____

3. _____
_____
_____
_____

I tried these three new things in 2021:

1. _____
_____
_____

2. _____
_____
_____

3. _____
_____

My favorite part of 2021 was

_____
_____
_____
_____
_____
_____
_____

My hope for next year is _____
_____
_____
_____

JANUARY

PAGE 8: JANUARY 4, 1896

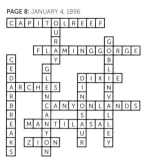

Crossword answers:
CAPITOLREEF, CUR, G, FLAMINGGORGE, C, Y, B, CED, G, DIXIE, L, ARCHES, I, I, N, R, N, N, V, B, CANYONLANDS, R, A, S, L, E, MANTILASAL, A, Y, L, E, K, ZION, U, R, Y, S, N

PAGE 9: JANUARY 15, 2001
1. 5
2. 495 MILLION
3. 4.4 MILLION
4. 15
5. 287

PAGE 10: HARLEM GLOBETROTTERS DAY

PAGE 11: WINTER UNIVERSIADE
1. SKI ORIENTEERING
2. SNOWBOARDING
3. ICE HOCKEY
4. FIGURE SKATING
5. CURLING
6. BIATHLON
7. SHORT TRACK SPEED SKATING
8. CROSS-COUNTRY SKIING
9. ALPINE SKIING
10. FREESTYLE SKIING

PAGE 12: NATIONAL SCIENCE FICTION DAY
Isaac Asimov coined the term *ROBOTICS* in his 1941 short story "Liar!"

PAGE 13: NATIONAL THESAURUS DAY

PAGE 15: NATIONAL POPCORN DAY

PAGE 18: NEW YEAR'S DAY

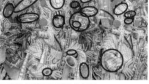

PAGE 19: PASS THE LUCK, PLEASE!
1. UNITED STATES
2. GREECE
3. ITALY
4. SPAIN
5. JAPAN

PAGE 21: MORSE CODE
The first telegraphic message was transmitted in 1844 between *WASHINGTON* and *BALTIMORE*.

PAGE 21: TIN CAN DAY
1. CANYON
2. CANDLE
3. PECAN
4. TOUCAN
5. VOLCANO

PAGE 22: NATIONAL TRIVIA DAY
1. A; 2. A; 3. B; 4. A

PAGE 22: NATIONAL HAT DAY

PAGE 23: NATIONAL PUZZLE DAY

PAGE 24: SAINT KNUT'S DAY (SWEDEN)
julstjärna = Christmas star
julklappsstrumpa = Christmas stocking
julgranskula = Christmas ornament
julgransbelysning = Christmas tree lights

PAGE 25: TU BISHVAT (ISRAEL)

FEBRUARY

PAGE 29: NATIONAL BIRD-FEEDING MONTH

PAGE 29: BIRD SEARCH

PAGE 30: NATIONAL LIBRARY LOVERS' MONTH

PAGE 30: AUTHOR AUTHOR!
1. D; 2. E; 3. C; 4. F; 5. A ; 6. B; 7. I; 8. J; 9. G; 10. H.

PAGE 30: SPELL CHECK
WHERE THE WILD THINGS ARE
THE PHANTOM TOLLBOOTH
THE CAT IN THE HAT
GREEN EGGS AND HAM
GOODNIGHT MOON
HARRIET THE SPY
WINNIE-THE-POOH

PAGE 31: CHILDREN'S DENTAL HEALTH MONTH

PAGE 31: RIDDLE SUDOKU

C	O	S	N	W	R
W	R	N	S	O	C
S	W	O	C	R	N
N	C	R	W	S	O
O	S	C	R	N	W
R	N	W	O	C	S

Why do Kings and Queens go to the dentist?
TO GET *CROWNS*

PAGE 32: FEBRUARY 5, 1971

JOHNYOUNG, EDGARMITCHELL, DAVIDSCOTT, HARRISONSCHMITT, BUZZALDRIN, PETECONRAD, ALANSHEPARD, EUGENECERNAN

The *APOLLO* space program sent these men to the moon.

PAGE 33: FEBRUARY 23, 1863

PAGE 34: NATIONAL GIRLS & WOMEN IN SPORTS DAY

1. B; 2. C; 3. A; 4. A; 5. C; 6. B; 7. B; 8. A; 9. C; 10. A

ALEX FINISHES FIRST!

PAGE 35: SUPER BOWL LV

What do football champions put their cereal in?
SUPER BOWLS

PAGE 35: SUPER BOWL SUPER STATS

1. C; 2. A; 3. B; 4. A

PAGE 36: OPERA DAY

BOLSHOI THEATRE: RUSSIA
LA SCALA: ITALY
METROPOLITAN OPERA HOUSE: UNITED STATES
NHÀ HÁT LỚN HÀ NỘI: VIETNAM
PALAIS GARNIER: FRANCE
SYDNEY OPERA HOUSE: AUSTRALIA
TEATRO COLÓN: ARGENTINA
WIENER STAATSOPER: AUSTRIA

PAGE 37: GET OUT YOUR GUITAR DAY

PAGE 37: NAME THAT GUITAR

WILLIE NELSON: TRIGGER
B.B. KING: LUCILLE
ERIC CLAPTON: BLACKIE
EDDIE VAN HALEN: FRANKENSTRAT
BRIAN MAY: RED SPECIAL

PAGE 38: PANCAKE DAY
What kind of exercises do pancakes do?
JUMPING FLAPJACKS

Who flies through the air
covered with maple syrup?
PETER PANCAKE

How is a baseball team like
a pancake?
THEY BOTH NEED A GOOD BATTER.

What do cow boys put on
their pancakes?
MAPLE STIRRUP

PAGE 39: CHILI DAY

PAGE 40: GROUNDHOG DAY

PAGE 41: VALENTINE'S DAY

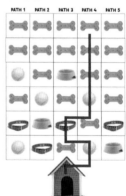

BONUS: CAULIFLOWER

PAGE 42: WASHINGTON'S BIRTHDAY

HOOVER: HOOVER DAM
KENNEDY: KENNEDY SPACE CENTER
(THEODORE) ROOSEVELT: TEDDY BEAR
LINCOLN: LINCOLN MEMORIAL
JEFFERSON: JEFFERSON MEMORIAL
WASHINGTON: WASHINGTON MONUMENT

They served in this order: Washington (1st president), Jefferson (3rd), Lincoln (16th), T. Roosevelt (26th), Hoover (31st), and Kennedy (35th).

PAGE 44: WORLD WETLANDS DAY

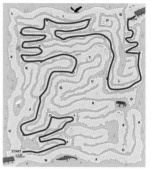

The *FLORIDA PANTHER* is an endangered Everglades animal.

PAGE 45: NATIONAL PERIODIC TABLE DAY
BaCoN   MoUSe
BaNaNa   HeLiCoPtEr
CaNdY   FUN
AmErICa

PAGE 47: WORLD WHALE DAY

What do you call a whale that talks a lot?
A BLUBBER MOUTH

PAGE 47: WHIRLED WHALES
BLUE   GRAY
BELUGA   FIN
RIGHT   MINKE
HUMPBACK   NARWHAL

PAGE 47: INTERNATIONAL DOG BISCUIT APPRECIATION DAY

PAGE 48: CHINESE NEW YEAR (CHINA)

PAGE 49: NAVAM FULL MOON
POYA DAY (SRI LANKA)

MARCH

PAGE 52: WOMEN'S HISTORY MONTH
1. Marie Curie
2. Amelia Earhart
3. Valentina Tereshkova
4. Junko Tabei
5. Sandra Day O'Connor
6. Aretha Franklin
7. Danica Patrick
8. Kathryn Bigelow
9. Mo'ne Davis

PAGE 53: NATIONAL UMBRELLA MONTH

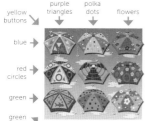

PAGE 53: NATIONAL MUSIC IN OUR
SCHOOLS MONTH

PAGE 54: NATIONAL NOODLE MONTH
T; F; T; F, T; F; T

PAGE 56: MARCH 3, 1931
*O say, can you see, by the dawn's early **light**,*
What so proudly we hailed
*at the **twilight's** last gleaming?*
*Whose broad **stripes** and bright stars,*
through the perilous fight,
*O'er the **ramparts** we watched,*
were so gallantly streaming?
*And the rockets' **red** glare,*
the bombs bursting in air,
*Gave **proof** through the night*
that our flag was still there.
*O **say**, does that star-spangled **banner** yet wave*
*O'er the land of the **free** and the **home** of*
the brave?

PAGE 57: MARCH 13, 1781

PAGES 58–59: MARCH MADNESS

PAGE 58: BASKETBALL OR BASEBALL?
1. BASKETBALL
2. BASKETBALL
3. BASEBALL
4. BASKETBALL
5. BASEBALL
6. BASKETBALL
7. BASEBALL
8. BASKETBALL

PAGE 59: WORLD BASEBALL CLASSIC
1. UNITED STATES
2. PUERTO RICO
3. JAPAN
4. NETHERLANDS

PAGE 60: READ ACROSS AMERICA DAY
Darryl checked out eight history books.
Keiko checked out two sports books.
Gunner checked out four outer space books.
Ximena checked out six animal books.

PAGE 61: TOP ACT
1. *BEAUTY AND THE BEAST*
2. *THE ADDAMS FAMILY*
3. *THE LITTLE MERMAID*
4. *INTO THE WOODS*
8. *LITTLE SHOP OF HORRORS*
9. *THE WIZARD OF OZ*

PAGE 62: NATIONAL PI DAY

PAGE 64: SAINT PATRICK'S DAY

PAGE 68: WORLD METEOROLOGICAL DAY
1. MORE
2. GERM
3. OGRE
4. MOTOR
5. GROOM
6. GOOEY
7. MOTEL
8. GLOOMY
9. OMELET
10. GEOMETRY

PAGE 69: EARTH HOUR
CHINA, 1:30 A.M.; UKRAINE, 7:30 P.M.;
NEPAL, 11:15 P.M.; MALI, 5:30 P.M.

PAGE 70: LEARN ABOUT BUTTERFLIES DAY
1. A; 2. C; 3. A; 4. B; 5. C

PAGE 70: NATIONAL PUPPY DAY

PAGE 71: TAKE A WALK IN THE PARK DAY
1. E; 2. C; 3. B; 4. F; 5. A; 6. D

PAGE 72:
INDEPENDENCE
DAY (GHANA)

PAGE 73: HOLI (INDIA)

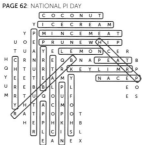

APRIL

PAGE 76: NATIONAL KITE MONTH

PAGE 77: PUNCH-LINE CONFUSION
1. D; 2. B; 3. A; 4. C

PAGE 79: 24 TO THE DOOR

9 + 12	2 x 11	15 + 9	17 + 7
7 + 15	35 - 11	8 x 3	25 - 2
3 x 4	6 x 4	20 + 3	18 + 7
18 + 6	40 - 16	5 x 7	33 - 10

PAGE 79: SUM FUN!
1. 7
2. 8
3. 29
4. 64
5. 7
6. 3,600
7. 10

BONUS: The world's largest box of chocolates weighed 3,725 pounds and was created by Thorntons, a chocolate company in England.

PAGE 80: OTTER-LY OUTSTANDING OLYMPICS

PAGE 80: OLYMPIC NUMBERS
1. C; 2. E; 3. H; 4. A; 5. F; 6. B; 7. G; 8. D

PAGE 80: ODDITIES AT THE OLYMPICS
THE SPORTS THAT HAVE NEVER MADE OLYMPIC STATUS ARE 3. BILLIARDS, 5. CORNHOLE, 6. WIFFLE BALL, 9. VIDEO GAMING, AND 10. BREAKDANCING.

PAGE 81: APRIL 12, 1961
1. U.S.S.R.
2. U.S.S.R.
3. U.S.
4. U.S.S.R.
5. U.S.
6. U.S.S.R.
7. U.S.
8. U.S.S.R.
9. U.S.
10. U.S.S.R.

PAGE 81: AN OUT-OF-THIS-WORLD WORD SEARCH

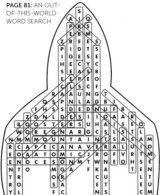

MISSION CONTROL SAYS, "BLAST OFF!"

PAGE 82: PLAY BALL!
1. CODY
2. HECTOR
3. CLAUDIA
4. SETH
5. JACOB
6. ARIEL
7. TROY
8. LINDSEY
9. LAURA

PAGE 82: HOME RUN!

PAGE 83: WORLD TABLE TENNIS DAY

PAGE 83: THE BOSTON MARATHON

PAGE 84: SHELF SCRAMBLE

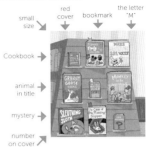

PAGE 84: BOOK SMART
ANNE OF GREEN GABLES
CHARLOTTE'S WEB
A WRINKLE IN TIME
DIARY OF A WIMPY KID
THE LION, THE WITCH AND THE WARDROBE
HARRY POTTER AND THE SORCERER'S STONE
CHARLIE AND THE CHOCOLATE FACTORY
THE ADVENTURES OF CAPTAIN UNDERPANTS
WHERE THE SIDEWALK ENDS
THE LITTLE HOUSE ON THE PRAIRIE

PAGE 84: JUST WING IT

PAGE 85: CRAYON HUNT

PAGE 86: BOBBIE'S BURRITOS
The order should be F, C, E, A, B, D.

PAGE 87: PRETZEL PATH

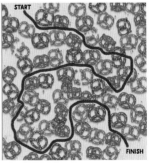

PAGE 89: ENVIRONMENTAL IQ TEST
1. B; 2. A; 3. C; 4. A; 5. B; 6. B; 7. C; 8. C; 9. B; 10. A

PAGE 89: EARTH DAY CLEANUP

PAGE 90: A VERY YUMMY EASTER

CARLY: STRAWBERRY MUFFINS
ANTHONY: APPLE TART
KIERA: COCONUT CUPCAKE
DAN: LEMON PIE

PAGE 91: JELLY BEAN PIECES

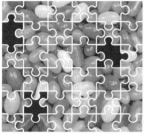

PAGE 91: GLOBAL EASTER TRADITIONS
Manchester, England, is the made-up tradition.

PAGE 92: ZOOKEEPER'S BYE-BYE

1. CROCODILE
2. BABOON
3. BUFFALO
4. SHEEP
5. GECKO
6. BLUTTERFLY
7. KANGAROO
8. POLAR BEAR
9. CHIMPANZEE
10. RATTLESNAKE

PAGE 93: TREEMONTON TOWERS

PAGE 94: NATIONAL UNICORN DAY

PAGE 95: TAKE OUR SONS AND DAUGHTERS TO WORK DAY

THE ARTIST HASN'T ARRIVED YET.

PAGE 95: SUPER SAVERS

PAGE 96: DO YOU KNOW THAT DRAGON? (ENGLAND)

1. F; 2. C; 3. E; 4. A; 5. D; 6. H; 7. B; 8. G.

PAGE 97: FLY IT HIGH (SIERRA LEONE)

MAY

PAGE 100: ASIAN/PACIFIC AMERICAN HERITAGE MONTH

1. Chloe Kim
2. Maya Lin
3. George Takei
4. Michelle Kwan
5. Jose Antonio Vargas
6. Duke Kahanamoku
7. Patsy Mink
8. Kalpana Chawla

PAGE 101: NATIONAL BIKE MONTH

PAGE 102: DRUM MATCH

1. E; 2. C; 3. B; 4. G; 5. A; 6. F; 7. D

PAGE 103: NATIONAL PET MONTH

PAGE 103: NATIONAL PET MONTH

PAGE 104: MAY 1, 1931

PAGE 105: MAY 22, 1906

PAGE 106: KENTUCKY DERBY

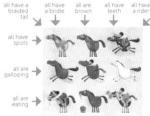

PAGE 108: NATIONAL CARTOONISTS DAY

Here are the captions written by the original cartoonists.

PAGE 109: NATIONAL TAP DANCE DAY

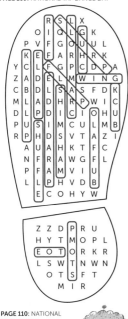

PAGE 110: NATIONAL HOAGIE DAY

PAGE 111: NATIONAL HAMBURGER DAY

What did Mr. and Mrs. Hamburger name their daughter? *PATTY*

How do you make a hamburger laugh? *PICKLE IT!*

What kind of dance does a hamburger go to? *A MEATBALL*

PAGE 112: CINCO DE MAYO
1.D; 2. A; 3. F; 4. B; 5. E; 6. C

PAGE 113: MOM MATCH

PAGE 114: EID AL-FITR
A *fanous* is a *LANTERN*.

PAGE 115: MEMORIAL DAY

PAGE 116: SPACE DAY

STAR, MOON, and *MARS* can be found in *astronomy*.

1. A; 2. C; 3. B; 4. C; 5. A; 6. B

PAGE 117: NATIONAL LEARN ABOUT COMPOSTING DAY

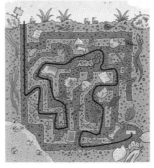

PAGE 118: MAY DAY AND LEI DAY

PAGE 118: NATIONAL LEMONADE DAY

It costs Lydia 40 cents to make each cup of lemonade ($20.00 ÷ 50 = .40). So she is selling each cup for 10 cents more than each cup cost. Lydia needs to sell 40 cups at 50 cents before she will make a profit ($20.00 ÷ .50 = 40). If she sells all 50 cups, she will make a profit of $5 (50 x .50 = $25.00; $25.00 - $20.00 = $5.00).

PAGE 119: NO SOCKS DAY

PAGE 119: NATIONAL FROG-JUMPING DAY

JORDAN: POLLIE, THIRD PLACE
SKYLER: HOPPY, FIRST PLACE
RILEY: TAD, SECOND PLACE

PAGE 121: VICTORY DAY (RUSSIA)

JUNE

PAGE 124: NATIONAL OCEAN MONTH

PAGE 124: TRUE OR FALSE?

T; T; T; F; F

PAGE 125: AFRICAN AMERICAN MUSIC APPRECIATION MONTH

1. BANJO
2. TROMBONE
3. TUBA
4. SAXOPHONE
5. TRUMPET
6. CLARINET
7. PIANO
8. DRUMS
9. BASS
10. GUITAR

Why do farmers play soft jazz for their corn? IT'S EASY *ON THE EARS.*

PAGE 126: NATIONAL FRESH FRUIT AND VEGETABLE MONTH

1. In the showroom, a **car** rot**ated** on a platform.
2. Maya looked **up each** book Liam recommended.
3. The dog's **bark ale**rted the cat.
4. "I'm getting a new bicycle **Monday,**" said Darnell.
5. Adrianna gets **up ear**ly every morning.
6. I bought a tea**pot at O**scar's sale.
7. Pete and his mom baked his tea**cher rye** bread.
8. That clown can **spin a chair** on his hand.

PAGE 127: FISHING FOR HIDDEN WORDS

PAGE 128: JUNE 4, 1896

PAGE 129: JUNE 6, 1946

BOSTON CELTICS
CHICAGO STAGS
CLEVELAND REBELS
DETROIT FALCONS
NEW YORK KNICKERBOCKERS
PHILADELPHIA WARRIORS
PROVIDENCE STEAMROLLERS
ST. LOUIS BOMBERS
TORONTO HUSKIES
WASHINGTON CAPITOLS

PAGE 130: GO SKATEBOARDING DAY

PAGE 130: SKATEBOARDING TRICKS OR FAKES?

These are the real tricks: airwalk, goofy foot, kickflip, McTwist, ollie.

PAGE 131: NATIONAL HOCKEY LEAGUE STANLEY CUP FINAL

1. B; 2. A; 3. C; 4. B; 5. A

PAGE 132: NATURE PHOTOGRAPHY DAY

PAGE 133: WORLD MUSIC DAY

What do brass instruments wear in the ocean?
TUBA GEAR

PAGE 134: NATIONAL DOUGHNUT DAY

PAGE 135: NATIONAL CHEESE DAY

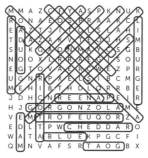

PAGE 140: WORLD GIRAFFE DAY

PAGE 143: NATIONAL SUNGLASSES DAY

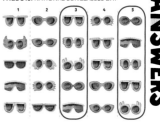

PAGE 144: DIA DOS NAMORADOS (BRAZIL)

JULY

PAGE 148: ICE CREAM MONTH

1. VANILLA
2. CHOCOLATE
3. COOKIES AND CREAM
4. MINT CHOCOLATE CHIP
5. CHOCOLATE CHIP COOKIE DOUGH
6. BUTTER PECAN
7. COOKIE DOUGH
8. STRAWBERRY
9. MOOSE TRACKS
10. NEAPOLITAN

PAGE 150: NATIONAL BISON MONTH

Bison trails were later used for *RAILROADS*.

PAGE 150: MAKE A MATCH

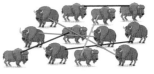

PAGE 151: NATIONAL PARK AND RECREATION MONTH

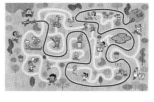

PAGE 151: PLASTIC-FREE JULY

1. paperback
2. paperweight
3. dishcloth
4. tablecloth
5. eyeglass
6. hourglass

PAGE 152: ELECTION SELECTION

TANYA: PRESIDENT
RAY: VICE PRESIDENT
TADASHI: TREASURER
LIZ: SECRETARY

PAGE 153: JULY 9, 1981

Why are cats good at video games?
THEY ALL HAVE NINE LIVES.

PAGES 154–155: THE WORLD GAMES 2021

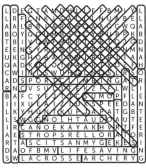

PAGE 156: NATIONAL MERRY-GO-ROUND DAY

PAGE 157: NATIONAL DANCE DAY

PAGE 160: INDEPENDENCE DAY
Vermont was not one of the 13 original colonies.

PAGE 164: WORLD EMOJI DAY

PAGE 165: NATIONAL WATERPARK DAY

PAGE 166: LA FÊTE NATIONALE (FRANCE)

PAGE 167: INDEPENDENCE DAY (LIBERIA)

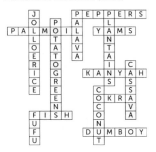

Liberia's capital city is *MONROVIA*.

AUGUST

PAGE 172: NATIONAL CRAYON COLLECTION MONTH

PAGE 172: FAMILY FUN MONTH

HIKE
MOVIES
GAME NIGHT
BAKE
BARBECUE
CAMP
BONFIRE
FISH
BIKE
CRAFT

PAGE 173: NATIONAL SANDWICH MONTH

PAGE 174: AUGUST 12, 1851

PAGE 175: AUGUST 12, 1981

1. What do you call a computer superhero?
   A SCREEN SAVER
2. Where do computers go to dance?
   THE DISC-O
3. Why did the computer cross the road?
   TO GET A BYTE TO EAT

PAGE 176: NATIONAL GOLF MONTH
1. C, 2. B, 3. A

PAGE 178: NATIONAL CLOWN WEEK!

PAGE 178: CIRCUS LINGO
1. F; 2. H; 3. A; 4. E; 5. G; 6. D; 7. B; 8. C

PAGE 179: NATIONAL TELL-A-JOKE DAY

What do elephants wear on their legs?
ELEPANTS

Why do elephants have trunks?
THEY LOVE TO TRAVEL

PAGE 180: CAMPFIRE DAY AND NIGHT

PAGE 181: EAT OUTSIDE DAY

We found these things that rhyme with grill and eat: windowsill, spill, daffodil, quill, windmill, anthill, duck bill, pepper mill, gill, sheet, tweet, feet, cleat, meat, parakeet, dog treat, beet, sweet, wheat, seat, street. You may have found others.

PAGE 182: NATIONAL WATERMELON DAY

PAGE 184: HURRICANE SEASON

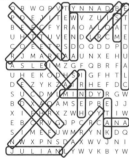

PAGE 186: NATIONAL BOWLING DAY

PAGE 187: NATIONAL ROLLER COASTER DAY

PAGE 188: ROYAL EDINBURG MILITARY TATTOO

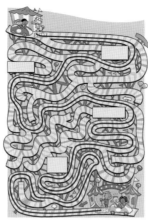

SEPTEMBER

PAGE 190: NATIONAL HISPANIC HERITAGE MONTH

1. Octaviano Ambrosio Larrazolo
2. Roberto Clemente
3. Rita Moreno
4. Franklin Chang-Diaz
5. Dr. Antonia Novello
6. Dolores Huerta
7. Carlos Santana
8. Sonia Sotomayor

PAGE 191: NATIONAL CHICKEN MONTH

Which birds are sad?
BLUE JAYS

What can turkeys use to play an instrument?
DRUMSTICKS

What do you give a sick bird?
TWEETMENT

What are smarter than talking birds?
SPELLING BEES

What do you get when you cross centipedes with parrots?
WALKIE-TALKIES

PAGE 192: BETTER BREAKFAST MONTH

PAGE 193: HAPPY HEALTHY CAT MONTH

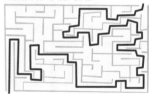

PAGE 193: PET-SITTER EDUCATION MONTH
Lucy eats liver.
Bailey eats beef.
Luna eats tuna.
Peanut eats chicken.

PAGE 194: SEPTEMBER 4, 1781

PAGE 195: SEPTEMBER 23, 1986
Columns 3 and 5 have the same roses.

PAGE 197: U.S. OPEN TENNIS FINALS

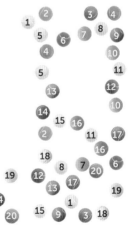

PAGE 190 maze

PAGE 198: NATIONAL COLORING DAY

PAGE 199: INTERNATIONAL COUNTRY MUSIC DAY

PAGE 200: NATIONAL CHEESE PIZZA DAY

PAGE 200: TOP 10 MOST POPULAR TOPPINGS

1. PEPPERONI
2. MUSHROOMS
3. ONIONS
4. SAUSAGE
5. BACON
6. EXTRA CHEESE
7. BLACK OLIVES
8. GREEN PEPPERS
9. PINEAPPLE
10. SPINACH

PAGE 201: INTERNATIONAL CHOCOLATE DAY

1. 400
2. 90
3. 5
4. 50 MILLION
5. 1.5 MILLION
6. 40
7. 35

PAGE 202: LABOR DAY

A "SHEAR" PLEASURE. (HAIRDRESSER)

I'M DRAWN TO IT. (ARTIST)

IT'S A PIECE OF CAKE! (BAKER)

OUT OF THIS WORLD! (ASTRONAUT)

I GET A KICK OUT OF IT! (SOCCCER PLAYER)

MOVING RIGHT ALONG. (TRAFFIC OFFICER)

AN APPLE A DAY COULDN'T KEEP ME AWAY! (DOCTOR)

PAGE 203: NATIONAL GRANDPARENTS DAY

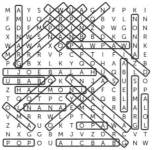

PAGE 205: FIRST DAY OF FALL

PAGE 207: WORLD RHINO DAY

PAGE 208: NATIONAL SKYSCRAPER DAY
1. A; 2. C; 3. B; 4. B; 5. C; 6. A

PAGE 208: NATIONAL AMPERSAND DAY

1. JELLY, 2. LIGHTNING, 3. SOCKS, 4. EGGS, 5. ROLL, 6. THE BEAST, 7. CHEESE, 8. CRAFTS, 9. PEPPER

PAGE 209: INTERNATIONAL SUDOKU DAY

F	S	N	T	R	A
A	R	T	S	F	N
N	F	A	R	S	T
R	T	S	N	A	F
S	N	F	R	T	R
T	A	R	F	N	S

Where do bugs go on vacation?
FRANTS

PAGE 209: INTERNATIONAL TALK LIKE A PIRATE DAY

What kind of socks does a pirate wear?
ARRRGYLE

PAGE 210: ENKUTATASH (ETHIOPIA)

PAGE 211: FIESTAS PATRIAS (CHILE)

GUITAR
HARP
PIANO
ACCORDION
TAMBOURINE

OCTOBER

PAGE 214: EAT BETTER, EAT TOGETHER MONTH

PAGE 216: GLOBAL DIVERSITY AWARENESS MONTH

1. CHINA
2. INDONESIA
3. JAPAN
4. NORWAY
5. GREECE

PAGE 217: ITALIAN AMERICAN HERITAGE MONTH

PAGE 218: ALBUQUERQUE INTERNATIONAL BALLOON FIESTA

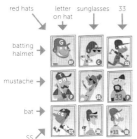

PAGE 220: RECORD SETTERS

5,714 STRIKEOUTS: NOLAN RYAN
4,256 HITS: PETE ROSE
511 WINS: CY YOUNG
1,406 STOLEN BASES: RICKEY HENDERSON
14 WORLD SERIES APPEARANCES: YOGI BERRA

PAGE 221: WORLD SERIES CHAMPIONSHIP

What baseball team does a joker like best?
THE NEW YORK PRANKEES

PAGE 221: TIC TAC ROW

PAGE 221: FLY CATCHER

PAGE 223: DICTIONARY DAY

1. TOY
2. ANT
3. CORN
4. DIRT
5. RAIN
6. TRAIN
7. CARTON

PAGE 223: NATIONAL COLOR DAY

1. RED
2. BLUE
3. BROWN
4. YELLOW
5. GREEN
6. PURPLE
7. ORANGE
8. BLACK

PAGE 225: NATIONAL PUMPKIN DAY

PAGE 228: NATIONAL BUTTERFLY AND HUMMINGBIRD DAY

1. B; 2. D; 3. A; 4. C

PAGE 229: INTERNATIONAL SLOTH DAY

It is 6:00 P.M.

PAGE 230: NATIONAL BATHTUB DAY

PAGE 230: ADA LOVELACE DAY

Ada created a poster about Hedy Lamarr.

Charles made a scale model about Katherine Johnson.

Marie wrote a book report about Dorothy Hodgkin.

Eli made a diorama about Edith Clarke.

PAGE 233: REPUBLIC DAY (TURKEY)

NOVEMBER

PAGE 236: NATIONAL NATIVE AMERICAN HERITAGE MONTH

PAGE 237: NATIONAL MODEL RAILROAD MONTH

What do you call a locomotive that sneezes?
AH-CHOO-CHOO TRAIN

PAGE 239: HISTORIC BRIDGE AWARENESS MONTH

PAGE 241: NOVEMBER 14, 1981

PAGE 242: NATIONAL TAKE A HIKE DAY

1. Emma planned the route.
2. We stopped to sketch at the bridge.
3. Two squirrels came racing along a log!
4. The whole crew ate raisins for energy.
5. We came upon chopped trees near a beaver dam.
6. Our pace had to slow at challenging, rocky parts of the trail

There are 10 squirrels in the scene.

PAGE 242: COMPASS CODE

Where's the best place to eat while hiking?
WHERE THERE'S *A FORK IN THE ROAD*

PAGE 243: NATIONAL SQUARE DANCE DAY

297

PAGE 245: NATIONAL SANDWICH DAY

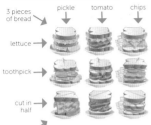

3 pieces of bread — pickle / tomato / chips

lettuce →

toothpick →

cut in half →

cheese →

PAGE 245: MENU MIX-UP
1. F; 2. E; 3. B; 4. D; 5. A; 6. C

PAGE 247: TURKEY TROT

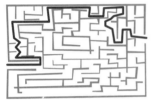

PAGE 247: MAKE A MATCH

PAGE 247: FAVORITE FOODS
1. PIE
2. STUFFING
3. GRAVY
4. SWEET POTATOES
5. HAM
6. MASHED POTATOES
7. MAC AND CHEESE
8. GREEN BEAN CASSEROLE
9. CORN BREAD
10. TURKEY

PAGE 248: WHOLE LOTTA LATKES
$24.43

PAGE 249: DREIDEL DILEMMA
Aaron is the winner.

PAGE 250: WORLD JELLYFISH DAY

1. B; 2. C; 3. B; 4. C; 5. A; 6. A; 7. B; 8. D

PAGE 251: WORLD RADIOGRAPHY DAY

Xavier ate too many *DOUGHNUTS*!

PAGE 251: BONE UP:
The ULNA, RADIUS, and HUMERUS are located in your arm.

PAGE 253: NATIONAL BUTTON DAY

PAGE 254: DÍA DE LOS MUERTOS (MEXICO)

PAGE 255: SAINT MARTIN'S DAY (GERMANY)

DECEMBER

PAGE 259: PENCIL PATHS

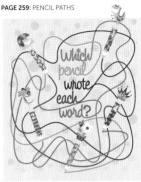

PAGE 260: LEARN A FOREIGN LANGUAGE MONTH
1. SPANISH
2. JAPANESE
3. GERMAN
4. RUSSIAN
5. FRENCH
6. ITALIAN
7. SWAHILI
8. CHINESE

PAGE 261: READ A NEW BOOK MONTH

PAGE 262: DECEMBER 7, 1941

PAGE 263: DECEMBER 21, 1891

PAGE 264: NATIONAL VIOLIN DAY

PAGE 266: NATIONAL COOKIE DAY

MACAROON

LEMON BAR

SUGAR

FORTUNE

GINGERSNAP

SHORTBREAD

OATMEAL RAISIN

PEANUT BUTTER

CHOCOLATE CHIP

SNICKERDOODLE

What did the gingerbread man use to trim his fingernails?
A COOKIE CUTTER

PAGE 270: A TREE FULL OF TREATS

PAGE 270: TRICKY TREES

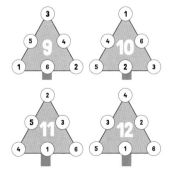

PAGE 271: GLEEFUL GIFTS

MASON: BASKETBALL

JAVIER: BOOKS

CHARLOTTE: VIDEO GAME

BODHI: SKATEBOARD

AMELIA: PUZZLE

PAGE 273: GOBS OF GIBBLES

PAGE 274: NATIONAL GINGERBREAD HOUSE DAY

PAGE 275: NATIONAL VISIT THE ZOO DAY

PAGE 276: ST. NICHOLAS DAY (BELGIUM)

PAGE 277: BOXING DAY
(COMMONWEALTH COUNTRIES)

Abbreviations: GI: Getty Images; SS: Shutterstock.com; WC: Wikimedia Commons

Photo Credits: -ELIKA-/GI (72); -lvinst-/GI (49); 00one/GI (116); 101cats/GI (188); 111chemodan111/GI (213); 3DMAVR/GI (16); 400tmax/GI (87); _Vilor/GI (26, 168); AbbieImages/GI (143); Abbus Acastra/Alamy Stock Photo (190); ac_bnphotos/GI (224); adogslifephoto/GI (3, 245); AdShooter/GI (86); Aeya/GI (51); agaliza/GI (90); agcuesta/GI (264); ajansen/GI (104); alenaohneva/GI (138); alexkava/GI (2); AlexLMX/GI (91, 239); alisafarov/GI (90); Allan Grant/GI (28); AlonzoDesign/GI (50); Alst/GI (180); aluxum/GI (119); Amy_Lv/GI (212); AnastasiaNurullina/GI (216); Anastasiia_M/GI (211); AnatolyM/GI (74); Andreas Rentz/GI (255); Andrey Zhuravlev/GI (248); Aneese/GI (218); Anna Pogrebkova/GI (186); anna1311/GI (5, 26); anopdesignstock/GI (82); ansonsaw/GI (111, 225); Antagain/GI (5); AnthiaCumming/GI (35); antonbelo/GI (188); Anurak Sirithep/GI (96); Ariel Skelley/GI (152); aristotoo/GI (137); asbe/GI (103); assalve/GI (112); Aukid/GI (207); AVNphotolab/GI (213); AYImages/GI (134); Azure-Dragon/GI (5); barbaramarini/GI (198); Bartosz Hadyniak/GI (73); Basilios1/GI (38); bastiennewentzel/GI (24); Batareykin/GI (82); bazilfoto/GI (29); Beano5/GI (264); Bedo/GI (23); bergamont/GI (35, 74, 86, BC); Betelgejze/GI (171); bhofack2/GI (87, 213, 216); Bigmouse108/GI (46); Bill Oxford/GI (220); bizoo_n/GI (24); blue_rain/GI (210); blueenayim/GI (43); BlueLemonPhoto/GI (147); bob_sato_1973/GI (FC, 264); BOLDG/GI (146); Bombaert/GI (130); bonchan/GI (43, 244); Boonchuay1970/GI (87, 180, 189); borchee/GI (256); bortonia/GI (51, 189); Bozena_Fulawka/GI (123); Bryan Reynolds (228); bsd555/GI (90); bubaone/GI (213); burwellphotography/GI (5, 135); by_nicholas/GI (197, 264); capemaydesign/GI (3); CasPhotography/GI (13); Cathy Murphy/GI (190); Cesare Ferrari/GI (264); Che_Tina_Plant/GI (206); chengyuzheng/GI (103, 159, 180); Chereliss/GI (66); cherezoff/GI (123); Chicago Tribune/GI (56); Childzy/WC (156); Chris Elise/GI (129); ChrisGorgio/GI (96); chrupka/GI (110); Coldmoon_photo/GI (123, 169); Collection of the Supreme Court of the United States, Steve Petteway/WC (190); Comstock/GI (269); coopder1/GI (197); CoreyFord/GI (250); corozco/GI (254); Corporation for National and Community Service (16); creisinger/GI (254); Cristian Storto Fotografia/GI (36); cveltri/GI (80); cynoclub/GI (122); DaddyBit/GI (140, BC); damedeeso/GI (132); dandanian/GI (264); daniel_wiedemann/GI (91); Dash_med/GI (134); DawnPoland/GI (256); dcdp/GI (38); deepblue4you/GI (125); Department of State of the United States of America/WC (28); DiamondGalaxy/GI (256); Diana Taliun/GI (138); Diane Macdonald/GI (6); diane555/GI (93); Dimitris66/GI (FC, 74, 118); DmitriyBurlakov/GI (274); DNY59/GI (82, 123); DonNichols/GI (123); dontbelievethehype/GI (216); dottedhippo/GI (189); Double Eagle V at the Albuquerque Balloon Museum, AAAIBM Staff Photo (241); duntaro/GI (45); DuxX/GI (197); DWithers/GI (164); EasyBuy4u/GI (224); Ekaterina Chudakova/GI (26); Ekely/GI (121); ElementalImaging/GI (76); Elen11/GI (FC, 27); Elenarts/GI (62); enot-poloskun/GI (25); Everett Collection/SS (52); EXACTOSTOCK/SUPERSTOCK (170); ExFlow/GI (73); FabrikaCr/GI (74); farosofa/GI (56, 79); fcafotodigital/GI (118, 267); FDR Presidential Library & Museum/WC (260); FedotovAnatoly/GI (168, 245); fermate/GI (125); FilippoBacci/GI (134, 217); filistimlyanin/GI (134); filo/GI (2, 25, 27, 51, 169); FineArtCraig/GI (IFC); fizkes/GI (196); Flavio Vallenari/GI (233); Freder/GI (272); fstop123/GI (199); Furtseff/GI (7, 125); gaetan stoffel/GI (216); Galeria del Ministerio de Defensa del Perú/WC (167); Galyna_P/GI (FC, 1); GaryTalton/GI (37); GCShutter/GI (114); Gearstd/GI (74, 129); Gene J Puskar/AP/SS (52); General Post Office of the United Kingdom of Great Britain and Ireland/WC (99); Georgina198/GI (266); Gianluca Fabrizio/GI (189); Girl Scouts logo (51) used with permission of the GIRL SCOUTS OF THE UNITED STATES OF AMERICA; girlfrommars/GI (50); Givaga/GI (120);

gkrphoto/GI (244); GlobalP/GI (27, 40, 86, 103, 147, 207, 245, 253); gmnicholas/GI (235); goir/GI (134); gojak/GI (63, 212); Granamour Weems Collection/Alamy Stock Photo (28); grandriver/GI (236); Grassetto/GI (99, 189); gresei/GI (87, 137); GrishaL/GI (147); gsol/GI (223); Guy Cali Associates, Inc. (40, 48, 54, 55, 65, 86, 110, 113, 120, 126, 137, 143, 159, 178, 204, 210, 222, 224, 246, 255, 269); gvictoria/GI (189); Gyzele/GI (123); hanapon1002/GI (46); Hank Schneider (4, 19, 41, 65, 67, 112, 136, 162, 181, 204, 222, 248, 249, 270, 277, BC); hdere/GI (148); heywoody/GI (20); HHLtDave5/GI (87); hkuchera/GI (19); Igor Ilnitckii/GI (145); Igor_Kali/GI (26); IgorDutina/GI (26); Ihor Deyneka/GI (69); ilbusca/GI (153); Image Source/GI (158); impactimage/GI (146); IMS Photo Archive (107); IngerEriksen/GI (71); instamatics/GI (224); ISerg/GI (107); istarif/GI (5); ivanastar/GI (2, 228); ivstiv/GI (256); J. Fusco for VISIT PHILADELPHIA® / ©VISIT PHILADELPHIA® (18); Jaan Künnap/WC (52); jack0m/GI (25–26, 48–49, 72–73, 75, 96–97, 120–121, 144–145, 166–167, 186, 210–211, 232–233, 254–255, 276–277); James Keyser/GI (28); jamesbenet/GI (257); Jane_Kelly/GI (24, 25, 48, 49, 72, 73, 96, 97, 120, 121, 144, 145, 166, 167, 186, 187, 210, 211, 232, 233, 254, 255, 276, 277); janeff/GI (244); Janine Lamontagne/GI (151); Janoj/GI (38, 69); janrysavy/GI (257); ©Jason Clark/Southcreek Global/Zuma/Alamy Stock Photo (52); JC Olivera/GI (100); jclegg/GI (47); jenifoto/GI (2, 159); Jenniveve84/GI (38); jgroup/GI (61); Jim Filipski, Guy Cali Associates, Inc. (14, 88, 91, 105, 140, 204, 245, 258, 267, 268); jirkaejc/GI (122); John Ferguson/WC (190); johnandersonphoto/GI (229); JohnGollop/GI (99); JohnnyGreig/GI (47); JPC-PROD/GI (99); jsolie/GI (203); Juanmonino/GI (94, 122); Jui-Chi Chan/GI (232); JuliaKa/GI (114); Jupiterimages/GI (32, 118, 244); k_samurkas/GI (75, 220); kaanates/GI (234); kaisphoto/GI (195); kanyakits/GI (211); karandaev/GI (39, 107); Karl Denham/Alamy Stock Photo (98); Kathy Hutchins/SS (100); Kativ/GI (272); Kazuharu Harada/GI (257); KenCanning/GI (206); keport/GI (30); Keystone-France/GI (81); khai9000/GI (31); kiboka/GI (5); kickstand/GI (234); Kintarapong/GI (75); Kirkikis/GI (125); Ko Hong-Wei/GI (169); KoBoZaa/GI (106); koya79/GI (176, 219); Krasimir Kanchev/GI (272); KrimKate/GI (123); Kritchanut/GI (88); krysteq/GI (50); ksushsh/GI (98); Kuzmik_A/GI (111); kyoshino/GI (151, 201); Laures/GI (213); LauriPatterson/GI (50); LdF/GI (26); Lebazele/GI (21); leekris/GI (137); Leezsnow/GI (241); lev radin/SS (28); Library of Congress, Prints and Photographs Division: LC-DIG-ds-11820 (28); LC-DIG-ppbd- 00603 (28); LC-DIG-ggbain-07682 (52); LC-DIG-hec-40747 (52); LC-USZ62-86846 (52); LC-USZC4-3812 (108); LC-USZC2-3565 (166); LC-DIG-ppmsca-12373 (190); LC-DIG-ds-11693 (194); LC-USZ62-33530 (202); LC-DIG-ggbain-33189 (220); LC-USZ62-62136 (240); LC-USW34- 017109-B (262); Liliboas/GI (99, 195); LindasPhotography/GI (19); linearcurves/GI (156); Litvalifa/GI (26); Louis Requena/Stringer/GI (190); lovell35/GI (250); LPETTET/GI (249); Lucerne 2021 Winter Universiade / ©WinterUniversiade 2021 (11); lucielang/GI (FC); LysenkoAlexander/GI (82); Madam Walker Family Archives/A'Lelia Bundles (28); Magone/GI (110, 224); MahirAtes/GI (63, 253); Makidotvn/GI (216); malerapaso/GI (39, 127, 253); Marcutti/GI (195); Marius Igas Photography/GI (217); MARKA/Alamy Stock Photo (52); Massed Pipes & Drums ©The Royal Edinburgh Military Tattoo (186); mayur_gala777/GI (150); mbbirdy/GI (29); mediaphotos/GI (101); MediaProduction/GI (207); Merinka/GI (276); meunierd/SS (131); mg7/GI (146); mgkaya/GI (9); Michael Burrell/GI (82, 88, 152); Michael Ver Sprill/GI (132); michelangelus/GI (66); mightyisland/GI (2); MikeyGen73/GI (256); mikheewnik/GI (98, 188, 212); mikimad/GI (273); milanfoto/GI (137); mipan/GI (272); MisterClips/GI (87); Momento Design/GI (50); Montgomery County Archives (28); monticellllo/GI (FC, 146); Moussa81/GI (98, 199); mphillips007/GI (FC, 38, 98, 208, 247); mtphoto19/GI (5); mustafagull/GI (256); mustafaU/GI (167); NAKphotos/GI (3); narvikk/GI (194); NASA (28, 100, 141, 190); Nastco/GI (134); Natalie Ruffing/GI (93);

Published by Highlights Press
815 Church Street
Honesdale, Pennsylvania 18431
ISBN: 978-1-68437-922-4

Manufactured in Marceline, MO, USA
Mfg. 03/2020

First edition
Visit our website at highlights.com.
10 9 8 7 6 5 4 3 2 1

Design and Art Direction by Colleen Pidel
Cover Design by Red Herring Design
Pre-Media Production by David Pearson